Revolting Librarians
Redux

Revolting Librarians Redux

Radical Librarians Speak Out

EDITED BY Katia Roberto
AND Jessamyn West

Introduction by Celeste West

ILLUSTRATIONS BY KATHERINE WEST

McFarland & Company, Inc., Publishers
Jefferson, North Carolina, and London

SELECTED LIBRARY OF CONGRESS ONLINE CATALOG DATA

Revolting librarians redux : radical librarians speak out / edited by Katia
  Roberto and Jessamyn West ; introduction by Celeste West ; illustrations
  by Katherine West.
     p. cm.
  Includes [bibliographical references and] index.
  1. Library Science — Philosophy. 2. Librarians. 3. Libraries.
  4. Libraries — United States. 5. Radicalism. I. Roberto, Katia, 1975–
  II. West, Jessamyn, 1968–
  Z665.R44 2003
  020'.01 — dc21   2003009927

ALTERNATIVE CATALOGUING-IN-PUBLICATION DATA

Revolting librarians redux: radical librarians speak out. Edited by Katia
  Roberto and Jessamyn West. Introduction by Celeste West. Illustrations
  by Katherine West.
     Jefferson, N.C.: McFarland & Company, Inc., Publishers, copyright 2003.
     Illustrated with comic strips and line drawings by Alison Bechdel, Cathy
  Camper, Jennier Camper, and Katherine West.
     Includes critiques of library and information science programs, firsthand
  accounts of work experiences, original fiction, poetry, and art.
     PARTIAL CONTENTS: Still revolting after all these years: voices from
  the original revolters.— Library school is revolting.— Sex, drugs, and will
  you please be quiet:our revolting jobs.— Creatively revolting self-expres-
  sion.— Our revolting issues.— Day to revolting day: our stories.— Unclas-
  sifiable.
     1. Library science. 2. Libraries. 3. West, Celeste. Revolting librari-
  ans — Sequels. 4. Librarians — Social responsibility. 5. Radical librarians. 6. Library humor. 7. Librarians — Personal narratives. 8. Women
  librarians. 9. Image of librarians. 10. Alternative press. I. Roberto,
  Katia, 1975– , editor. II. West, Jessamyn, 1968– , editor.

ISBN-13: 978-0-7864-1608-0 (softcover : 50# alkaline paper) ∞

British Library cataloguing data are available

Designed by Robert Franklin
Cover photograph by Jessamyn West

Manufactured in the United States of America

*McFarland & Company, Inc., Publishers
  Box 611, Jefferson, North Carolina 28640
  www.mcfarlandpub.com*

ACKNOWLEDGMENTS

"The front of a book is a vast literary moonscape not worth exploring."
— John Maxwell Hamilton

Katia: This book would have never happened without the Internet, heaven help us all. Jessamyn offered to co-edit via email, we sent out the call for submissions via email (and on a few websites), the bulk of our submissions were received via email, and we pestered our editor via email. Three cheers for technology.

As far as actual people go, many of them deserve thanks as well. Jessamyn is the best co-editor ever, of course. I discovered that several of my coworkers—Daren Callahan, Katie Salzmann, and Cristy "Slugger" Stupegia—were very good at making sympathetic noises about my various book-related woes. R.J. and Di always asked how the book was going and always managed to listen to my lengthy and sometimes incoherent replies. Sandy Berman received a lot of phone calls and always offered good advice. James P. Danky graciously sent us the release forms used for *Alternative Library Literature* to use as a model for our forms. Chris Dodge and Christopher H. Walker offered plenty of reassurance. Anna Claire Amundson, Ericka Bailie, Toby Beauchamp, Riley Demland, Devon King, Angela Kostenko, and Lindsey Morrison were supportive and never told me to shut up. Brian Hasenstab lived with me throughout the entire process and still likes me anyway.

Of course, this book would have never happened if there weren't any contributors, and it wouldn't have been a sequel if *Revolting Librarians* had never been published in the first place. I'm incredibly grateful to everyone involved.

Jessamyn: Katia and I live over a thousand miles apart and had only one face-to-face retreat-type meeting thing over the year or so that we worked on this book. Almost all the work we did occurred over email, a few phone calls, and a well placed letter or two. My working email box for this project contains over 1200 messages, many of them quite amusing in their sarcastic wit and frustrated acting out. So, I must acknowledge the one higher power without whom none of this would have been possible: I am referring, of course, to the Internet. I have to give a big hand to Katia since I hear she actually held down a *job* while she worked on this book; I have no such excuses. She is a peach, don't let her tell you different.

As far as living breathing collaborators, there is my sister the nifty illustrator who did some high quality work over a very brief period of time. She is the West I am related to, Celeste is the West I am not related to. Bill Altreuter <http://www.out-sidethelaw.com/> gave us sound advice and early encouragement to give the high stakes world of publishing a try. My Mom preceded me in the writer biz; she has always been an inspiration and was available at the other end of the phone when I felt like I was in over my head. My Seattle roommates—Hahn, Drew, Jasper, William and the Brown Clown — gave me support and did not roll their eyes when I told them I was "working on my book" for days on end in the living room. My Seattle librarian buddy Dawn matched my whirlwind pace in many things and showed me that I wasn't alone in my wacky librarianness. My Vermont roommate and boyfriend, Greg, had more faith in my own abilities than I sometimes did, and makes a mean pesto.

 All of our contributors have been some kind of wonderful or, at the very least, kept us on our toes. May there be a special place in heaven for you for all the efforts you've expended.

TABLE OF CONTENTS

*Haiku on part title pages are provided by Kathleen Kern.

IV. Creatively Revolting Self-Expression   72

V. Our Revolting Issues   87

VI. Day to Revolting Day: Our Stories   147

VII. Unclassifiable   176

PREFACE: DON'T BLAME US; OR, WE LIKE YOU ALL IN DIFFERENT WAYS

Katia Roberto *and* Jessamyn West

Is thirty years too late for a sequel?

We don't think so. Both of us were deeply influenced by *Revolting Librarians* in library school and both of us have tried hard to further the revolting tradition, such as it is.

It all started in the shower. Katia spent most of 2001 thinking about possible research topics for the publications necessary to make sufficient progress towards tenure as an academic librarian. One day, while performing ablutions in preparation for another day in libraryland, she realized that it had been almost 30 years since *Revolting Librarians* was published. She briefly contemplated being involved in such a project, but it didn't fit neatly into the "writing research articles in peer-reviewed journals" model that is usually recommended to achieve tenure. (Admittedly, Katia is used to a life where nothing fits neatly, but there's always hope.) She decided that co-authoring articles would be a good idea, and asked Sandy Berman if he wanted to write something. Sandy asked what she'd had in mind, and after discussing cataloging minutiae, she mentioned this silly *Revolting Librarians* sequel idea. Sandy, in typical exuberant fashion, thought this was a brilliant idea, and immediately began making suggestions. After talking with various radical librarian types, Jessamyn offered her co-editor services, Katia took her up on it, and here we are.

We first met in the back of an audience at a SRRT meeting, trying and failing to keep from making wiseass comments as the speaker was droning on and on about some very, *very* important topic. Every venerable tradition — the radical tradition, the library tradition, the intellectual tradition — has its adherents, its detractors, the staunch supporters, and the peanut gallery. The main question we got when writing this book was, almost surprisingly, "What is a revolting librarian?" (The second most often asked question was, "What is heteronormativity?") Like all good ill-defined terms, we could reply that we know it when we see it, but there's more to it than that. The revolting tradition means not taking the status quo as a given. While this may be a foregone conclusion when the status quo is tomb-silent libraries, persnickety librarians and sensible shoes, the status quo can be pervasive and pernicious. Status quo in libraries is the American Library Association. Status quo in the U.S. government is pro-business, anti-terror, and has a mixed opinion on freedom. Status quo in radical librarianship is still fraught with interminable committees, petty infighting, and masculine posturing. We're not saying we are against all these things — well, maybe we are — but we're trying to say that they deserve examination.

Our authors investigate these issues, rail against them, beat their chests in their defense, create new paradigms, dash old ones. The path to revolting librarianship is never easy and you'll notice that some of our articles aren't even consistent with each other. This is a fact of the movement, not an oversight on our part. When we put out the call for writers, we were mainly looking for "readable and interesting" critiques of traditional library topics. We turned away very few articles based on content, and lost out on a few more due to the ever-present reality of deadlines and jobs. Sadly, many of our more vocal contributors preferred to be pseudonymous due to pressure from work or peers to toe the line or not rock the boat. At our final tally, our female-to-male ratio was roughly three to two. We have librarians from several non–U.S. countries and many different facets of the profession. We have no article about cats, but we have several about globalization. We have one or two pieces that use the word "bun." At least one of those is facetious. Some of our contributors have been accused of behaving unprofessionally and not taking librarianship entirely seriously. If expressing anger, frustration, hope, and pride is unprofessional, please burn our American Library Association membership cards in effigy.

You'll notice we have yet to address the question of what a revolting librarian is. This may be because the precise definition doesn't really matter. Revolting librarians aren't defined by what they are; they are defined by what they do. In fact, it's not even what they do, but how they do it. As with every generalization, this one misses some people, but we think that the focus of the matter, the real crux of the biscuit, is this: dissent sparks change. Informed dissent creates inspired changes. Thoughtful, imaginative, forward-looking dissent generates concrete, progressive, and bountiful change. Being able to have clear sight about the problem is nearly useless unless you can formulate how things might be better. (For the record, we're not implying that all change is good; if the present situation is bad, properly stewarded change can lead to improvement.)

Some of these ideas have been interminably batted about in the alternative library press: pay raises, humane subject headings, sensible classification schemes, alternative collection development, justice and equality through technology, and service to the poor, the underserved, the unserved, the undeserved, the masses, and the individual. Above all this is the understanding that while change may not always necessarily come from within, it may not come at all unless we lobby for it, talk about it, harangue, testify, beat our chests, and write our representatives.

Join us.

Katia Roberto and Jessamyn West
West Topsham, Vermont

INTRODUCTION: *REVOLTING LIBRARIANS* RIDES AGAIN

Celeste West

Revolting Librarians Rampant!

Heartiest welcome: first to you older riders of the purple sage who rallied in 1972 as our writers, artists, and readers of the earnest Chautauqua and frolicsome detours that became *Revolting Librarians*. How propitious that the editors of *Revolting Librarians Redux* gathered a full coven of Spirit of '72 campaigners to ride again. Other notable events of 1972: Watergate break-in adds the suffix *-gate* to nefarious deeds exposed, and wicked toad J. Edgar Hoover drops dead. So rejoin me in flashing the old peace sign as we continue to uphold such ramblin' roses of sweet anarchy as library worker self-direction/self-management, and social responsibility/festivity.

Let's re-celebrate the blooming centerpiece for each Revolting Librarian: free inquiry. Free inquiry is the fertile valley that nurtures the roses of the open quest, open dissent, open advocacy, open universities—not to mention open source code and free broadband. I never tire of the fragrant clarity of such roses' attar, and then of how to resolve the sharing of the flowers and fruits of our libraryland's Free Inquiry Commons.* By now, most of us veterans have experienced how each wild rose must also use its briars of self-defense in order to sustain our creative gestation. Let's help each other to honor and to sharpen the brambles we seem to require, backlash after backlash.

In this organic *RLR* module you can touch or this *RLR* whirl of electrons that has somehow run free to touch you, we have four living generations of Revolting Librarians to potentiate our vision and social activism. Creatively hybridizing the social values of our different comings of age, we can together revitalize the "profess" in the professional calling of librarianship. So I especially rejoice to welcome new generations of Revolting Librarians who are shouting out for peace and social justice, while continuing our dance with diversity: you IT gal/guy, you data hunter, you knowledge gatherer, you wisdom sharer — and you odd-bird Gen X and Nexster antiquarians who enjoy being under the covers, choosing to still curate, browse, and propagate book pollen.

We come together at a critical time. A U.S. presidential putsch has occurred. The Bush [rhymes with "putsch"] Coup now declares war on human rights and foments new laws to make democracy illegal. As the data smog exponentially increases, civil society requires authentic information editors in its library workers. Check out the so-called "Patriot Act," especially Section 215 on library records, and "Operation Tips" hurling us from the Information Age into an Informant Age. Revolting Librarians must use consummate tracking skills to expose the Bush Coup as it suppresses public information such as the entire Reagan Archives, Freedom of Information Act documents, memos of cabinet-corporate collusion, and juridical rationales for arbitrary and infinite detention. Every Revolting Librarian must also sustain the energetic clarity to shovel through all the disinformation the Bush Coup churns out via its mislabeled categories: "Axis of Evil" (actually Bush–Cheney– Ashcroft); "terrorist" as a code word for dissident; "enemy combatant" to strip a soldier or any freedom fighter of Geneva Convention protections; and other propagandistic rhetoric.

Libraries are also manipulated by a corporate mass media and e-content-ers ever more consolidated — swallowing government lines and infotainment garbage as they bottom-feed on advertising. Conglomerate "menstream" media doesn't overtly tell us what to think as much as it tells us what to think about. Besides preserving accurate history and providing current, "non-spun" information, the Revolting Librarian's pro-active media selection policies focus on the reportage of dissent. Let's divert funds from the panderers who continuously mass mediate us as consumers, stupid ones at that, and rarely address us as concerned citizenry. It is up to the Revolting Librarian to support and supply the independent voices that actually inform citizens of a true democracy, especially the little publicized, valuable reports of the non-governmental agencies such as Amnesty International, Institute for Policy Studies, Global Exchange and many others. Let's also publish more of our own expertise in Revolting Librarian resource lists, search tools, 'zines, and books like this.

Let me complete my editors' assignment to stroll with you in the moonshine of memory. Because I was co-editor of the *über-RL* thirty years ago, I was asked to highlight a few of our adventures with the old campaigner so you can better see where we've been, what bears repeating, and which new frontiers beckon. As soon as I accepted my current job at the San Francisco Zen Center Library on April Fool's Day 1989, I dove into the piece Reva Basch (née Landy) wrote in *RL #1*, "Reflections of a Head Librarian." I too am a "head" staff of one: the Director and CFO (Chief Freedom Officer), Supervisor of Small Change, Head of Reference & Acquisitions & Cataloging & Janitorial Services & Who Shall I Be Today? My autocracy is both sweet and a bit lonely. I actually joined the Special Libraries Association in hopes of meeting another church basement library worker. SLA does enable me to give really good jargon. The leading SLA verb seems to be "deploy," as in: "To measure the return on information investment, deploy high-value business intelligence." I do like my group's acronym: MAHD (Museum and Humanities Division.)

I believe some tech talk facility is essential if the Revolting Librarian is to forestall the following scenario:

"Click 'OK.'"

"But it is not OK!"

"Click it anyway."

I did find one buddy, the director of the elegant and intellectual Jung Institute Library. She was fortunate to have resigned just before the Y2K bug blew her library's once renowned search service to beejeezus. Luckily for me, each year the Zen Center Library Technical Advisory Board just "sits with" digitizing our 15,000 volume card catalog. Lacking "deployment" impetus, the ZC Library has saved hundreds of my hours and thousands of ZC dollars in "knowledge economy" upgrades, subscription fees, and crashes. The Zennas continue to revel in the 96-drawer oaken and brass card catalog scavenged from a U.C.–Berkeley library for $100 by my favorite scholar and gentleman, Bill Redican. Such an antique is now worth more like $100 per drawer; people prize the old catalogs for "deploying" tape cassettes, wine bottles, and nostalgia. I do realize that the digital tape worm, in its pixilated cave, tolls for me. So, if someone out there who has served an apprenticeship with nature will volunteer to be our Taoist Techie, you are hired. You may have any title you want, as well as fabulous lunches, but no coin of the realm or stock options.

My prime benefit through the three decades of *RL #1* ripples is that I am still blessed with the stalwart friendship of my very first library co-worker, contributor Judy ("Jubilee") Hadley, as well as that of my merry word-wife on *RL*, indefatigable co-editor Elizabeth Katz. I also met two prima lovers via *RL*, which is probably the best reason to write a book. I recommend it highly. I suspect the digerati's blog format is a great flirtation station too. *Revolting Librarians* was such an effortless success, I got the nerve to go full-tilt into book publishing and packaging, to create material as well as serve it in libraries.

The hippie, yippie, skippy Elizabeth Katz found me via the magazine *Synergy* that I was editing for the Bay Area Reference Center (BARC) at San Francisco Public Library. I had arrived at BARC in 1968, largely because of our tax dollars at work. You will perceive the leit-motif throughout my story is: "taxes for books, not bullets." In the Great Society days, the feds provided not indentured loans but full, truly munificent scholarships. To get 3,000 miles away from a particularly violent man, I simply applied for a "ride," as the jocks say, and it worked. *The Lord of the Rings* was my guide (talk about *redux*): "You must go quickly and you must go soon."

Rutgers School of Library and Information Science was both high seas and home for me. Several of my professors were kind and erudite humanists. They and many of my co-students were quite investigative regarding the dynamics of power: Who were the information haves and the have-nots, and how and why so? We debated and participated in much of the politics, sexuality, and culture publicized in the lively underground media. Our late sixties milieu viewed librarianship as a perfect launch for activist social work.

This was fine with me. I had been previously unhired as a social worker for the sole reason that I did not have a driver's license. I told my apologetic supervisor that a poetic license certainly was called for, and that everything I knew about social work I had learned on mass transit. So I rode my bus a few stops farther and became a "paraprofessional" for a couple of years in the Portland State University Library. At the first whiff of my domestic contretemps, the two wonderful librarians I para'd for bought me a copy of Constance Winchell's five-pound *Guide to Reference Books* and sent me off to Rutgers to become a safely registered information steward, "lost" in the New York City metropolitan area. (Until feminist activism, domestic violence was neither acknowledged nor deterred. Domestic terrorism against women still accounts for 40 percent of police calls in the U.S.)

At library school, several male students were preparing for library work in Canada to avoid being drafted and issued their U.S. license to kill. Old generals and eager boys, plus the preying Military-Industrial Complex, had led the United States into a terrorist war against most of Southeast Asia's living creatures and habitats. With friends at Rutgers, I traveled to NYC for the Columbia University student sit-in and to the Pentagon for massive protests. This tumultuous period, as the sixties became the seventies, I now realize was the tail-end of the Golden Age of Capitalism. The U.S. was still investing substantial funds in butter as well as in guns. During the seventies, U.S. working people's real incomes were higher than they are now, for which we labored fewer hours! The assets gap between the wealthy and the poor and the CEO and the worker was neither as wide nor increasing as it is today. Accounting firms had not gone completely rogue, nor had housing prices. The bulky remains of our throw-away culture, as well as its chemical and nuclear residuals and military-base toxins, were still buried mainly out of sight.

Soon after completing my MLIS degree, I watched the police riots on TV at the Democratic Convention. Bloodied political protestors were re-framed by officials and establishment media as civilian terrorists ("The Chicago Conspiracy"). From the uniformed racist brutality of the civil rights decades, we were now confronting police violence and juridical perversion in the face of citizen efforts to stop the war machine. The FBI intervened as the secret police of dirty tricks via its COINTELPRO. Such FBI political policing had previously been waged against the labor movement, the "Red Menace," and the Free Speech Movement, as it would later be used against eco-activists, peace workers, feminists and _____ (fill in the blank for current and future dissidents … Revolting Librarians?).

Since library jobs abounded, I decided to head for the San Francisco I had visited in the 1967 "Summer of Love." (Be still, my heart.) The City of Saint Francis continued as epicenter of a counter-culture where political and anti-war activism were high, while joyful living still flowered. The opium poppy — with accompanying mob/cop violence — was only beginning to overwhelm the Haight-Ashbury. This heroin came largely from the "golden triangle" of Southeast Asia. The eighties' U.S. invasions against Central and South American countries brought in loads of coca. Now, U.S. poppy is mainly from the "golden crescent" of Central Asia. Per usual, the U.S. government wars for drugs and against civilians partner one another. Add poverty and racism to the mix for a really bum trip, to use the vernacular of *RL #1*. Bush foreign policy today ignites this sorry brew with oil and religious fanaticism for catastrophic suffering.

Back in 1968, I landed a job at San Francisco Public Library's federally funded Bay Area Reference Center. BARC was a vibrant, loving, if hipoisie, group of reference librarians whose job it was to solve the "out of bibliographical control" and time-consuming reference queries from nine Bay Area library systems. Though we operated from the central branch of San Francisco Public Library, we acted like cheerleaders running all over town and countryside, mining data bases from the test labs at *Sunset Magazine* to the brown-rice communes. There were hazards. BARC librarian Carol Brown broke her tooth while personally researching the macrobiotic diet. The special library at Gallo ("drink the blood of the farm workers") demanded enormous market research from us, but it wouldn't provide one pip of info when BARC received a viniculture query.

In researching "women's liberation" and attending a consciousness-raising group, it dawned on me that the power struggle I kept having with even nice guys was structural, not personal, and that (shock!) that I was ignoring half of the human race as sensual beings. I decided to make up for lost time. I only mention the latter revelation in enumerating research hazards because I, due to lesbian "congress," was sued for my house in 1987 (I won) and again in 2001 (pending). A lesbian owning a piece of the rock can spark greed. Or maybe it is that an anarchist attracts lawyers the way an atheist attracts evangelicals?

But back to BARC. We realized we should publish, for libraryland at large, the precious resources we were finding on grassroots social, cultural and political stirrings. So we founded a 'zine, *Synergy*, to run news and source material on such phenomena as the Black Panther movement, communes, student strikes, prison reform, etc. I became editor. Topics formerly dubbed underground, unworthy, and discreditable by the prudish and status quo were not only appearing in polite company, but were being clamored for by patrons. BARC danced with inspiration and ideas, and immersion in democratizing resource access beyond the Muggles' bestseller list. How to collect and organize completely new areas such as ethnic, women's, and gay studies? *Synergy* offered a narrative by, for, and about the informationally marginalized. The five-thousand-year era of a patriarchal dominator culture, with its scarcity economies (have/have-nots), power hierarchies (winner/losers), and its defining colonial language was no longer the only game in town. The Tower was falling.

For one look at the Bay Area's tribal movements with dazzlingly creative, sharing way of life, see the 2002 film renaissance of another 1972 phenomenon, "The Cockettes." Fayette Houser, one of the three women artists in the performance troupe's glittering dozen, sums up the milieu that birthed *Revolting Librarians*: "We were living in a parallel universe of myth, fantasy, self-exploration, and high drag. What mattered was enlightenment. A new idea was valued like currency." Sure, the Cockettes were total glam, but they also opposed predatory capitalism to its rotten core, with the spirit that not only does "information want to be free," so does food, art, clothing, gender, and the whole hokey pokey...

Virtually all the professions from architects to educators and physicists—even lawyers—began envisioning how their vocations could help free people from the suffering inherent in old dominator conditioning. Seeking answers, professionals birthed their own radical caucuses with alternate publications, in vivid contrast to staid journals and inbred organizations that had ceased questing. When free from such conditioned maladies as bigotry, unearned privilege, and hypocrisy, we could be free to, well, kick up our heels like the Cockettes, and "treat each other like gods and so become gods."

Meanwhile, "radical spiritualities" were doing an end run around the ruling notion of God/He monotheism. Mr. Mono was so rife with cosmic contradiction, mundane prudery, and murderous contrariness that a thousand and one religions, from new cults to the classics, were sending beams into mass consciousness. Authentic spiritual questions such as "Who am I?" and "How shall I live in order to leave the world a better place?" naturally touched the workplaces where most of our life hours are spent.

National and state library associations formed various radical caucuses (women's, ethnic, gay, peace, independent press, etc.), often called "Social Responsibilities Round Tables." As the caucuses synergized, *Synergy* grew in circulation and clitzpah, winning library awards for innovative text and graphics. But, as usual, with success came backlash. BARC began to feel SFPL administrative disapproval. Then, California Governor Ronald Reagan's newly appointed state librarian, who administered BARC's federal monies, ordered the SFPL administration to bury *Synergy*.

Among other *grotesquerie*, I had been running some particularly candid Nixon photos from a newspaper morgue which had been donated to SFPL. I coped with being censored in *Synergy* by submitting over-the-top photos to use as bargaining chips, thereby perhaps to retain other controversial copy about which I really cared. Surprisingly, a few suggestive Nixon photos slipped through. *Synergy* was also rising in print cost as demand increased; our circulation was capped when we reached 2,000. I realized I'd better make hay before the twister hit.

I met *RL #1* co-editor-to-be Elizabeth Katz while she was a freelance librarian part-timing in the Mechanics Institute Library. She had got her taste of office politics with Madalyn Murray O'Hair and Barbara Mikulski as a social worker in Baltimore. Elizabeth had dropped out of a history Ph.D. program at the University of Minnesota to journey to San Francisco during the Summer of Love. She obtained her first acid in the famous lesbian bar "Maud's." So equipped, she worked as a paraprofessional in academic libraries until she got her MLS at SUNY–Albany.

I, by choice, was job-sharing at BARC with a single mom. Part-time work offered us the requisite hours to branch out, be creative, and refuel. So, Elizabeth, I, and my first lesbian love, Sue Critchfield, also a librarian at BARC, formed a triple play to gather all the Revolting Librarians we could find under the covers. We would use *Synergy* and the various SRRT groups to put out a national call for change-agent librarians' impassioned ideas. We would publish their true-life, uncensored adventure stories. Our opening salvo for *RL #1*, on an otherwise blank first page, was from the great Italian anarchist Antonio Gramsci: "To tell the truth is revolutionary." The printer scrambled the first four pages, so Mr. Gramsci appears on page iii, instead of page i, of *RL*'s first printing. After a big battle with the printer, we got reparations for their misplacing Mr. G. Our first run of *RL* therefore cost only around 30¢ per copy to manufacture and then about 20¢ in 1972 postage rates to mail.

Elizabeth and Sue and I hoped a totally unfettered and widely circulated book could encourage and inform isolated progressives out in libraryland. We especially hoped the book might inspire library school students who would, after all, be shaping the future of our seemingly embattled profession. We wanted *RL #1* round-priced at a low $2 for students, new librarians, and support staff. We couldn't decide whether to take proffered contracts with Harcourt Brace or with the American Library Association. Then Harcourt Brace found we were flirting with ALA, and dropped us. The act of "multiple submission" was taboo, although photocopiers were supplanting an author's limited copies of manuscripts possible via carbon paper (one carbon copy for back-up and one to "submit" to publisher after publisher for years).

When we got to terms, we were too uppity for ALA. We wanted a $2 cover price, no ©, and a $1 per copy royalty (50 percent). I have nothing but respect for ALA senior editor Herb Bloom; we later agreed to allow ALA to distribute one printing for their payment to us of $1 per copy. ALA, however, couldn't resist in its advertising banner line for *RL #1*: "Revolting? Revolutionary? Or ... Tomorrow's Establishment?" (Oh, dear! I forgot to join the Establishment! ... I instead became a woman who runs with the Silver Panthers.)

I discovered the only way to retain artistic, economic, and marketing control is to roll yr own incense and wave the smoke where you can. Happily, Sue Critchfield loaned our newly created Booklegger Publishing $1,098 to get the first 3,000 *Revolting Librarians* printed. She also provided the labor of keyboarding the entire book on an IBM Selectric typewriter, which she also helped finance. The Selectric, along with offset printing (in contrast to laborious letterpress), was our era's amazing do-it-yourself tool of desktop publishing. Elizabeth and I acted as acquisition, content, and copy editors. I designed *RL* with the brilliant Nan Parsons' deliciously esoteric cover art and her whimsical chapter title graphics. We sent Nan our descriptions of the art we needed, and she mailed her originals from Montana. Nan is now a famed artist activist in Montana, where she still lives without electricity. (Nan, did you ever go solar-power digital? Will you go 3G wireless, or shall we continue communicating through the cats?)

Although only Elizabeth kept cats during the first *Revolting Librarians*, I had somehow developed a feline mode of shamelessly poaching any line drawing I fancied. Like Alice in Wonderland, I wonder, "What is a book without pictures and conversations?" The entire underground press pirated text and graphics, with almost the same abandon as Netizens. I have other rationalizations for my appropriations, but no excuse. When my own material is used without permission, I may have a flash of anger, but the applause meter takes over; I mainly feel gratified at the increase in number of readers per hour of effort. I now, however, go forth and graphically sin no more. I took the pledge never again to appropriate art without going the limits to obtain its creator's proper blessing and credit line.

Actually, the only piece of art in *RL #1* that we were taken to task for was a full-page spread of a woman's nude torso rising from a pair of not-quite fastened, or pantied, 501s. Stare in *samadi*, and her belly button winks. At the woman's breasts there is a bumper sticker with strategic shadowing. The bumper sticker, printed by union labor for the SFPL Librarians Guild, reads: "Happiness is an Uncensored Library." Several feminists emphatically responded that they felt the photo exploited the woman, objectifying her body to the male gaze. Discussions were fruitful. I was the model (feeling unexploited and laughing as I had set up the shot), and SFPL librarian Dennis Maness was the photographer (feeling I-know-not-what, but his conduct as an artist was impeccable.) Actually Dennis owns the rights, and I wasn't paid, but Dennis agreed never to show or accept money for my photos either. It might be fun now to scan a copyright circle into my belly button to further layer messages.

The other *RL* contributors were also a joy to work with. Librarians tend to be lively writers because we read so much. *RL #1* had to run one piece anonymously, so the tart Ph.D. candidate would not be forever excised from academia. It was dangerous for another writer to come out as lesbian where she lived and worked, so we used a pseudonym. Our revolution truly will have succeeded when all workers may safely express their truths according to their lights.

As I look through my *RL #1* archives, the responses of the readers and reviewers were rousing, as good as love letters and corsages. One of my favorite Revolting Librarians of all time, LaVonne Jacobsen, even designed another great cover for *RL* on an antique letterpress. We were intending to do a second edition of *RL* as our 15,000 first edition ran out, in around three years.

By this time, I had left SFPL after filing a grievance against the administration. I won my case with the help of the union. We established that a supervisor cannot file a "reprimand" against a librarian without the target being given equal time and space to rebut. This is crucial in political disagreements, such as mine. The reprimand against me was withdrawn; it had been instituted for going to my readers and the library media to prevent *Synergy* from being killed. I also received substantial back pay for the years I had never received raises; management had denied me raises because I worked half-time. I was more concerned with the double-censorship of *Synergy* and myself, but the union couldn't revive *Synergy*, despite pleas from its readers. I archived their fan letters as well, always a great tonic for any setback. Never underestimate the power of supportive mail in sustaining ideals. Thanks, folks.

So I began my own 'zine, *Booklegger Magazine*, named for "the home of *Revolting Librarians*." I managed to sneak a full-page ad for it in the last issue of the doomed *Synergy*, so that our subscription base was set. I had a glorious time with *Booklegger*. I worked with Sue again and with my first Valkyrie, Valerie Wheat, as well as the marvelous Carole Leita. Carole went on to organize Women Library Workers, found the annual *SHARE Directory*, and become known as "the librarians' librarian" for her creation of the *Librarians' Index to the Internet* <http://www.lii.org>.

Booklegger Magazine was pre-digitalia, and we ceased after three years because we could no longer service the mailing list of 5,000 by hand. We couldn't farm-out mailing due to the starvation budget we maintained as hippie purists who would not take ads or use an "angel." We depended solely on subscription income. "Unbossed and unbought" carried a little too far. My leisurely side was also getting worn away by a periodical's frequent and ceaseless deadlines.

With some regret, I left the library field to earn a living by writing and editing books. *Revolting Librarians* had been pleasant and successful, as were Booklegger's *Women's Films in Print* and then *Positive Images: A Guide to Non-Sexist Films for Young People*. But I knew book publishing would not be a cinch. We had ended *Booklegger Magazine* with a fat special issue, *The Passionate Perils of Publishing*, funded by a generous government grant from NEA. It unleashed one of the first articles to chart "The Literary-Industrial Complex" on the dangers and extent of media monopolization. My report spun off to become a four-page tabloid, selling for a dollar, which, to my delight, was framed in the loo of Old Wives Tales Bookstore.

I lived lightly as a freelance journalist, editor, and agent for fifteen years. Valerie went on to teach at U.C.–Berkeley Library School. Elizabeth became a legal researcher and writer for the San Francisco City Attorney, also teaching legal research at San Francisco State University. She then got a massage certificate from Body Electric to become a masseuse on the AIDS ward at San Francisco General. In 1990, Elizabeth moved to my home town, Portland, and met the woman of her dreams. She was hired to set up the library for inmates at the Washington County Jail and is now designing services in various Jewish libraries. For a workout, she shelves for eight hours at the Lake Oswego Public Library.

My beautiful Sue died of cancer in 1986. What a national outrage that 50,000 women are still dying of breast cancer each year!

Whenever I *really* need to know about a topic, I still write a book about it, thus subsidizing my curiosity. My curios are *Words in Our Pockets: The Feminist Writers Guild Handbook on How to Gain Power, Get Published and Get Paid* (now pirated by Rudolph Steiner Publishers, of all people!, but I still have a case of the magnificent hardback edition if you want one); *ELSA: I Come with My Songs*, the story of Elsa Gidlow (1898–1987), the poet-warrior with whom I fell in love; *A Lesbian Love Advisor* (my "best seller," which in the USA is any book selling more than 50,000 copies); and my most controversial book, the one which every feminist publisher and even a printer rejected, *Lesbian Polyfidelity: How to Keep Nonmonogamy Safe, Sane, Honest, and Laughing, You Rogue!*

Thus I lived simply, in great abundance. After all, I still had another federal grant. This time it was in the form of USDA food stamps, which enabled me to fearlessly pursue my art — and civil disobedience, as events dictated. I was in jail three times, and am pleased to say that after our massive arrests to protest the Diablo nuclear power plant, no nuclear power plant would ever be built in the USA again. Listen up, Prince George!

Finally, however, I was forced to drop my USDA largesse under the welfare "deforms" of Reaganomics. To continue to qualify, I would have had to sell my old house and rent a hovel, or have babies. Instead, by some act of grace, I got a part-time job managing the Zen Center Library and its then amazing collection of Soto silverfish. Because I earn but $10.50 an hour as "Library Director," I negotiated for free meals at ZC, and I can also take leftovers to my neighbors. Since ZC founded Green's Restaurant, one of the most famous in all of San Francisco's culinary crown, this is no small benefit. To write well, one must eat well — except for people like Isak Dinesen or Simone Weil, of course.

Running Zen Center's "Library of the Rising Sun" — which quite outruns me — provides a host of other benefits and challenges. In my life I have labored picking crops, in retail, in academia, for corporatocracy and bureaucracy, but *nothing* is like being a keeper of the sutras in a Zen Buddhocracy. The inside of my skull is shaved. The only library position left for me to attain would be librarian at the renowned Clown Conservatory, the one full-curriculum clown school in North America — Ringling Brothers and Clown College having recently been downsized. I am not at present a career Buddhist, i.e., on the priest track. Best for me to be a butterfly in the Zen Center pagoda.

But because I am utterly intoxicated with the Buddha Dharma, thereby breaking Buddhism's fifth cardinal precept of "Be not intoxicated…," I, per my habit, am making a book about the antics of this librarian as Dharma Wheel turns. A Revolving Librarian? My book's working title is *Laughing Buddha Maria, Lumine Us, Good Faeries All*. It is a novel because, for me, Buddhism is more art than philosophy or religion. My main characters rise like archetypical absolutes, noble truths, only to shimmer and dissolve in numinous patterns flowing into realms now here, nowhere. But you may not see *LBM* for awhile because she insists imprinting on hemp paper to save trees. She says the best books remain in trees. *Laughing Buddha Maria* wants to light up as a $1 e-book too. More anon.

Meantide, for any of you who also work in a church library, I will send you my one-page manifesta that has survived four years in the Zen Center Library. It was posted on the door after censorious outbursts by those whom I call "the lost priests." As my practice leader reminded me at my first brush with these unenlightened, "A monastery is just like the real world, only more so." The magnanimous gain in magnanimity, and the pusillanimous usually remain so. Email me at Bookleggerpubl@aol.com for "Freedom of Spiritual Inquiry: Zen Center Library Staff Statement."

Luckily, the Zennas and Taoist eccentrics at Zen Center hold a lovely ceremony each full moon. Our outburst of Buddeo-paganism is a special time for us *Homo-not-*

so-sapiens— a chance to engage in self-evaluation and to mark our sincere intention to let go and compost any "ancient, twisted karma, born of greed, hate, and delusion." We are thus emboldened to set our burdens down in order to renew and nourish the lovely pursuits of clarity and kindness, both always on the alert for useful compost. As I await the full moon to once again reset my yin-yang compass and regroup my moral — and especially my mortal — bearings, why not review, renew and set forth my Revolting Librarian Vows here, for all to play with? Despite the lack of fashion in making vows (or laments), I hereby commit to practice the following seven vows in honor of Revolting Librarians in All Realms, All Generations.

Revolting Librarian, Awaken

1. Each one teach one. Each protégée become a mentor. Each mentor become a dare-devil's apprentice.
2. Be cyber-skeptic, while art-directed. Reward analog, anomaly, and high concept, high touch, low-cost anything. (Example: Install non-binary software in "Bubbleator" format. No learning curve! No wait for tech support! No patch or virus ever! No worrisome private property contracts! Crashes and pops, sure, but this is bubble magick!)
3. Remember, integrity needs no masters. Don't wait for leaders; do it alone, together.
4. People are more important than paper or pixels. But if patrons run on for more than twenty minutes, stay in present tense and put 'em to work.
5. Boycott conglomerate media, which manhandle the news we can use. Be a free distribution depot for revolving indys such as <http://www.war-times.org>, <http://www.jimhightower.com>, and the Buddhist Peace Fellowship at <http://-www.bpf.org>. For the growing list of indys to love and to feed the body politic, see *Utne Reader*, November–December 2001:78 <http://www.utne.com/globalization>.
6. Let the critics criticize and the players play.
7. What if the hokey-pokey *is* what it's all about?

May you, Revolting Librarian, select and reject all data/dada with the utmost awareness, knowing, that when organized, such information has life and must be cared for. Allow information to blend with experience to become knowledge, and knowledge to transcend into wisdoms ... quite beyond these words.

Please join our revolutions whenever you can. Especially, go out and make some of your own! May a mighty secure server be watching your back.

with L & K,

Celeste West
San Francisco, Summer 2002

1000 Blossoms of Gratitude to my colleagues who vetted "Revolting Librarians Rides Again" with their love & vigor: Darlene Cohen, Jocelyn Cohen, Judy Hadley, Elizabeth Katz, Jamie McGrath, and Bill Redican

*For a list of my books, broadsides, notions & novelties (including *RL #1*, signed!), contact Booklegger Publishing, Box 460654, San Francisco 94146 (415–642–7569). Bookleggerpubl@aol.com. You'll be glad you did.

I. Still Revolting After All These Years: Words from the Original Contributors

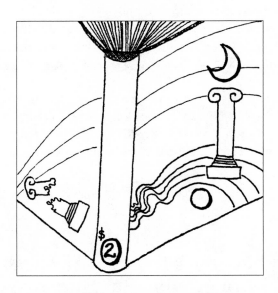

saplings sprout, leaves fall
birds build nests in the great trees—
does the forest change?
—Kathleen Kern

The following pieces are newly written by contributors to the original 1972 *Revolting Librarians* (those contributions are specified in the headings).

Elizabeth Katz, co-editor of *Revolting Librarians*

I remember the process of working on the original book with Celeste very fondly, but I'm not sure I have much more to say about it. I think the book itself pretty much describes the process.

As for my time since then, I switched from library work to legal work in 1978. I was the first legal assistant hired by the San Francisco City Attorney's Office and started work just days after the Moscone-Milk assassinations. I was very fortunate in being given the opportunity to specialize in legal research and writing rather than in litigation, and in working with an attorney who encouraged me to work at a level usually reserved for attorneys.

I also taught legal research and writing for the paralegal program at San Francisco State, where I had completed my own training.

I became involved in AIDS work early on, first as an emotional support person for Shanti, then as a compassionate touch volunteer for Visiting Nurses and Hospice and the AIDS ward at San Francisco General Hospital. This work led me to connect with my Jewish heritage and to begin to study and practice Judaism.

In 1990, I moved to Portland, Oregon. Seven and a half years ago, I met the woman I'd been looking for all my life. We recently registered as domestic partners and bought a condominium on the shores of Lake Oswego, about 10 miles south of Portland.

I'm semi-retired now, but I'm working and volunteering in libraries again. In 1998, I set up a library and library service for inmates in the then new Washington County Jail. It was a really wonderful experience and one that gave me an opportunity to put many of the ideas set forth in *Revolting Librarians* into practice.

Marilyn Gell Mason, author of "The Passing of the Unicorn, A Fable" (as Marilyn Gell)

It's hard to believe that it's been 30 years. My submission to *Revolting Librarians* was my first publication and still holds a special place in my heart and on my bookshelf. It's also hard to imagine what could possibly be considered radical these days given the vast changes that have taken place and are continuing to take place in libraries.

Since 1972, I have had the opportunity to contribute to the profession and the people we serve in many different ways. In 1979, I was the Director of the first White House Conference on Library and Information Services. Since then I have been director of two major urban libraries: Cleveland and Atlanta-Fulton. Although my article in *Revolting Librarians* was my first publication, it was not my last. I have written several books and many articles. Occasionally someone even tells me that one of them has made a difference. I've had the great good fortune to work with outstanding colleagues in professional associates and through service on the boards of OCLC, the Council on Library and Information Resources, and the National Commission on Libraries and Information Services.

After retiring as the director of the Cleveland Public Library in 1999 to join my husband in Tallahassee, I have served on a National Academies Committee to study the knotty group of issues involving children, the Internet, and sexually explicit material. I also serve as the chair of the library advisory board for my local public library in Leon County, Florida.

Most recently, the Gates Foundation has awarded OCLC a grant to create a public access computing portal for libraries and other community organizations. I will be program director for this effort. It is an exciting opportunity to help public libraries take another step in the continuing evolution of service to the public.

I love my life. There is nothing better than to be with people you love and do work you think is important.

Art Plotnik, author of "The Liberation of Sweet Library Lips"

I've now looked at my 1972 *RL* piece about the NO SILENCE sign. Some of what I said about library noise being cool still rings true; some of it seems like hippie posturing to impress flower babes.

I visited my regional library yesterday just to check the noise level and how I felt about it. I liked the steady, moderate level of kids chatting, the slamming of books and video cassette cases at the checkouts, keyboards clacking, copiers pumping out lousy copies, reference librarians wording up, and so on.

I'm less comfortable in stone silence, and I'm bugged by irregular disruptive sounds like dorky laughter. But we never believed libraries should be video arcades. The real impetus for the NO SILENCE sign was to put a dent in the shushing-librarian stereotype — which for one brief shining moment we seemed to do. Silences being imposed on libraries lately have less to do with sound than with content and privacy rights, and are much scarier.

Sanford Berman, author of "Libraries to the People!"

Thirty years ago I ranted mainly about narrow, unresponsive collection policies and unhelpful, inadequate cataloging of library resources. How much have those sorry situations changed in the meantime? These two recent homilies update the selection and access scenes:

Libraries "Dumbing Down?"

Psychologists can maybe explain *why*, but there's no doubt about the *what*: library administrators and "leaders" are increasingly gripped by—in Jim Danky's words—"adoration of the mainstream, the corporate mainstream." They readily embrace such "business values" and practices as making money, downsizing, outsourcing, stealthy decision-making, contempt for individuality and dissent, a "we-know-what's-better-for-you-than-you-do" attitude toward the public, and product-merchandising that emphasizes celebrity, faddishness, and pure image.

Too many of today's library managers really wanna be CEOs. Too many book selectors really wanna be Borders or Barnes & Noble superstore buyers. Too many have forgotten — if they ever knew — the essential public library ethos and mission: To freely provide materials and information in a variety of formats, representing widely divergent opinions, experiences, and perspectives — and to do so in a noncommercial, "neutral" environment for the entertainment, enlightenment, and both intellectual and spiritual growth of the whole population, unlimited by age, income, sex, disability, ethnicity, or occupation. The public library, unlike the bottom-line-driven superstore or corporate media, is precisely where citizens should expect to find challenging, vital, unusual, and unorthodox books, magazines, videos, and CDs, works both old and new that may never make "bestseller" lists, but nonetheless satisfy human cravings for knowledge and excitement and beauty.

The bizness-oriented wannabes now dominating many libraries don't agonize much over knowledge, excitement, and beauty. They demand ever-higher circulation numbers to impress their funders and emulate their corporate models. They passionately embrace digitization — of nearly everything — as the irrepressible wave of the future, even if that means the severe reduction or possible elimination of traditional print and AV resources, as well as the diminution of the library as a place, a physical space to gather, talk, browse, read, hear, and think. Perhaps suffering from a deep-seated inferiority complex, they fervently welcome and uncritically promote every piece of fluff or drive their commercial mentors lay on them. Having abandoned the long-touted objective to be the "people's university" and a partner in "lifelong learning," the wannabes are now managing institutions where the most intellectually and spiritually challenging materials available to library users may soon be artificially-hyped "blockbusters" and the collected works of Martha Stewart, attractively displayed alongside the expanding banks and towers of buzzing computers.

Think this is a fevered, delusional rant? Well:

- Children's book selectors have been told not to bother examining the publisher's review copies because everything necessary to place orders is already online. No need to look at the books.

- Subscriptions to alternative review media like *MultiCultural Review, Counterpoise, Small Press Review,* and *Women's Review of Books*— the gateways to vast treasures of human activity and ideas— are either never placed, scaled back, or totally dropped. After all, who needs more than Baker & Taylor's online "best lists"?

- Potentially valuable government documents are not added to collections because cataloging staff has been cut.

- Libraries order hundreds of copies of conglomerate-produced "best sellers" that within six to eight months will be sold for 25¢ apiece in the used bookstore. Worse, mega-copies may be ordered of titles that haven't even been published yet — and occasionally haven't been *written* yet! Why? Because Random House or Simon & Schuster announced that it will spend Big Bucks on hyping the new Grisham or Mary Higgins Clark novel or celebrity memoir. Quality, relevance, accuracy, style? None of that's as important as sales and hype.

- One director wannabe, convinced that his system was subscribing to far more journals than other comparably-sized operations, did not regard this excellence as something to be proud of, but rather decided — unilaterally — to flatten the periodical collection by extracting some $80,000 from the magazine budget, these "savings" to be expended on DVDs, more e-resources, and other "popular" (i.e., circ-inflating) materials. Some 1,120 current periodical subscriptions were slated for cancellation, about 340 or those *not* being available online and another 170 not received by a neighboring metro-area library. Further, standard professional and review titles like *Library Journal, Booklist, Choice,* and *PW* were to be restricted to a staff library, no longer cited in the catalog nor accessible to ordinary readers and library school students. Among the axed items are such business, cultural, scientific, and political staples— as well as stimulating out-of-the-mainstream mags— as *Science, New Scientist, Lancet, Advertising Age, Human Events, Spotlight, Z Magazine, Monthly Review, Index on Censorship, American Economic Review, Dollars & Sense, U.S. Banker, Journal of Business, African Arts, Rock & Rap Confidential, Big Beautiful Woman* (but not *Glamour* or *Cosmopolitan*), *Off Our Backs, Film Quarterly, Public Art Review, Yale Review, American Journal of Public Health, Journal of American Indian Education, Labor's Heritage,* and *Playboy.*

- An ongoing epidemic of wanton, mindless weeding often consigns worthwhile, frequently unique items to the dumpster, remote storage, or used bookstore.

Common reasons: they lost their dust jackets, appear slightly tattered or dog-eared, or — worst of all defects — they haven't circulated for the past four to five months. (For more on this biblio-wipeout, see "The Weeding Epidemic in American Libraries," *The U*N*A*B*A*S*H*E*D Librarian* 118: 17, and my "'Inside' Censorship," *Sanford Berman Website*: <http://web.library.uiuc.edu/ahx/ead/ala/9701040a/berman/intro.html>.)

- Pervasive self-censorship effectively excludes whole genres — like comics, zines, and small press fiction and poetry — plus multitudes of labor, ethnic, free thought, erotic, and radical titles from library shelves. (For details on this underreported phenomenon, see James P. Danky, "Libraries: They Would Have Been A Good Idea," in *Alternative Library Literature, 1996/1997* (Jefferson, N.C.: McFarland, 1998): 3–6; "Self-Censorship: Librarianship's 'Dirty Little Secret,'" *U*N*A*B*A*S*H*E*D Librarian* 119: 23–24; and "'Inside' Censorship.")

So what's the remedy for this "dumbing down" malaise? Not easy, but library users and frontline staff must resist the degradation and warping of America's once-premier democratic institution. And it would be helpful if the wannabes underwent Reparative Therapy. Or submitted job applications to Wal-Mart.

(Reprinted with permission from *NewBreed Librarian* <http://www.newbreed-librarian.org>, June 2001.)

Why Catalog?

Issues of cataloging inadequacy and reform can't be meaningfully addressed in a vacuum. So I propose this credo or "mission" as context:

- Cataloging should identify and make accessible a library's resources — in all formats. That identification and access should be swift and painless. The language and structure of catalog entries should be familiar and comprehensible. And catalogers should recognize that they do what they do not to please bosses and not to mindlessly adhere to rules and protocols, but to serve their information desk colleagues and the public. That's who they're working for.

Given such a mission or function, which incidentally coincides nicely with Ranganathan's famous admonition to "save the time of the reader," how does today's reality stack up?

Libraries tend to trumpet how easily and helpfully their wares can be accessed. Some really seem to think that just because they have "push-de-button" online catalogs with keyword searching, everything is findable and the bib-records are invariably useful. Well, as I've argued and demonstrated in many writings (most recently, "Jackdaws Strut in Peacock's Feathers: the Sham of 'Standard Cataloging'," in the

June 1998 *Librarians At Liberty*, and "Good Luck, Folks! Finding Material on 'Those People' (And Their Concerns) in Library Catalogs," in the June 2000 *MultiCultural Review*), basic, national cataloging records–whether created at the Library of Congress or in the LC manner–provide too few subject and access points, seldom include searchable and clarifying notes, and continue to employ abbreviations and other bibliographic conventions (like slashes, dashes and brackets) that most people don't understand.

What's more, many topics are still not recognized by LC. (Try searching for CORPORATE WELFARE, PSEUDOSCIENCE, SECULAR HUMANISM, WORKING POOR PEOPLE, CYBERCULTURE, MANAGEMENT FADS, CONSPIRACY THEORIES, CULTURE WARS, ANTIRACISM, NATIVE AMERICAN HOLOCAUST (1492–1900), or CLASSISM.) Some subjects are rendered in such an arcane, unfamiliar form that almost no one would search for them that way (and too many libraries don't make necessary cross-references); as examples: ABNORMALITIES, HUMAN instead of BIRTH DEFECTS; CESTODA rather than TAPEWORMS; INTERVERTEBRAL DISK DISPLACEMENT for SLIPPED DISC; and, believe it or not–CANADA. TREATIES, ETC. 1992 OCT. 7 instead of NAFTA or NORTH AMERICAN FREE TRADE AGREEMENT.

Other topics are constructed in an indisputably biased or inaccurate fashion that may misinform or prejudice catalog users against either the materials or the subjects; for instance: MANPOWER, CRO-MAGNON MAN, and SWORDSMEN instead of the more inclusive HUMAN RESOURCES, CRO-MAGNONS, and SWORDFIGHTERS; GYPSIES rather than the self-preferred ethnonym ROMA; UNTOUCHABLES rather than the widely-accepted and nonpejorative DALITS; SIAMESE-TWINS for the medically-sanctioned and much more precise CONJOINED TWINS; and a distinct preference for Christianity in scores of religion-related forms.

A further actuality, perhaps spawned in part by increasingly reduced quality control in LC's Cataloging-in-Publication (CIP) program, is mistakes. Sometimes Big Ones. In classification and subject analysis. Like Chris Kreski's *Life Lessons from Xena, Warrior Princess: A Guide to Happiness, Success, and Body Armor* (Andrews McNeel, 1998), clearly denoted "a parody" on the cover, which got soberly classed in self-help psychology and assigned the single, misleading descriptor, SUCCESS–PSYCHOLOGICAL ASPECTS.

Why catalog in-house? Why catalog locally? And why not outsource the whole operation? Because critical, creative catalogers within individual systems are the last and only bulwarks against the often error-laden, access-limiting, and alienating records produced by giant, distant, and essentially unaccountable networks and vendors.

(Copyright 2000, *The U*N*A*B*A*S*H*E*D Librarian, the "How I Run My Library Good" letter,* P.O. Box 325, Mt. Kisco, NY 10549. Reprinted with permission from issue #116.)

Jana Varlejs, author of "Continuing It?"
(Associate Professor, Rutgers–The State University of New Jersey, School of Communication, Information and Library Studies)

Where Has All the Passion Gone? or, Time for Another Revolution?

Unlike the early days of the social responsibilities movement in librarianship, recent decades have seen more passion spent on narrowly defining what issues are germane to the profession than on promoting "progressive" causes. At least there are still a few people who are passionate about *something* pertinent to the social role of librarians and libraries! The American Library Association Council discussions never generate as much heat as when someone proposes a resolution that others see as irrelevant to libraries. Those crying "not relevant" bring greater sound and fury to the floor, and seem to prevail more often than did the young Turk librarians some thirty years ago, promoting such concerns as peace and information to the people. It is not difficult to find reasons for this shift, and I do not have any surprising insights to offer on this state of affairs. What I do want to argue, however, is that the dominant conservative, technocentric ethos among the profession has obscured many of the tenets espoused by the 1960s/1970s generation, and therefore more recent recruits to librarianship seldom confront the old social responsibility issues. This is regrettable, because many of those issues are still with us.

To be fair, lately I have detected signs of an incipient social consciousness among some of our students. An increasing number enter the MLIS program seeking an alternative career in the same spirit as many of my late 1960s cohorts. These students are less enchanted with technology, corporate glamour, and financial rewards than those who were entering classes just a few semesters ago. They want to make a difference in people's lives, and this is not just an aftereffect of 9/11. As students learn to look critically at library services in the places where they are users, employees, or interns, they see where changes need to be made. Staffs are still largely comprised of white, middle-aged, underpaid females, while the public is increasingly diverse in ethnicity, language, age, and information needs. There is actually less effort to discover and acquire materials appropriate for this changing clientele; rather, there is greater reliance on vendors and jobbers, resulting in homogeneous collections. Commendable programs to help users learn to use computers and electronic information systems are often undermined by librarians' overconfidence in their own knowledge and skills, coupled with underestimation of learners' abilities, especially if young or elderly. Despite a great deal of technological innovation and cooperative resource expansion, the human aspects of library services have not changed that much. Students observe poor interactions among staff and between staff and patrons. When asked what proportion of potential users are actually reached by a library in some way, no one seems to have a ready answer. It is clear that a small minority account for the bulk of library use, even though the percentage of the population that claims to use the library at some point during a year has increased dramatically over the decades. It is also clear that the poorest communities that need good library and information services the most are the least likely to have adequate funding.

These things are fairly obvious to students today, and I sense that there is a genuine desire to change them for the better. The barriers that stand in the way of effecting change are formidable, however. Among these are job security, current trends in library education, and socialization into the profession.

The current job market is tight, and that means that newly employed MLIS graduates are not going to be great risk takers. Most library administrators that I can think of have been in their positions for a long time, and are not likely to welcome activism at the grassroots level in their own back yards. Even if a recent graduate wanted to risk disturbing the landscape, she or he has received little preparation for an activist role. It is rare that they encounter real change agents as role models in their pre-professional exposure to librarianship. In their MLIS classes, they encounter, for the most part, professors whose academic personae project a dispassionate, neutral stance. It is the job of the scholar to question, to collect data, and to analyze. Most of my colleagues would eschew advocacy on behalf of underserved users or promotion of any particular philosophy of library service, and avoid discussion of librarians' political perspectives on how access to information is affected by socioeconomic factors. The role of professional associations in the lives of students and recent graduates can be powerful at the local level, where they are welcomed and invited to become involved, but it is hard for newer members to be appointed or elected to positions of influence. While it was easy for us in the 1960s and 1970s to get an American Library Association committee appointment, that is no longer true. Even if today's aspiring librarians get their foot in the door, where are the leaders who can set an example for potential activists and help them to navigate an organization's structural and political mazes? The new member is more likely to hear a measured, let-us-watch-out-for-our-best-interests talk, than revolutionary incitement.

The reason that I am focusing on students and recent graduates is because as an educator, I feel some responsibility for their readiness to contribute to the profession. Moreover, many of the "revolting librarians" of the 1960s/1970s were not long out of library school, and the "revolution" would not have happened without them. At Rutgers we do a good job of instilling a service orientation and user-centered approach to information work, but we are less successful in getting students fired up to campaign for "information to the people." My class on outreach services attracts very few, relative to the hordes who take the technology courses, although those who do take it are enthusiastic and some actually pursue careers in this specialty. There is no history of librarianship course, and there is very limited opportunity to introduce students to the recurring issues in the field or to permit them the luxury of in depth discussion of current hot topics such as how librarians' tenets are threatened in new ways in the digital age. For the most part, students graduate without enough exposure to the history and ideology of the field to form their own philosophy and develop confidence in their own judgment about what role the profession should play in society and how best to assert that role. The standard thirty-six credit program is too short, and our students are generally too harried and overloaded to take advantage of the extra opportunities that are provided. Most hold down jobs and have family responsibilities in addition to taking courses. Many have long commutes. Given all these factors, it is understandable that they are not out on the ramparts advocating services for New Jersey's migrant workers—yes, we still have them — or running teach-ins on the Middle East.

Still, I confess to a deep disappointment that the passions and activism of yesterday are so seldom reflected today. Perhaps this is sheer nostalgia, for there are many librarians who are not content with the status quo and are trying to reach out and do more to help the entire range of the population take advantage of what libraries and librarians have to offer. Perhaps the problem is that these efforts are individual, isolated, and unpublicized. There is no "movement," no ruckus at New Jersey Library Association, let alone American Library Association conferences, and no marches on Washington by busloads of librarians.

It is saddening to think about how few of us are still around of those who were involved as major or minor players (or groupies) in the early days of the conglomerate of Congress for Change and Social Responsibilities people. Some were driven out of the profession by conservative employers or communities, some chose careers where they thought they could make a greater difference, some just dropped out. But others became part of "the establishment" and actually have made a difference through their leadership in the American Library Association, major library institutions, and library education. It is high time for them to be challenged by the next wave of revolting librarians!

Judy Hadley, author of "Trials of a Paraprofessional"

There and Back Again

I did leave academic libraryland shortly after *RL* was published, but not without some anguish. Many years later, I still dreamed of answering scholarly reference questions, always certain I was the only one who knew where the introduction to *Beilstein's* was shelved. My contribution to *RL* had been received with a cool disdain by my colleagues (is it any wonder?), and I had decided it was time to move on. After a twenty-year tour of duty in the social service jungle, I woke up to find myself employed as a library assistant again in a fairly large, pulsing, electric public library.

Nothing quite prepared me for the shock of the new. Electrification eliminated the need to search for purloined catalog cards, the tussle over subject drawers and miraculously spelled the end of those legendary bleeding hangnails. This was the good news. The bad news was that it seemed that the software side of life was about to consume all of the library's hard copy resources. Lately, it appears that either/or arguments have somewhat subsided and that balance has begun to be struck. Now, however, I find the talk has turned to the imminent death of the library as an institution. An unholy movement to compete with retail style establishments for "customers" alarms and perplexes our staff. The fear that public service personnel will no longer be needed is mounting. Seniority is basically non-operative except for lay-offs and rehires. Experienced personnel can no longer expect automatic promotion to a supervisory level. Everyone must apply formally, and librarians now hold most management positions. The very existence of this entire system is subject to the limits of public funding, of course.

Automation has forever changed the face of library service. We reference people spend a good deal of our desk duty running Internet use violators to Earth, troubleshooting hardware and software problems, and instructing patrons at the public search terminals. Sophistication of computer program design has made it possible to search any topic a good deal more thoroughly, creating an imperative need for intensive one-on-one instruction. Advanced searching takes up at least 20% of our service time. That's only with regards to the collection; we also have to try to keep up with everything else. In order to polish our skills, study of Internet services, coupled with daily practice and applications, are mandatory. Service preparedness expectations have gone through the roof. Reference staff must continue to specialize, but need to be generalists, too.

Lots of other changes happened while I was away. Materials are less often archived than removed to make way for the fresh and new. Book distributors have pre-selected the majority of the items in our collection, with considerable impact on its shape. These jobbers have eliminated many of the tasks that library workers performed in the past. A movement is afoot to forego as much of the "detail" work as possible, some of which work supports the very foundations of information organization and retrieval that used to define a library's mission statement. Part of this sentiment can be linked to the continuing search for a new library identity. Our chignons have been shorn (I know I no longer wear one) in favor of no one knows exactly what. It's a profile in transition. The majority of staff is still white and female. The good news today is that the female majority extends to management staff as well. I also notice that I am one of the only persons here who still uses a pencil, a habit hard to break after being threatened with death for using pen in my previous library life.

Volunteer labor plays a larger role in our workforce. A cadre of volunteers now complete duties which used to be performed by paraprofessionals: simple mending, labelmaking, clerical support, and helping with children's homework.

The library has discovered the merits of applying customer service techniques to public contacts. Some of these efforts have produced surprising results, such as hefty increases in visitor and circulation statistics. So hefty, in fact, that the library cannot easily absorb the financial costs of this bonanza. The human stress outcomes have yet to be completely determined.

So, what's new with paraprofessionals in particular? The lines between classifications of all unionized staff have blurred a good deal in the past few years. Paras, mainly "library assistants" (LA), have remarkably similar job descriptions to professional staff for considerably less money. Our duties may be parallel, for limited periods, to those of children's librarians, reference librarians, or even supervisory staff. Tasks may include, but are not limited to, storytelling, collection development, and temporary management. Candidates for library assistant jobs can be bona fide degreed librarians-in-waiting for professional positions to open up, clerks, or pages who have passed the LA test to work as subs. You just never know. And, although you cannot tell the players without a program, in terms of the end result, the difference may be as much as $5.00 an hour in pay. Relations are much more relaxed between paras and professionals than I remember, except cross-departmentally. There are the usual tensions, but they stem mostly from the wrestling of the medieval versus the contemporaneous mind. Both make their good points. Every employee wants to be a reference person whether they're trained for it or not. Several people attend library school online and work full-time. Paraprofessionals still make up the majority of library workers.

In the past, full-time employment was the norm; now it is no longer a given. Part-time employees comprise a significant percentage of this workplace. 40-hours-per-week positions are basically viewed as promotional. Supplementing employment has become usual for those who work less than 40 hours. Some employees work only as substitutes. This means they have taken their place on the bottom rung of the organizational ladder without representation, benefits, or job security.

Currently it happens to be a particularly scary time for all of us public servants, but then it's always been a bit of a taffy pull. We've entered the time of famine after much feasting, so I've come up with a few survival suggestions for paraprofessionals:

- Develop a formal mentoring program for new and old hires to insure success and continued achievement. This program could be developed in conjunction with any evaluation process already in place. Although we are all expected to be generalists, we could learn more about sub-specialties with expert tutoring.

- Lobby for more pay in exchange for more responsibilities at all classification levels. Make your union more perfect. If you don't have one, start one.

- Use caution in asking volunteers to do our chores. They should be used for jobs that are truly outside our job descriptions or time commitments. Volunteers should not be used to perform duties that we just don't want to do.

- Support and enhance any efforts to increase diversity in staffing, including people with disabilities.

- Design and promote our own professional organization and standards. It's great if we get recognition from library professionals. We welcome their support and return it in kind, but we can't wait around for that to happen. There's a lot to be done for ourselves, and we can bestow our own awards.

- Finally, be actively involved in the discussion of what a library is. Digital technocrats have been calling the tune far too long. We need to be part of the reconstruction, not the deconstruction of its identity.

Elspeth Pope (on behalf of Jim Holly, author of "Tribal Processes")

In 1972, when Jim wrote "Tribal Processes," The Evergreen State College had just admitted its first class, joining Sangamon State, Governors State, and others in major curriculum innovation. It still survives with its basic principles intact. There are still no departments (only programs), no ranks (only faculty, staff or student), no tenure (only evaluation), and no letter grades. One major dereliction, however, took place. It has been almost 30 years since Jim Holly was fired as founding Dean of The Evergreen State College Library. "First hired, first fired," he would answer when asked. His dream of what an academic library should be and the president's goal of building a mini–Harvard University library were far from compatible. However, the three years he spent putting his philosophy into practice were sufficient because the library still reflects the main goal he had — of making the library an integral part of the whole educational experience, not just a warehouse for books. Evergreen librarians are faculty in the true meaning of the word. Every three years a reference librarian has to rotate into a program and teach with that team for three quarters. At the same time, a faculty member rotates into the library, learning how to help students and colleagues find the best sources of information, in all forms and in all places. That faculty clamor to experience library service attests to the acceptance of this experience by all.

Back to Jim. What do you do when you are 58, out of a job, and wish to stay in a small town? You follow another dream and open a wine, cheese and fine coffee store, offering only those items which originate in Washington State. Of course there was a bookcase filled with books about wine; history, growing and what to serve with what food was an important focus. The shop was called The Asterisk* & Cheese Library. It was supposed to be called the Wine & Cheese Library but the state did not permit any alcoholic term in a store's name, so in true library censorship tradition, the censored word was replaced by a series of asterisks. Two years later, when Jim turned 60 and began drawing his army pension, he turned the store over to his younger son and started off on his journey of doing all the things he had put off doing until later, as many of us do.

Peg, Jim's first wife, died in 1975. In 1983, I took early retirement from teaching in the University of South Carolina's library school, and we married and I moved to Olympia. I brought my small letterpress shop with me so Jim could finally indulge in his love of the book arts, particularly printing. We added a Vandercook press and over time we printed ephemera, broadsides, small books, and one very fine monograph. Jim wrote much of what we printed, mostly poetry as an antidote to the years of professional writing he did before. He also learned papermaking, binding, paper marbling, and box making to protect the fine press books he continued to collect.

Jim's appreciation for fine printing began much earlier when he was dean of the library at Macalester College. He became a good friend of Walter Hamady of The Perishable Press Ltd. fame and one of the first things he did as dean of the Evergreen College library was to set up a standing order with this press and other fine letter presses. After he left, this collection developed more slowly but a core of finely printed books was another of his lasting contributions. In the spring of 1995 the present dean of the library wrote Jim to tell him that they had moved this collection out of storage into a fine room and it had been named the James F. Holly Rare Book Collection. This collection now continues to grow, thanks to the support of the present library administration, the Friends of the Library, and many of the fine printing friends Jim made. Two years ago, a major gift was given to the collection by Martha Jane and Edward Zachert. This gift added a sizable collection of miniature books and monographs, primarily by women fine printers, both modern and historic. It makes the James F. Holly Room truly special.

In 1991, feeling his energy ebbing, he was told that he had a degenerative lung condition. They had no idea how quickly his lung capacity would hold up, but he did wonderfully until almost the last two months before he died on November 26, 1995. His goal was to reach 80 and die in his own home — another of his goals he reached.

Reva Basch, author of "Reflections of a 'Head' Librarian" (as Reva Landy)

Still "Heady" After All These Years

Revolting librarians: what a concept. In 1971, when I graduated from library school and fell into my first professional job, Berkeley was synonymous with revolution. Of course librarians were revolting; everybody else was, too. In our case, the revolution had an internal component as well. We were determined to bust the controlled, conservative image foisted on us by the media and perpetuated in library school and even by some of our colleagues.

That first job — starting and running a library in a small, private engineering technology college — and what I did, hoped to do, and had given up on doing there, was the subject of my contribution to the original *Revolting Librarians*. Rereading that essay is embarrassing yet validating. At 24, I knew everything. Engineers were the Other. Computers were soulless, scary, and depersonalizing; at Cal, I'd unhesitatingly chosen Children's Lit over Computerized Bibliographic Retrieval.

Oh, but I loved the autonomy of being my own boss. I still do. In fact, that first job laid down the dominant themes — technology, solo practice and entrepreneurship — on which my subsequent career played some intriguing variations. My next two positions were in engineering libraries, too — one large operation with two branches, followed by another small, one-person startup. I learned that engineers were not (all) alien life forms. Reader, I married one — one after another, in fact. I also discovered a taste for techie talk and, when Dialog came along, a bent for Boolean logic, both of which I'd successfully avoided during my Eng Lit undergrad years and my sojourn in South Hall. Talk about empowerment. Online searching was like mudwrestling with the machine, going one-on-one with the ones and zeros. My college protest generation had demonized computers, making punch cards a symbol of batch-processed humanity: "Do not fold, spindle or mutilate — me." By the late '70s, information scientists and practitioners had transformed the "impersonal and dehumanizing" technology into yet another tool for doing what we'd always done — gathering, organizing and disseminating knowledge to our patrons and clients.

We'd never called them "clients" in library school. In fact, some of my instructors disdained special libraries, as if plying our trade on behalf of corporate interests was a form of prostitution. If that was the case, then Information on Demand, which turned out to be my dream employer, was probably their worst nightmare. IOD would take on just about any research project, as long as it was legal, seemed doable and the client was willing to pay. The company, and the concept, had plenty of detractors — revolted librarians, aghast at the prospect of charging for information that they nobly gave away for free. It wasn't the information we were charging for, it was our expertise in finding, evaluating, and analyzing that information in a manner more timely and complete than our clients could do themselves. IOD's research staff — five or six black-belt lapsed librarians — took on projects far more complex than any public or academic reference desk was equipped to handle. Even corporate libraries, used to providing their own in-depth research for management and R&D, hired us for projects that fell outside their core competencies, overtaxed their staff, or that required a shield of anonymity or an impartial investigative approach.

Sue Rugge, IOD's founder, was the quintessential revolting librarian. She worked in conventional library settings for years before launching her own business, although she'd never received her high school diploma, let alone earned an MLS. Sue was not an online searcher, but her telephone research was unparalleled; I sat right outside her office and could eavesdrop on her calls. In addition, Sue possessed two crucial qualities that many librarians today still lack — an unerring marketing sense, and a remarkable ability to relate and respond to people.

At IOD, the technological and the entrepreneurial threads came together. I honed my multitasking skills by juggling reference interviews, budget negotiations and online and manual research, and tracking dozens of disparate research projects in various stages of completion. Phone calls, books, periodicals, databases — we'd query whatever source, in whatever format, it took to fill our clients' research needs. When I left work in the evening, my mind was a blur of fascinating factoids, insights, and conversations. I loved that job. It was a turning point for me. I could never go back to working in a traditional library.

I did, however, remain a wage slave for a couple of years after I left IOD, lured to the vendor side by obscene amounts of money (way before the dot-com years) and the promise of stock options. There I learned technical writing, user interface design, and how to communicate, in a rudimentary fashion, with programmers. But research still called, as did actual clients who'd tracked me down from IOD.

I considered myself an unlikely entrepreneur. I was risk-averse, and hated marketing. However, I knew by this point that I had little tolerance for administrivia and even less for authority. With a guaranteed flow of subcontract work from Sue — who by this time had sold IOD and started another independent research company — and generous support on the domestic front, I launched my own business full-time in 1988.

That venture has morphed, over the years, from providing online research via Dialog, Nexis and Dow Jones — and eventually, of course, the Internet — to research plus writing and consulting, to the mélange of writing, editing, and speaking that I do today. I laid off my last research client several years ago. I suppose I don't qualify as a librarian anymore, strictly speaking, but I do follow the profession and relate to its concerns. It's from that perspective, looking back at my contribution to *Revolting Librarians* in 1972, that I'll offer three closing observations.

1. As a solo librarian, brand-new at my profession, I was aware that I was working in a vacuum. I had no opportunity to network with my colleagues. I barely knew where to buy library supplies. Email was born about the time *Revolting Librarians* was published. The Web was not even a gleam in Tim Berners-Lee's mind. Three decades later, the Internet has revolutionized our professional and personal lives. Think about what we could have done with it back then.

2. *Revolting Librarians* was born in part to mess with standard preconceptions about what libraries and librarians were supposed to be — to combat our conventional image. More than thirty years down the road, we're still fighting that battle. Sites like *The Lipstick Librarian, NewBreed Librarian, Progressive Librarian, The Rogue Librarian, Renegade Librarian, Naked Librarians,*

Street Librarian, The Laughing Librarian, Warrior Librarian Weekly, Librarian Avengers, Bellydancing Librarian, Barbarian Librarian and *The [Body-]Modified Librarian,* wonderful as they are — as well as the sequel to *RL* that you're holding in your hands — demonstrate by their very existence that the need for such correction persists. Why, oh why? My theory is that the root of the problem is the word "librarian" itself. But that's a whole 'nother essay.

3. One last personal note: My contribution to the original *Revolting Librarians* was my first professional publication. Since then, I've written hundreds of articles, columns, books and portions of books, and edited a couple of dozen more. Research is grand fun, but writing is what I love most. Thank you, Katia and Jessamyn, for offering the close-parens to match the set that Celeste and Elizabeth opened for me thirty years ago.

Noel Peattie, author of "Sipapu: A Tunnel Between Two Worlds"

I'm proud of what I contributed many years ago, of my participation in other struggles, and of over 25 years of publishing *Sipapu*. I capped the whole achievement with *The Freedom to Lie* (Jefferson, N.C.: McFarland, 1989) with my co-author John C. Swan, dead now for many years of ALS. In subsequent years, I have been less involved with library issues and have been only an occasional visitor to ALA / CLA meetings. My last confrontation with library problems (now, mercifully out of date, but [even better!] not out of print!) was *Amy Rose,* a novel available from Regent Press in Oakland, California. It's a naughty, skeptical tale about the loves and lives of a couple of young librarians — one a widow, one a divorcée, whose adventures take them to China and back. Wanna know what it's all about? Read it and giggle. I have also published three poetry books with Regent Press and am working on a fourth; my principal study and concern is with contemporary American poetry.

Paul Axel-Lute, author of "Notes on a Utopian Information System" (as Paul Axel)

I must confess that I found this piece embarrassing enough to leave it off of my résumé for most of the last thirty years. Rereading it now, I still like most of the ideas. Some of the technological predictions seem to be coming true sooner than anticipated–though not, of course, in the centralized system that I envisioned. Most of the social and political ideas seem even remoter from reality than they did then.

II. LIBRARY SCHOOL IS REVOLTING

in the sunny brook
trout do not expect the bear —
how does one prepare?
—KATHLEEN KERN

Getting the Letters: Library School Redux

Moe Giust

In the twinkling of an eye, thirty years have passed since Volume I of *Revolting Librarians* emerged from the ad hoc, offset bed of Booklegger Press, scratched itself crudely, and wagged its sassy way through the mails into the hands of every library malcontent with eight sticky quarters to spare. Much has changed, and, of course, much has not. Eight quarters will not even buy you a serious cup of coffee any more in some places—but it's better coffee than it was, if it does.

Rereading the three original essays about library school, as I teeter on the brink of graduating from an equivalent program in 2002, is sobering but instructive. Some of the problems these writers encountered have indeed gone away, but not because library schools have changed, only because society has.

As C. Sumner Spalding explained to Steve Wolf about subject headings, the library world is seldom in the vanguard of social change. Bianca Guttag wrote about being hassled in library school for being a lesbian, and felt that she needed to go through the mummery of passing for straight in order to graduate. *That* nonsense is all over and done with. Rampant and unapologetic homophobia in library schools seems to be gone, if mine is typical. Bianca herself (if she was who I think she was; the pseudonym is not difficult to pierce) did yeoperson's work to drag the profession along not *too* far in the wake of social progress on that—once she had a job.

A job. There's the still-rotten core of the apple: that business about the relationship between jobs and staff stratification (see Judy Hadley's wailed "Trials of a Paraprofessional," in the original volume; not an iota of *that* has changed), and the meal-ticket pretensions of the master's degree. Eighty years after the *Williamson Reports*, the profession is still struggling with the knowledge that most library work can be learned better on the job than in a classroom, but scrambling nevertheless to reserve the jobs that offer a living wage and a fragment of professional respect for holders of the degree. In the years since the publication of volume I of *Revolting Librarians*, SLIS schools have contorted themselves into reinvented pretzels, changing names, curricula, and jargon to protect the illusion that the degree is valuable, up-to-date, and necessary.

Harleigh Kyson wrote, in the first *Revolting Librarians*, that "the MLS is about as useless as Confederate money;" but that part has changed. He wrote in a year when inflation was high and so was unemployment. At that time, students were being cynically lured into university programs that led nowhere in order to postpone their entry into an overcrowded job market. Nowadays, you can't get a job digging ditches behind the library without one. It does have functional utility now, which is why, after years of protesting that I thought they were about as useful as tits on a chair, I finally started one.

Harleigh went on that the MLS amounts to inflated, "spurious credentialing," peculiarly ridiculous when based on a program made up of courses that, for the most part, have "less content than the void of interstellar space." Having just come through this harrowing experience, I can confirm that thirty years later the content is still thin, to the point where I felt guilty for shoplifting graduate-level credit for the high school-level classes I was taking. The curriculum has shifted to become more techno-focused, but it is still the same steeplechase of pointless hurdles and busywork assignments. The most laborious challenge in most classes is the effort to keep a straight face, and to suppress a sneer during class discussions of the jargon-armored pap that passes for professional literature.

That, too, has changed. In 1972, Kyson congratulated the field of librarianship for not clogging the shelves with pseudo-scientific treatises. These days, the advent of information science journals provides the dispiriting spectacle of reinvented librarians making half-hearted attempts to spin a few misbegotten germs of common sense, tarted up with the tinsel of buzzwords, into a "publications" quadrant for the writer's curriculum vitae. Virtually none of it has the logical consistency of a soap bubble, and none of it has the charm. A key to its purely perfunctory ambitions can be noted in the popularity, for info science journals, of the APA style sheet, which cites authors by surname and first initial only. God forbid we should actually be able to *identify* the writers of this glop. It contains few ideas; when it does contain an idea, the writer invariably avoids taking responsibility for it, by casting the whole thing in the passive voice. "It has been found that..." "Keyword searches were preferred by..." "The study was designed to..." "Three subjects were recruited, in order to assure diversity."

The program I slogged through, actually one of the highly ranked ones, still offers a headless, legless, dying vestigial MLS, Siamese-twinned with an MIS program that absorbs all the new faculty lines, all the resources, and all the attention. It is a little bewildering, since the MIS program is the one that duplicates, with unimportant variations, the curricula offered in half a dozen adjacent faculties of the university. They'll give you graduate credit for mastering application software that will be obsolete before you finish your degree. It's the techno-flummery equivalent of a high school shop class, but with less pragmatic value. People major in this, and snap up the better-paying jobs.

Why did I, an experienced paraprofessional, enroll, then? I enrolled because when a job came open, at a sister institution, doing exactly what I do (better than they do it there, as I know from seeing their records in OCLC), I contacted the supervisor and asked him if he could keep my résumé from getting slushed by their HR department. "I do the same work here," I said, naming the high-prestige institution where I was working at the time, "but the ad says MLS, and I don't have one."

"If you don't have an MLS," he told me, "I'm not interested in your résumé."

Unable to move even sideways, crab-fashion, without the union card, I capitulated. Fifteen years of high-quality work and hard-won expertise in a demanding profession (and fairly fluent command of four foreign languages) could not get my foot in the door any longer. So be it. The bitterness came from the reflection that, once I have the damned degree, it's still my experience and the languages that are going to get me onto search and screening committees' short lists. The MLS only gets me past the Cerberus that winnows the pile of résumés in Human Resources.

Questioning this, however, is sacrilege. Whether in the hope of concealing from other educated people the watery substance behind an MLS or an MIS degree, or in compliance with some form of Stockholm Syndrome, it is considered a serious offense, after completing a professional degree in our field, to allude to its flyweight status as an academic credential. I don't think other people with real graduate degrees are fooled, but such are the pieties. I do want to land a job when I graduate, so I will follow the precedent of Anonymous and Bianca Guttag from the first volume, by offering this to the editors of *Revolting Librarians Redux* under a pseudonym.

I thought of Bride of Coatlique, because the three years I spent finishing the ugly program I'm just escaping from reminds me, rather, of the sacrifices made to the Mesoamerican goddess with a necklace of human hearts; but I think her brides ended up drowned in a deep well. I just want an academic librarianship in a Dilbert-like cubicle. So sign me

Moe Giust

ACCREDITATION: WHAT'S ALL THE FUSS?

A. Librarian, MLS

Reference Librarian, Assistant Professor of Library Science
Academic Library, Regional University

I'm a promising young librarian finishing my third year in a tenure-track position at a small university library. By any measure, I'm doing well. For two years running, I've received service awards from the university for both my dedication to students and my hours spent on non-library activities. I've developed good relationships with the teaching faculty and am much sought after for my bibliographic instruction abilities. In the larger world of the library profession, I'm already a committee chairperson in my state library association and will soon assume control of an ALA committee. I regularly publish reviews and articles in my state library journal and have even managed a peer-reviewed publication that was based on my capstone project from library school. I'm also a regular presenter at state and regional library conferences and have made contacts that will serve me well throughout my career. There's just one catch: officially, I'm not qualified for my job. Yes, I have a master's degree in library science, but I didn't attend an ALA-accredited program.

How did this happen? Was I in a rush when I applied to library schools, forgetting to check their accreditation status? Maybe I'm a thrill seeker, someone who always stands on the bus and never grabs a strap, even when turning a corner? Am I a rebel, always ignoring recommendations and deliberately choosing the unapproved stuff, like my non–ADA approved toothpaste that has no fluoride but 26 grams of sugar per serving? Was I too dumb for an accredited school? With a 3.7 GPA from my undergraduate career and a 2160 on the GRE, I don't think so—ask any of my friends and they'll say I'm smart, as will my mom and dad. So, why did I end up at an unaccredited school?

First, I made a bad assumption when I moved to my current state of residence. I came from a place where most state universities had a library program and thought that my new home in a major metropolitan area would follow that pattern. Wrong. When I felt settled enough to add graduate school into the mix of work and home, I found that there was no locally-based library program in the area.

Second, I had, and still have, a life. With a significant other and our shared menagerie settled in our new home, I was not about to spend months away in another state when I made the decision to get a library degree.

Third, I'm a people person. I didn't want to do an online degree program because I like to see people and engage in discussions. For all the wonders of chat rooms and other technologies, online classes are not for me.

Finally, I looked at a local university's program (in which I eventually enrolled) and felt that it would do a fine job of preparing me for the wonderful world of librarianship, despite the fact that it was not accredited. Though there's more I could say about the school, greater detail would make the school's identity obvious and political considerations prevent full disclosure, so let's call it Polytechnic University.

What did I learn at good ol' Poly U.? Well, based on my perusal of other library school course offerings, I took the same classes as students in an accredited program: reference, cataloging, professional ethics, information technologies, information psychology, collection management, administration, etc. As a bonus, I've found that the topics and techniques covered in these classes are occasionally applicable to my professional life. From my readings about the value of library school, it sounds like my experience is similar to the majority of library school graduates. How were my instructors? Most were excellent; a few were adequate. Again, I suspect the same could be said about instructors in any accredited program. Do I think that my school prepared me to be a good librarian? Absolutely. Of course, preparation is only part of the recipe for success. Perhaps it's just because I'm so gosh-darned special that, despite my inferior education, I'm managing to survive (or, if you believe my last rank-and-tenure review, I'm actually "outstanding"). No, I'm really not that special. Let's look at the jobs of my classmates, shall we?

Government documents librarian at a university library. Associate director for technical services for a large public library district. Collection development specialist for a large city school district. Director of a small suburban out-of-state public library. Access services librarian for a medical library. Associate director of a research organization. Independent information professionals. A veritable horde of public reference librarians and catalogers. One was the Web librarian at a large public library, but was just promoted to the assistant head of reference services. Must I go on?

It's not just me. My unaccredited classmates are also doing well and are poised for leadership roles across the state when our bosses retire in the next five to ten years. Could we be an anomalous cohort that would have succeeded regardless of where we went to school? Again, I don't think we're unique. Sure, we're a bright bunch, but no brighter than the folks with whom we work (well, maybe a little brighter than the folks who haven't been promoted as quickly). Like any other graduating class, we have some folks who haven't landed a professional job, but even with an accredited degree, these people would have a hard time.

So, what does this mean? Based on the success of its graduates, should the Poly U. library school join the august ranks of those with the ALA stamp of approval? After all, how else do you measure the success of an educational program if not by examining the products of said program? If going to an unaccredited school didn't prevent us from becoming good librarians, why should accreditation matter? I'll tell you why: the "ALA-accredited MLS" conspiracy. Take a look at most job ads and you'll see that little phrase heading the list of requirements.

What's the point of requiring an accredited MLS? Although this system may have originated to ensure that degreed professionals were hired for librarian positions, it's devolved into a union card that you must have if you want to get your foot in the door. Rather than ensure quality applicants, the current accreditation system ensures the continued dominance of existing library schools, stifling innovation and rewarding adherence to form over all else. (No, I'm not bitter.) The ALA Office for Accreditation website has a collection of frequently-asked questions that includes this one:

"Q: Why should I go to an accredited program?

A: Graduating from an ALA-accredited program provides greater flexibility in the types of libraries and jobs you can apply for and enhances your career mobility. Most employers require an ALA-accredited master's for most professional level positions and some states require an ALA-accredited degree to work as a professional librarian in public or school libraries. ALA accreditation indicates that the program has undergone a self-evaluation process, been reviewed by peers, and meets the Standards established by the American Library Association and Committee on Accreditation" [*Frequently Asked Questions* <http://www.ala.org/alaorg/oa/faq.html#q7>].

Though the latter part of the answer refers to "Standards" that would imply some sort of quality control, notice how the initial response is related to your marketability, not your ability. If accreditation really represented something other than a union card, then the first part of that answer should be, "You'll get a better education and be a better librarian if you graduate from an accredited program." After all, being a better librarian should be the reason why you go to library school in the first place. As long as the requirement for an "ALA-accredited MLS" is still the norm, a piece of paper will be privileged over a person's abilities.

(Side note: My quote would have been more persuasive if I hadn't included the answer's section on standards, selective quoting being perfectly normal in academe.

However, my unaccredited ethics told me that I should be fair and tell the whole story if I'm going to quote ALA. Would I have made the same decision based on an accredited education? Discuss amongst yourselves for 5 minutes.)

With the "ALA-accredited MLS" system in place, how did we unaccredited librarians get our jobs? Some of us work for libraries that dropped the "ALA-accredited" requirement long ago. Others made it very clear where we went to school, but were granted an exception to the "ALA-accredited" requirement based on the strength of our interviews and past job history. Still others have ignored the traditional library job market and are working in lucrative positions for organizations that don't care about accreditation status, but just want a skilled professional.

If Poly U. did a poorer job of preparing us for our careers than an accredited institution would have done, then why have we been so successful at what we do? Could it be that accreditation has no bearing on the success or failure of a program's graduates? If that's the case, then accreditation is failing at its central purpose of weeding out the good from the bad. Why is it still around, other than to reward the library schools that it keeps in power? I suspect it has something to do with the library profession's collective low self-esteem.

All good professions have some mechanism to ensure that the practitioners are qualified and this often involves an accrediting body. However, professionals in other fields (doctors, teachers, and accountants, to name a few) all have to pass some sort of certification process that measures the achievement of the individual. If librarians want to count themselves among the other professions, then why not institute a national certification exam that would separate the wheat from the chaff? Could it be that we're afraid we're not smart enough for such an exam? Instead of focusing on programs, why not have accreditation focus on people? After all, people go to librarians for help, not library schools.

The ALA is already talking about how to rethink professional education, but the discussion is stalled in task forces and committees and will likely go around in circles for years without making changes. One of the concerns is that the "prestige" of an ALA-accredited degree would be lost if we changed the current system. ALA could still be involved as the logical organization to administer this exam, so the "ALA-accredited" phrase could still exist, but attached to a person instead of a school. This doesn't mean that ALA shouldn't create standards for library education to serve as a guideline for library schools, but ALA's primary focus in accreditation would be to ensure the abilities of individual practitioners, improving both the quality and image of librarians at the same time.

If an individual exam is the way to go, we have a long time to wait before a change of such magnitude will take place (possibly for all eternity). In the meantime, my colleagues and I will continue to work hard and provide good service despite the absence of a central professional qualification. As I think about this, it's likely that we're going out of our way to prove we're worthy as a form of compensation for the non–"ALA-accredited" MLS. Call me crazy, call me a dreamer, but maybe if all librarians had to work this hard to prove their worth, accreditation wouldn't be an issue.

DYKES TO WATCH OUT FOR:
FOOD FOR THOUGHT

Alison Bechdel

WHY MO IS GOING TO LIBRARY SCHOOL

Alison Bechdel

To be perfectly honest, sending my character Mo to library school was not my idea. I was speaking at the University of Illinois at Urbana-Champaign a couple years ago, and met Christine Jenkins, who teaches there at the Graduate School of Library and Information Science. She said she had this great idea for Mo. I'd been intimating in the strip that Madwimmin, the feminist bookstore where she works, was struggling and perhaps not going to last much longer. Christine thought Mo's logical next career step should be to become a librarian. It sounded perfect to me at the time, but I didn't know how perfect until I learned more about what librarians do. Since I began this story line, I've been besieged by email from subversive librarians all over the country deluging me with information (URLs, books, dissertations! Help!) on just what that is.

WHAT I REALLY LEARNED IN LIBRARY SCHOOL

Karen Elliott

Creativity is prized only if it will get you future employment.
Working in teams is good. Autonomy is bad.
Never assist your classmates with homework assignments if you are not specifically told to work in groups.
Looking in two or three sources is not enough to sufficiently answer a reference question.
Trying at least two print sources, two websites, and perhaps a Dialog search is ideal.
Sucking up really does get you somewhere.
Libraries are never about politics.
Libraries are always about politics.

Taking a business administration approach to librarianship is to be desired.

All intelligent and talented librarians invariably wind up working in the private sector, as well they should.

If you feel like you're in an MBA program instead of an MLS program, it must be a good school.

"Librarian" might be a dirty word. Use "information professional" to be on the safe side.

If you don't want to learn programming or how to implement databases, you have no ambition.

If you don't want to go into administration, you have no ambition.

Reference librarians answer over 50% of reference questions incorrectly because they didn't go to *our* school.

All good reference librarians want to become information brokers or information consultants.

All good catalogers want to catalog Internet sources and nothing else. They should also be experts in SGML and metadata, otherwise they are not to be taken seriously.

Outsourcing the cataloging of all printed materials is a good idea.

Children's librarians are masochists. Nobody understands them and nobody wants to.

Anyone without an MLS who calls herself a librarian has delusions of grandeur.

Taking yourself and your chosen profession less than seriously is *verboten*.

Distinguish yourself only by scholastic achievements and not by personality traits.

Collection development is all about balancing budgets and dealing with vendors. No intellectual activity should be required.

Filtering the Internet is bad unless: a) it's the children's section, or b) your library board wants it.

While corporate librarianship is ideal, academic librarianship can also be acceptable if it is in an ARL institution and you are tenure-track faculty.

Political activism isn't allowed at work. Unless you win.

If you can't quote Ranganathan's five laws of library science verbatim, you suck.

Don't wonder (aloud) why the techies in your department aren't in computer science degree programs.

Don't expect any of your professors to have worked in an actual library any time in the past 20 years.

Don't expect any of your professors to have worked in an actual library any time *ever*.

(Reprinted with permission from *MSRRT Newsletter*, Spring 1999.)

What Library Schools Still Aren't Teaching Us

Jess Nevins

Library schools are good at educating future librarians and teaching them the technical skills they need to do their jobs. The teachers in library schools are for the most part well-educated, articulate, and highly-trained professionals who are very good at passing on the information, skills, and enthusiasm new librarians will need to help on their jobs. Library schools usually have current library literature as well as new technology, so that students in library school can learn about contemporary issues in librarianship and the proper use of modern technology. Students in library school are usually intelligent, well-educated, and enthusiastic about their chosen profession.

So why are so many librarians unprepared for the realities of the job when they leave library school? Why is the first day, and the first week, and the first month, so often a shock to new graduates?

There is a critical disconnection between the day-to-day realities of librarianship and what library schools teach students about the profession. Changes need to be made to library schools' curricula, and additional and different kinds of training need to be offered to library students. In this article I will describe some of the gaps in library schools' curricula and conclude with a hypothetical course incorporating these ideas.

Little Things

The first gap, what might be called Little Things, are those skills that library schools do not teach but which nonetheless are very useful, even essential, in the workplace.

Office Skills. More than any other, the one job that seems to provoke the cry, "They didn't teach us about this in library school!" is fixing photocopiers and removing paper jams. It is a dirty, tedious job for which no librarian is trained, but that most of us need to do on a daily basis.

Fixing broken photocopiers is only symbolic of a larger skill set that is not taught in library schools: general office skills, which includes things like using and fixing photocopiers, using fax machines and phone systems, fixing broken faucets and clogged toilets, and so on.

These are skills that are required in most libraries, to a greater or lesser degree; corporate librarians will not often be called upon to exhibit the janitorial skills necessary to fix a clogged toilet, while most public librarians will face this odious task at least once a year. Corporate librarians, conversely, will make far more use of fax machines than public librarians. Some librarians come to the profession from other jobs where they will have learned these skills, but many librarians do not.

Secondary Librarian Skills. Another skill set that is not taught in library school but librarians need to use every day might be called Secondary Librarian Skills. These include the use of various integrated library systems, such as DRA, SIRSI, Innovative Interfaces, and NOTIS, for tasks beyond simply finding books. Other related skills are the evaluation of websites and databases, the writing of pathfinders for websites and databases; performing reader's advisory tasks, preparing and executing programs for children, and performing collection development. These skills are not as important to librarians as learning how to do research or catalog books, but their regular and required performance does demand that librarians learn how to do them. Like Office Skills, Secondary Librarian Skills are often learned on the job, but librarians need to know them before they are hired.

Dress and Hygiene. Just mentioning these to librarians is almost guaranteed to cause anger and offense, as can be seen by the tone of the letters published in *American Libraries* in 2000 following Mark Herring's "And We Wonder About Our Image!" article. But, loath though many librarians are to admit it, the truth is that we are judged, at least initially, by our appearance, both in our personal lives and in our professional lives. Dress codes requiring a certain minimum level of appearance are a part of most jobs. The reason for this is simple: a professional appearance signifies competence and engenders trust. Well-dressed and well-presented people are trusted more than those who are not, and most professions acknowledge this and use it.

Librarianship seems to be an exception. We tend to think of this exception as a good thing, as we can dress comfortably and cheaply. However, the end result is that librarians often appear very unprofessionally, in clothing that is ill-fitting, apparently uncomfortable, stained, torn, or simply dull and dowdy. Librarians' hygiene is likewise too often lacking, with librarians sometimes badly in need of a shower, bath, or deodorant. Librarians too often have haircuts that are unflattering, if they regularly get their hair cut at all, and male librarians too often need either a shave or to have their mustache or beard trimmed.

The obvious objection to this claim is that our appearance doesn't impede our ability to do our jobs. However, it hinders our ability to be taken seriously as professionals by our patrons and by fellow professionals in librarianship and out. If librarians are to be given respect as degreed professionals, we must make the effort to appear as professional as possible. How we look, from clothes to hygiene, is a basic part of that.

BIG THINGS

A second set of skills which library schools do not usually teach librarians might be called Big Things. These are skills which are more important to librarians and which are used more often than the Little Things described above. A lack of training in Big Things can directly affect our job performance.

Sensitivity Training. Sensitivity training is an established part of the corporate landscape, and many library schools devote at least a nominal amount of time to ensuring that librarians treat all their colleagues and patrons in a respectful fashion. The sort of sensitivity training that is required in the course of a librarian's job, however, goes beyond a simple awareness of ethnic and religious differences. Librarians need to be trained to be sensitive to the particular needs of their patrons. Librarians working in public libraries in areas with African-American populations will inevitably discover that there is a demand for romance novels written by African-Americans for African-Americans, whether by E. Lynn Harris, Eric Jerome Dickey, Rochelle Alers, or from BET Books/Arabesque or Genesis Press. Librarians entering academic librarianship may receive a thorough grounding in the basics of research, but on taking a job in an academic library they will find that the college or university's strengths are in areas like business or law which require subject-specific knowledge. Corporate librarians often find themselves faced with specialized databases such as Bloomberg, Choices II, Datastream, Dow Interactive, Gartner Intraweb, and Multex Investor, few of which are available or taught in library schools outside of the rare business reference course. Library schools often do not teach this kind of specialized information, and librarians are forced to discover these situations for themselves and to educate themselves in how best to deal with them. This does not serve the patron or the librarian's employer well. Library schools need to teach librarians how to research their specific patrons' needs, how to be sensitive to them and how to anticipate them.

Teaching Teaching. One of the largest parts of any librarian's job is teaching. Librarians are constantly called upon to teach their patrons how to do things, whether it is using a card catalog, using a database for research, using web browsers, or using books for research. Academic librarians often teach courses, whether single-class bibliographic instruction sessions or semester-long reference courses. Teaching well is a skill that can be learned, but most library schools do not teach librarians how to teach. Most of us are forced to learn on the job, with the result that our patrons are not always given the best information in the best manner. This is unfortunate, since teaching is a basic skill of the profession and one that most of us are in need of learning.

Book Purchasing. Another essential part of a librarian's job is purchasing materials for their library or collection. Most librarians buy material at least in their area of specialty, if not for their entire library. Unfortunately, library schools do not teach librarians about this process, leaving librarians to learn on the job. Each library has its own acquisitions procedures, and a wide variety of vendors and middlemen are used in book buying. No library school could hope to teach any one best method, but there is no one best way to do research, either. Library schools teach librarians a variety of research methods and equip them with the skills to learn others. The acquisitions process is often similarly structured in most libraries. Library schools could show librarians a number of examples of purchasing procedures in libraries of every field, from public to corporate. In this way, librarians would receive a solid grounding in the procedures of purchasing and be better prepared when they become professionals. Also, librarians should be taught how to bargain hunt, so that they know, for example, which distributors can be directly approached and bought from, rather than using a middleman vendor.

Professional Writing. Writing articles is, admittedly, not nearly as important for public and special librarians as it is for academic librarians. However, at some point in their careers, most librarians will be called upon to professionally write articles or grants. Library schools do not usually teach this skill; rather, students in library schools are expected to write as students. There are several differences between writing for a class and writing for publication, from the intended audience to the prose style. Most librarians learn how to write for publication the hard way: through experimentation with their articles, and by following editors' suggestions after the first submission. Library schools would do their students a great favor by teaching students how to write as professionals. Similarly, book review writing is an essential skill for librarians, even for those in special and corporate libraries. Writing book reviews gives a librarian a better understanding of what makes a book good or bad as well as about the library and the needs of the patrons. Library students should be instructed in the basics of good reviewing.

Public Relations. Something that surprises many new librarians is just how much publicizing of their library they will do in the course of their job. Public relations and the publicizing of the library's role in the life of its patrons is an essential part of the librarian's job. Examples include a school librarian speaking to parents, a public librarian helping a reporter from a local paper, a corporate librarian touting the virtues of the library to the company's CEO or CFO, or an academic librarian speaking to teaching faculty. There are preferred methods for public relations and for presenting the librarians and the libraries in the best possible light. Library schools do not teach these methods, leaving librarians to fend for themselves. This learning process can be awkward and can lead to many missed opportunities as well as to occasional damaging missteps.

Managerial Skills. Any librarian who spends a sufficient amount of time in the profession will inevitably be promoted into a managerial role. Even entry-level librarians are often put in charge of pages, student workers, paraprofessionals, and non-faculty library staff. As librarians are promoted, they are often placed in charge of sections, departments, and perhaps entire libraries. With these promotions come a host of varied new tasks for librarians: training, budgeting, writing office procedure manuals, writing and performing job evaluations, and disciplining employees. These bureaucratic tasks are not simple, but they are a part of many librarians' jobs. Most library schools do not teach these skills; some doctoral programs do, but most librarians do not get a Ph.D. before they enter the field.

Interviewing Skills. Librarians spend a significant percentage of their time conducting interviews. Sometimes, the interviews are for jobs, and those interviewed are support staff or other librarians. More often, the interviews are reference interviews, and those interviewed are our patrons. Most librarians have their own stories about reference interviews gone horribly wrong and, conversely, reference interviews in which the librarian found what the patron wanted with great efficiency and a minimum of wasted time. Librarians perform these interviews on a daily basis. Determining what our patrons want is a basic part of our job. Interviews of all kinds must be done correctly; a mishandled reference interview can be a disaster. Librarians need to know how to lead an interview, regardless of type. Library schools do not currently teach librarians how to do this, leaving librarians to learn — or mislearn — interviewing on their own.

PARADIGM SHIFTS

The following three items are, for lack of a better phrase, paradigm shifts: necessary changes in the basic assumptions of library schools; most notably, the assumption that librarians should wait in their libraries for their patrons to come to them. A basic paradigm of librarianship is for librarians to be reactive instead of proactive in response to patrons. This paradigm needs revision, and the three items below would be a good start.

Outreach. The essential mission of libraries — to provide information to patrons — has not significantly changed in the past several decades, and presumably will not change in the coming decades. There will always be a need for information, and librarians will remain useful as information providers.

How non-librarians perceive this need is another matter. Public libraries suffer from annually decreasing floor traffic and circulation. Increasing numbers of corporations, hospitals, and medical colleges decide that they can more easily teach a lawyer or medical student librarian skills than the reverse. More and more money-strapped companies decide that they don't need a librarian and that their employees can figure out the library on their own. Increasing numbers of students labor under the delusion that accessing their schools' databases from their dorm rooms eliminates the need to do any research at the library. Teachers on all levels do not consult with their local public or school librarians when designing curricula and individual assignments; these same teachers often allow their students to use any source found on the Internet. Public libraries find it increasingly hard to get adequate funding from their towns or counties; many public librarians can recount the story of Carter County, Kentucky, whose citizens decided not to build their first library on the grounds that it was unnecessary and too expensive. Too many non-librarians believe, say, and write that librarianship primarily entails shelving books.

This does not mean the need for libraries and librarians has decreased. This means that we have not done a good job of informing their real or potential patrons about the need for libraries and librarians. Librarians have not adequately demonstrated to our patrons what libraries can do. We have not sold our patrons on libraries. There are several reasons for this; I tend towards the explanation that librarians, as a group, are usually bookish, introverted types, and this kind of salesmanship is quite unnatural for us. There is a simple solution to this problem: librarians must become salespeople. We must learn how to actively promote ourselves and our libraries to our patrons, our patron institutions, the corporations that employ us, our non-librarian colleagues, and to the disinterested public. We must convince them that libraries can occupy an essential position in their lives. The days in which non-librarians automatically assumed that libraries and librarians would always be there are gone. It is up to us to let non-librarians know that libraries and librarians are essential. This can be done by active publicity.

Needless to say, this concept is not taught in library school. The idea that we must market ourselves, that our position of corporate and academic privilege is no more, is an unwelcome one. A sea change is undertaking the profession, and if aggressive and positive action is not taken, we may well be rendered an expensive luxury in the minds of those who need us most, and who we need most.

Ways in which we can promote ourselves are relatively simple. Library school students could meet with the students and faculties of business schools and show them what librarians can do for them. Regular meetings with and presentations to our academic and corporate colleagues will provide librarians with "face exposure" in addition to giving librarians the opportunity to expound on the resources available in the library. Promotional and instructional sessions with teachers will let them know how much we can assist them and their students if they work with us. Asking instructors for opportunities to speak with students at every level of education will help drill into students' minds that a library is more than a database, and that librarians are there to help them. Librarians should make every effort to leave their workplaces and visit their patrons instead of waiting for the patrons to come to the library. Whenever possible, librarians should give interviews to school papers to promote their local school and public libraries. Until library schools make a point of teaching future librarians to do these things, these things will only happen intermittently, which is not enough.

Bridging the Digital Divide. Librarians more than any other profession are acquainted with this cliché. Many of us groan and roll our eyes when we hear this phrase. It, along with "the information superhighway," is one of the most overused phrases of the computer age. That does not mean it is meaningless; the most recent U.S. Census data showed that 143 million Americans, or 54% of the population, used the Internet, including 90% of children between the ages of 5 and 17, 75% of 14–17 year-olds, and 65% of 10–13 year-olds. These are all encouraging numbers, but this still leaves millions of Americans who do not use the Internet. Although there are those who have no use for computers or the Internet, there are still tens of millions of children, adults, and the elderly who have never used the Internet and are ignorant of its use. Many of these people will never learn how to use the Internet and will never learn how to use computers. Most of these have-nots live in economically disadvantaged areas where the schools and public libraries, if there are any, can only afford a few old computers, if that.

Children who have limited exposure to personal computers and the Internet find themselves at a marked social and academic disadvantage to their peers upon entering high school and college. They will, in turn, become adults who enter with the workforce less skilled than their competitors in a world in which computer literacy is an increasingly required skill. Students and adults who are not comfortable with computers and the Internet will not be as good at performing research or at doing basic tasks on the job. These adults will not have as much in common with their more computer-savvy peers. A lack of familiarity with computers and the Internet is by no means a death sentence for these people, but it is a definite disadvantage. The Internet and computer skills can be learned as adults, but children learn computer skills faster and more easily than adults do and retain them longer.

It can be argued that this is a widespread societal problem and so should be solved by society as a whole, rather than by librarians. While this is true, librarians are a part of society, and we need to take action instead of waiting for others to do so. More importantly, librarians are in a unique position to act on this problem. We are a part of most communities, from the very affluent to the very poor. We are highly skilled, computer-literate, and experienced in teaching and passing on these skills to others. We have access to the equipment needed to train the computer-illiterate. And, perhaps uniquely among professionals, we have the flexibility to fit this kind of instruction into our schedules.

There is no guarantee that the children and teenagers and elderly who we teach will become patrons of our libraries, or any libraries. Strictly speaking, it is not within a corporate or special librarian's purview to teach children and the elderly how to use the Internet. Teaching children how to use computers appears on the job descriptions of very few librarians. Nonetheless, the job needs to be done. Librarians have the means and the opportunity to do this; we simply need the will.

This is what library schools should be teaching. For most part, library schools are vocational, teaching students the skills necessary to learn their trade. Library schools should have higher ideals than that, and librarians need to live up to those ideals outside the library as well as inside it.

Keeping Up with the Times. Finally, there is the issue of how prepared newly graduated librarians are to work in a field undergoing a constant, if slow, evolution. Most library schools do at least an adequate job in training library students to use new technology, especially personal computers and electronic resources. Most library schools devote some attention to the fact that the role of the library and the job of the librarian have changed. Most recently degreed librarians know that the library workplace is significantly different from both the common stereotype and the library experience as remembered from childhood.

This isn't good enough. Librarianship has changed over the past two decades and continues to change. Some of these changes include the advent of personal computers, videocassettes, and compact discs; the continuing decrease in reading among both adults and children; the rise in the availability and use of the Internet; and the decrease in a shared sense of community among the public. Other significant issues are the increasing hours most people spend working instead of reading, the increasing demands placed on corporate workers leading to increased demands for information and longer hours spent at work, and the increase in available media outlets and the corresponding explosion of available information and entertainment. All of these things have had an impact on librarianship and will continue to do so. Many librarians like to think of libraries as unchanging bulwarks against the tides of change, places in which the pell-mell rush of life is abated. This may be so, but unless libraries and librarians learn to adapt to these changes they will become outmoded.

The problem is that, as mentioned above, libraries and librarianship tend to be reactive. Librarianship doesn't usually anticipate new developments. Even today, there are public and academic libraries without public Internet terminals or automated catalogs. Library schools still graduate librarians who see the Internet as a despised competitor rather than a complement to books. Many public librarians are still hostile towards genres despite their popularity with the public: mysteries, science fiction, fantasy, romance, Westerns, and Oprah's Book Club. Concomitant with this hostility is ignorance, among both public and academic librarians, of current trends in various literary fields. This is in spite of the fact that many of these librarians have the responsibility of purchasing books in these fields. These librarians get their knowledge of hot young writers and recent developments and fashions from a few trade journals, many of which are late in noticing, if they do at all, various publishing trends.

There are still librarians who ignore library media specialists and electronic resources librarians and choose not to use the technological resources available to them. There are still librarians whose professional reading is limited to *Library Journal* or *Publishers Weekly* instead of reading any computer technology journals or visiting any technology news websites. There are still librarians who make no effort to get new technology for their libraries or even know how to update the library's web pages (if the library has any). There are still librarians who hate amazon.com for entirely the wrong reasons. There are still public librarians who resist buying videos, books on tape, or sound recordings for their collections. There are still librarians who will not write grant proposals.

These librarians are not keeping up with the field, and that's bad for their libraries and for librarianship. Life is speeding up, and expectations from the public are different from what they once were. The public wants more from libraries than books. The public wants new technology and access to electronic resources. The public is savvy about these things. They go online and find out about new technology. They hear about good new writers or bands. They go to amazon.com and check the readers' reviews. They often know more about these things than the librarians do.

This is an intolerable state of affairs.

What library schools fail to teach librarians is something that most academics and non-librarian professionals learn early on: professional self-improvement is a necessity. This is true more than ever because of the changing shape of librarianship. When librarians don't keep up with current trends, they are slow to give the technology-savvy public what it wants. This can only hurt library attendance. Librarians are also resistant to many of the changes in the field. Librarians need to evolve as professionals across the course of their careers; a librarian who learns a set of skills and practices those skills only across several decades is not helping his or her patrons. Library schools must inculcate into their students that learning as a librarian is a lifetime process that does not end after receiving the diploma. The alternative, to stay trapped at a level of development and knowledge that becomes increasingly antiquated as time passes, will further doom the profession.

AN IDEAL COURSE

I've spent the preceding thousands of words detailing what library schools are doing wrong. The following is my attempt at describing how library schools can solve these problems.

The best and easiest solution would be one course, perhaps entitled Library Skills, that would incorporate my suggestions. It would begin with those items most easily taught and grasped — the office skills — and proceed through increasingly difficult topics until the final few classes, which would deal with the philosophical issues of the role of the librarian and the library. This course would ideally place a heavy emphasis on skills, with library students visiting a number of different types of libraries and seeing the day-to-day realities of the job while also speaking with working librarians, who could offer their opinions about the matters discussed in the course. The course might also have a short (one day or one week) internship at the students' preferred places of eventual employment. This would enable the students to see the distance between what they are taught in library school and what librarians actually do.

I love being a librarian. I love helping people, I like my colleagues, and I think our job is a valuable one. But the field needs help, and the place to begin solving these problems is in library school.

III. Sex, Drugs, and Will You Please Be Quiet: Our Revolting Jobs

patron in corner
looking at pornography —
maybe researcher
—Kathleen Kern

Labia Lumps, Chunky Discharge, and Other Things They Never Taught Me in Library School

Barbara Bourrier-LaCroix

What's so great about email reference? It is somewhat new, and libraries, notably public and academic, are jumping on the bandwagon, providing some sort of email reference services to their patrons. Some librarians pontificate about the joys of providing email reference services, including the ability to reach far-flung users, and the leisurely pace when the patron isn't standing there, expecting a quick answer. Big sigh. I've been doing it for a year now, so I beg your indulgence — allow me to rant about some of the pitfalls, especially when one is dealing with health information.

I work for a national women's health organization. The clearinghouse department (i.e. me) offers a health information service to Canadian women. You can contact us by telephone, using our toll-free number, or fill out an online form. We answer only general health information requests, or we will assist researchers and other women's activists and advocates in locating pertinent information in women's health and the Canadian women's health movement. Our staff (again, yours truly) will get back to users in three business days. For the most part, questions come to us via the online form. At first, traffic was slow — two or three questions a week. We now average about 15 a week, and I suspect the number will continue to grow. I catalogue the questions I receive into three principal categories: Health Promotion; Health Research; and Health Stupid. Health Promotion questions are those sent to us by women who are looking for information on a specific disease or condition, or want to know how to keep healthy. On the surface, these health promotion questions look easy; repackage some information from books, find some related articles on our website, look for credible information from other websites, or find a women's health organization in their community that provides direct service. There are a few wee little problems, though. First of all, you can't conduct an effective reference interview by email. Generally, I'm lucky if the user types more than a sentence or two, so I really don't know WHY they're looking for the information, or what they plan to do with it. Those that do type more than a few sentences tend to completely ignore the rules of spelling and grammar, and often fail to mention what it is they're actually looking for. I have seen so many different variations of the word 'endometriosis' I can never remember how it is actually supposed to be spelled. Requests for clarification are generally ignored. I run the real risk of sending too much information or not enough. Online reference services are not the same as face-to-face encounters, so there's no feedback available to me. Rarely someone will send me a thank you, but most times I don't even know if I helped or not. Let's face it, we all need some sort of validation at some point or another. And let's not forget that people think because they send you an email, you will answer RIGHT AWAY!

Health Research questions are by far the most fun, and naturally, the most rare. These questions usually involve searching for articles or published research on women's health — not the typical bio-medical research, but research that also looks at the social factors that affect women's health. We collect a great deal of documents from various Canadian and international women's health agencies— most of which wouldn't be acquired by traditional public or academic libraries. Like most librarians, I enjoy the thrill of putting an obscure research publication into someone's hands.

Then we have the Health Stupid questions, a.k.a. 'I-can't-believe-these-people-can-dress-themselves.' These are the ones that generally make me either a) laugh out loud, b) hurl obscenities at my monitor, c) push me into a dark mood as I despair about the stupidity of the human race, or d) all of the above. Naturally, these health information requests comprise the majority of the questions I deal with. We have quite clear disclaimers posted on our website, stating that we do not provide diagnoses, or opinions on women's states of health. Our users seem to ignore these facts. So disclaimers don't work because most Internet users wouldn't be able to locate their asses, even if provided with a detailed map. We all know that people rarely read web pages word by word — they scan the page, picking out individual words and sentences. Teaching information literacy is very hard when you don't have direct contact with your users.

But what really gets me down are the women who email me, giving me their lists of symptoms, asking for a diagnosis or just plain help. A question regarding labia lumps was by far my personal favorite, followed closely by the woman who went into excruciating detail about her vaginal discharge. Other frequent examples include being asked my opinions on what drugs women should take for their various maladies. Or what herbs will make them better. Some days I laugh off these requests, shaking my head at the folly of humankind. Some days I feel like creating a gene elimination squad that would remove these dumbasses from the general population. I have to constantly remind myself that for the most part, these women are scared; scared of talking to their doctor, because as women, we're told very early on that our health problems are just in our heads. Scared that there will be something wrong with them that will require hospitalization or treatments, and who will look after them? Scared because there is no doctor in their community who is accepting new patients. Scared that someone in their small community (Bumfuck Nowhere, Canada) will find out about their sexual activities. Scared of a health care system that seems to slowly be sliding towards a two-tiered system, where women will usually be at the bottom.

So what do I do? Well, I'm not a health professional. I'm a librarian. I do what all good librarians do. I refer them to the right sources of information, their family physicians, while trying to remain empathetic to their plight. Along with my co-workers, we put together Frequently Asked Questions for the website or write articles in our magazine on hot topics in women's health, or on just how to communicate effectively with your doctor. Maybe we can make a difference. And maybe, just maybe, I'll go a whole week without wanting to kill someone!

THE OTHER SIDE
OF A BALANCED COLLECTION

W. Beauchamp

In mid–January, I ran across an Associated Press article about a public library in North Carolina that was struggling with whether or not to add a Ku Klux Klan videotape to its collection. In the face of community outrage and statements of objection from the local NAACP chapter, library officials were considering the addition of the videotape because "it could provide a viewpoint not currently represented in the library's collection." Three days later they'd decided not to include it, citing poor technical quality and undocumented content as major factors in turning down the tape. The library director noted that it was a difficult decision: "It's our responsibility to be courageous, not to run away from the controversial, but to give you the information that you need."

The original *Revolting Librarians* urged us to "balance" our collections with "pro-racist, sexist, violence material" but to "push the other, the human-hearted." Reading over these lines, I sometimes feel like Alice through the looking glass. I work as the information specialist at a non-profit progressive research center that monitors and analyzes the U.S. political Right. We take a broad definition of right wing: everything from the right wing of the Republican party to neo–Nazi groups. Our library is one of the most comprehensive special collections of books, videos, periodicals and direct mail by, about and from right-wing organizations. A look through our file cabinets reveals folders stuffed with articles about the Promise Keepers, newsletters from anti-immigrant groups, and catalogues from publishing houses for the Christian Right. Periodicals? We've got everything from James Dobson's *Focus on the Family* to the World Church of the Creator's *The Struggle*. Issues of the newspaper published by the National Association for the Advancement of White People dating back to the early 1980s. Phyllis Schlafly's newsletter? You betcha. And all of her books, too, along with several editions of *The Turner Diaries*, the complete collection of Tim LaHaye's apocalyptic novels, and an entire shelf of videos about the gay agenda.

So the concept of "balancing" the collection does an abrupt about-face. We make room for books by our progressive colleagues, reports published by the National Gay & Lesbian Task Force or People for the American Way, and enough left-wing theory and history to keep us feeling somewhat stable. I quickly learned to catalogue books in batches according to subject, spending half the day working through a shelf of anti-choice books and then devoting a few hours in the afternoon to the pro-choice volumes. In the pile of subscription renewal forms for periodicals that discuss the left-wing bias in media, give information about the annual white power picnic, and encourage gay men to repent and reform, progressive magazines can easily get lost. But over time, balancing becomes crucial not just in terms of the physical collection, but for my own psyche as I make my way through materials that run counter to every one of my political ideals. I have dreams about Jim Bakker and Timothy McVeigh, and think to myself, "I should stop reading our periodicals on my lunch break." When I discover that Topps is producing a set of Enduring Freedom trading cards, including cards for weapons, military aircraft, Condoleezza Rice and John Ashcroft, my first thought is "We need those for the library!"

The point of this collection is to aid progressive researchers, journalists and activists in their work, with the basic premise that progressives should know what right-wing leaders and movements are arguing, and should understand the nuances of right-wing strategies, in order to effectively counter them. I try to keep this in mind when I am cataloging shelves of books promoting white supremacy and condemning queers. But it is not really my job to "push" the more human-hearted materials. Patrons who visit our library to do research are not here to read through books of left-wing political theory, but rather to thumb through histories of the Nazi movement, autobiographies of anti-abortion activists, and back issues of periodicals about the Communist threat. When I fill information requests, I don't even make an effort to include progressive materials, because ultimately those are not the resources that our collection is here to provide. Sometimes I have tried to think of "balance" in broader terms, not simply within the collection I maintain, but relating to libraries overall. For progressive people needing accurate information by and about the Right, our collection of right-wing materials balances that of other libraries which deal mostly with mainstream or left-wing views of the Right. In this broad view, our collection represents what is often underrepresented. I often feel as though my decisions on what to add, what to weed out, and what to renew are the polar opposite of my progressive colleagues. And yet, my purpose in managing this collection is, like that of any other librarian or information specialist, "to give you the information that you need."

I am more likely to struggle with whether to renew a subscription to a left-wing periodical (which, in general, would not strengthen our collection in terms of content that is congruent with the subject matter we maintain) than to add a videotape by a white supremacist organization (which would likely be purchased without question). We do not, as the library director from North Carolina said, "run away from the controversial" on the contrary, we run towards it. We surround ourselves with it, with the hope that in doing so, we will better understand how to counter it.

FAILURES IN NEO-CORPORATISM: A RANDOM WALK THROUGH A UNIVERSITY LIBRARY

Tracy Brennan

Although I've recently escaped from the corporate world to find peaceful refuge in libraries, I remain an unrepentant capitalist (sorry if that statement was unexpectedly revolting), and I embrace the belief that a lot of good can arise from applying a corporate philosophy to institutions not traditionally grounded in capitalistic principles—such as academic libraries.

What I don't embrace are the recent misguided attempts by libraries to reinvent themselves by selectively adopting retreads of worn-out corporate strategies. Process Re-engineering, Creative Realignment, Quality Circles, Peanut Clusters, Taffy Pulls— they've all emerged as the next new thing. Even when enthusiastically adopted by corporations, their results are moderate and they tend to fade away. But when half-heartedly launched within non-corporate institutions, they are assuredly doomed to fail.

I haven't had time to conduct an in-depth study of this phenomenon across a statistically significant cross-section of libraries, but I have paid very close attention to what's been happening at my workplace — and I'm comfortable enough with my nonscientific method of research to assume that the behaviors and results that I've observed are not atypical.

My present workplace — the library at a prestigious nationally-ranked university — has, for the past several years, been restructuring itself into something quite different: the library whose workers attend a lot of meetings to discuss what it means to be librarians at a prestigious nationally-ranked university. In order to effect this transition, we've engaged the services of several consultants (insert your favorite acerbic observation about consultants here), and sought to formalize the process of self-examination.

The details are messy and uninteresting, but basically the process involves a superabundance of flip charts (approximately 7.4 per FTE); the creation of a new Strategic Focus (and its misbegotten spawns Team Formation and Team Building); and a new institutional Vision, closely followed by the inevitable Mission Statement. I am not invoking hyperbole when I state that I've actually engaged in discussions of several hours' duration (or at least been present at — to say 'engaged in' would misrepresent my tenuous hold on consciousness during these events) concerning the misperceptions that may ensue if our mission were stated as "to facilitate users' information gathering" rather than "to identify and resolve users' information needs"— and this is only after the debate over whether the word "users" is better expressed by the phrase "community of library patrons." Of course, the more time we spend naming them, the less time we spend actually helping them; more than once I've had to ignore pleas for assistance when rushing away from the reference desk — on my way to yet another meeting to talk about how to provide better reference assistance.

Notwithstanding the frequent logjams they create, these strategic exercises are informed by compellingly valid organization theory. Initially, we're invigorated by the notion of participatory management from a newly empowered workforce. It can even be thrilling to recognize the underlying anarchy that drives the flattening of the traditional hierarchical structure and the emergence of greater autonomy at all levels of management (or underlinghood).

But — like a comically befuddled misunderstanding at the reference desk — it seems as though the innovative organizational theories of management guru Rosabeth Moss Kanter have somehow become mixed up with the death-coping strategies described by the similarly-named theorist Elisabeth Kubler-Ross. So, as our enthusiasm for creative reorganization diminishes, we confront our restructuring and revisioning exercises with denial, anger, and depression — until at last we move beyond these stages and slouch, with a collective sigh of resignation, into reluctant acceptance.

To some extent, the library's excuses for failing to effect meaningful evolution resemble those in the corporate world. Internal resistance to change, for example, is pervasive across all organizations. But libraries may be doubly doomed to fail in these initiatives because we lack a profit motive. In the corporate world, workers are induced to restrategize with assurances that change and innovation will reduce production costs, enhance the bottom line, increase shareholder value. But academic libraries don't have shareholders, and interested parties ("stakeholders" in the neocorporate parlance) ascribe value to vague ideas that can't be measured by columns of numbers, if they can be measured at all (correct answers at the reference desk, for example, apparently have less value than incorrect answers pleasantly proffered).

Moreover, corporate workers are induced to innovate by organizational policies that recognize meritorious achievement. In academic libraries, where employees might have to labor for months over tasks such as Revisions to Intra-organizational Communications Charts, there seems to be an institutionalized aversion to acknowledging the timeless truth that monetary rewards might inspire meaningful actions. Consequently, innovations that might otherwise successfully be adopted by appropriately motivated workers are never given a chance to thrive.

On the surface, the result of our attempts to become more relevant (which spring from the mistaken premise that to be more "corporate" is to be more relevant) is just a lot of foolishness at the workplace. Scarce dollars are misspent on second-rate consultants; tragically out-of-focus vision exercises confuse rather than inspire us; and employees who were once eager and optimistic have been beaten into jaded cynics.

But these missteps also prompt us to consider a deeper question: is the corporatization of the academic library just another attempt to overcome the low self-esteem that's always afflicted our profession? Are we embarrassed by the nurturing soft-edged, non-aggressive (non-corporate) manner in which we do our best work? Are we too feminine? Too motherly? Are we worried that the librarianly stereotype is true, that our Inner Marian will be exposed?

Are we so ashamed by how we continue to be (mis)perceived by others that we'll go to great pains to corporatize the academic library—which only makes us more pathetic as we try (and inevitably fail) to become something we're not? Though it may seem cruelly unrevolting, perhaps we are better served by embracing rather than denying our traditional service-oriented focus.

TAKING A STAND

Daniel C. Tsang

In one sense, the post-9/11 world is no different from the one before it. There have always been acts of inhumanity, many perpetrated in our name (or at least in the name of the nation-state we reside in) and for activist library workers like ourselves, the issue has always been when to take a stand.

As a successful plaintiff in an ACLU-supported lawsuit[1] against the CIA for spying on me (I had indexed *CovertAction Information Bulletin*—now *Quarterly*, as well as several autobiographies of former intelligence officers), I am acutely aware that since 9/11, the erosions of our civil liberties have taken a quantum leap. Racial profiling is no longer taboo: People of certain nationalities are now officially the target of increased state scrutiny and surveillance, all in the name of "homeland security." The new restructuring of the U.S. federal bureaucracy and the creation of a department focusing on this topic may not result in better intelligence about suspected terrorists, but is already opening the floodgates for further domestic surveillance with the lifting of guidelines put in place after the intelligence abuses of the sixties. Libraries, for example, are cited as a specific venue where FBI agents are now free to troll or conduct fishing expeditions for basically anything.

One area where little has been heard in the progressive community is how library workers are directly affected by what has been done in the name of fighting the war on terrorism. More specifically, as a social science data librarian and archivist, my job is to provide access (wherever feasible) to as much data as possible for research and instructional use in the academy. Yet two troubling developments have gotten very little notice outside of those of us who deal with data or provide service on accessing such data.

Just a few months after 9/11, Congress rushed thru the so-called USA PATRIOT—

Uniting and Strengthening America by Providing Appropriate Tools Required to Intercept and Obstruct Terrorism — Act, an eclectic mish-mash of provisions permitting the sharing of intelligence information between the CIA and the FBI, allowing lengthier detentions of non-citizens, and making wiretapping easier. One troubling provision allowing the seizure of "business records" prompted the American Library Association to suggest that librarians can contact ALA's legal team if faced with a subpoena to say, produce circulation records on a patron. That response is lame at best. We should take a stand against the law itself.

Yet among its little-noticed provisions was one that many missed. This provision would henceforth allow FBI agents to receive the actual survey instrument filled in by a student — say from a Middle Eastern country — whom the FBI believes might be a terrorist. An entire section of the new draconian law mandates that the National Center for Educational Statistics (NCES) must turn over to law enforcement the raw data from any survey it compiles if the government so requests in court. And as you are well aware, judges are often too quick to acquiesce to the state in "national security" cases.

I understand there was resistance within the NCES to this provision, but how that played out or why the effort failed remains to be revealed. Important lessons could be learned from such a case history.

When I found out about it, I circulated information about the NCES provision to my data archivist/librarian colleagues on the IASSIST listserv (IASSIST — International Association for Social Science Information, Service and Technology — the data librarians and vendors group <http://www.iassistdata.org/>). One data archive, the Data and Program Library Service at the University of Wisconsin-Madison, subsequently wrote a succinct report on the provision, in the February 2002 issue of its *DPLS News* <http://dpls.dacc.wisc.edu/pubs/Newsletters/feb02news.html> :

"Among the expanded authorities granted by the act is a little-publicized clause that amends confidentiality requirements for statistical databases of student information. Section 508 of the USA-PATRIOT Act allows law enforcement to access the student data collected for the purpose of statistical research under the National Education Statistics Act (NESA), impacting data held by the National Center for Education Statistics (NCES). The new standard requires a simple court order, to be issued based on a certification that the records are relevant to an investigation.

"To date the new standards for NESA data have not been used, and it may prove that the subject will not come up. However, given the bad memories of the misuse of U.S. census data for internment of Japanese-Americans in World War II, it will be important to monitor the extent to which 'confidential' retains its meaning with regard to government survey data."

Notwithstanding this incredible violation of the hitherto inviolate principle of confidentiality relating to survey research or the chilling effect this will have on future data collection, this precedent suggests that other government agencies may well be ordered in a future USA PATRIOT Act II to turn over government records on individuals merely because some FBI agent (now under new guidelines, no longer constrained by any need to link a request for data to any criminal investigation) wants it.

In addition, the Israeli garrison state has, during the same period, beyond the slaughter of Palestinians in occupied territories, effectively destroyed the Palestinian Authority (PA) infrastructure. In one midnight raid in early December 2001, Israeli soldiers rampaged through the PA Central Bureau of Statistics headquarters in Ramallah, destroying computer hardware and software.

After Israel claimed it found evidence allegedly linking the PA to terrorism, the bureau's director, Hassan Abu-Libdeh, according to an account, "'Israeli' Army Raid Sets Dangerous New Precedent," on the website <http://www.moqawama.org/articles/doc_2001/dangerous.htm> retorted, "Our statistics are part of the public domain and until the beginning of the intifada, we were working closely with the Israeli Central Bureau of Statistics."

He also added, "This institution is financially supported by several donor countries such as Norway, Germany, Sweden, Switzerland and the EU. We also go through regular audits. If one adheres to the Israeli Army allegations, it would mean that European countries support terrorism?"

He continued: "The army was looking for something, thinking that we keep records on individuals and their political affiliation or a central database on Palestinian activists. This is naturally not the case since we only collect socio-economic and cultural statistics. Maybe the army thought that our 1997 population census or the list of the voting population would be of use, although again there is nothing political in these data."

Jean Breteche, the European Commission representative in the West Bank and Gaza, reacted as reported on the same website: "This is an act of vandalism.... I would be curious to see the evidence that the Israeli Army claims to have uncovered. PCBS was conducting very serious work which allowed us to follow the economic situation in the territories and help us in our planning efforts. It is incomprehensible that the army would set itself so vehemently against an agency that presents no security threat."

Our Wisconsin colleagues headlined the Israeli raid in a report in their newsletter, in the same February 2002 issue that carried the NCES story. It was headlined: "National Statistics in Troubled Times" and began as follows:

"In mid–December, word of a little-reported news story began to filter through the social science data world. The Palestinian Central Bureau of Statistics (PCBS) headquarters in Ramallah, in the West Bank, had been raided by Israeli Defense Force (IDF) soldiers on the night of December 5th.

"The PCBS came into being in 1993 in the wake of the Oslo accords. The agency was founded with donations from the EU, Norway, Germany, Switzerland, and Sweden. The U.S. made a much smaller contribution. The agency has continued on donated funding, although the Palestinian Authority did provide 30% of funding in 1999 and 2000.

Information about the PCBS and their work is available at their website at <http://www.pcbs.org>.

"From 1967 to 1993, the only source for census and social-survey information about Palestinians in the West Bank and Gaza had been the Israeli Central Bureau of Statistics, online at <http://www.cbs.gov.il/engindex.htm>. The establishment of a national statistics bureau for the Palestinian Authority with multinational backing provided an important new source for describing Palestinian demography, economy, and society.

"The overnight December 5th raid lasted six hours and involved every room of the five-story PCBS office headquarters. Israeli soldiers detained the Bureau's guards for the length of the incident. Photographs of the aftermath are available on the PCBS website at <http://www.pcbs.org/events/event4/photo.htm>"

The May 2002 issue of *DPLS News* <http://dpls.dacc.wisc.edu/pubs/Newsletters/May02news.html> also noted that other Palestinian Authority ministries had been subsequently raided. The newsletter deserves credit for sustaining the effort to inform the data librarian and data user communities of developments that impact on the collection and preservation of social science data.

A later report, "Operation Destroy the Data," in the Israeli daily, *Ha'aretz*, by its reporter based in Ramallah, Amira Hass (his name is misspelled in the copy of his article posted at <http://www.commondreams.org/views02/0424-03.htm> gives a succinct account of what was raided, and the implications of the raid:

"It's not merely the expense of the hardware that has to be replaced. The loss is immeasurable in shekels or dollars. Years of information built into knowledge, time spent thinking by thousands of people working to build their civil society and their future or trying to build a private sector that would bring a sense of economic stability to their country.

"These are the data banks developed in Palestinian Authority institutions like the Education Ministry, the Higher Education Ministry and the Health Ministry. These are the data banks of the non-governmental organizations and research institutes devoted to developing a modern health system, modern agricultural, environmental protection and water conservation. These are the data banks of human rights organizations, banks and private commercial enterprises, infirmaries, and supermarkets. They all were clearly the targets for destruction in the military operation called Defensive Shield."

Elsewhere, neither atrocity against civil society got much attention, beyond a few news articles, web notices, or email traffic on mailing lists. The *New York Times* finally mentioned the December raid four months after it happened.[2]

The UN and NGOs have spoken out against the Israeli raids, calling it "a humanitarian crisis without precedent in its destructive impact on the Palestinian people and its institutions." The joint statement, issued in Rome in April 2002, was signed by representatives of United Nations organizations, including UN Development Program, UN Population Fund, World Health Organization, UN High Commission for Refugees, and the International Federation of Red Cross and Red Crescent and UN Works and Relief Agency, among others. The statement is cited in a report that gives readers some idea of the scale of the destruction in the Israeli raids against dozens of government and non-governmental offices in occupied Palestine has been posted

on the web <http://www.palestinemonitor.org/Other%20Updates/list_of_destructions_
and_vandalism.htm> It is titled, "Destruction of Palestinian Institutions Preliminary
Report" by CODIP. CODIP is the Centrum voor Ontwikkeling, Documentatie en
Informatie Palestijnen <http://www.codip.be/> in Landen, Belgium. The report was
compiled by Rema Hammami, Birzeit University; Sari Hanafi, Palestinian Refugee
and Diaspora Centre, Shaml; and Elizabeth Taylor.

The head of the Netherlands-based International Statistical Institute, Dennis Tre-
win, did write to the Israeli Ambassador to protest the raid <http://www.cbs.nl/isi/
NLet021-01.htm> although the letter was marred by historical references that turned
out to be inaccurate.

Library workers, especially those dealing with government records or social science data, must awaken to the realization that this may well be just the beginning of
a process of further restriction of information or access to data in the service of the
state in the new move to seek "homeland security."

U.S. government documents librarians— who get the bulk of their "documents"
on deposit from the federal government — know all too well how what is given with
one hand can be taken back with another, as recent developments over the restriction of web-sites that show geographical information — deemed of interest to a potential terrorist — demonstrate.

We need more voices of protest over the PATRIOT Act section on survey research
from the NCES, or over the destruction of the Palestinian statistical bureau by Israeli
forces.

Library workers must take a stand against these intrusions by the state all in the
name of an endless War on Terrorism. Library workers spoke out in protest when
the FBI tried to use librarians to spy on Russians and other foreigners.[3] But since
9/11, we must not become silenced out of fear. Resisting the state is never more necessary. For once, resistance is fertile, not futile. And urgent.

Notes

1. See my op ed: "A CIA Target at Home in America," *Los Angeles Times*, January 18, 1998,
M2–M3 <http://sun3.lib.uci.edu/~dtsang/ciatarget.htm>; my "'Eyes Only': The Central Intelligence
Agency versus Daniel C. Tsang," *CovertAction Quarterly*; no. 65 (Fall, 1998), 60–63; and Kimberly
Kindy, "Prying Eyes Were Watching UCI's Library Activist," *Orange County Register*, January 25,
1998, 1, 22+. My lead attorney in the case, Kate Martin, of the Center for National Security Studies, spoke on the USA PATRIOT Act at ALA Midwinter Conference 2002 in New Orleans. The CIA
settled the case for $46,000 plus a dubious promise never to spy on my political activities again.

2. Serge Schmemann, "Palestinians Say Israeli Aim Was to Destroy Framework," *New York
Times*, April 16, 2002.

3. See: *FBI Counterintelligence Visits to Libraries : Hearings before the Subcommittee on Civil
and Constitutional Rights of the Committee on the Judiciary, House of Representatives*, One Hun-
dredth Congress, Second Session, June 20 and July 13, 1988 (Washington, D.C.: U.S. Government
Printing Office, 1989), and Herbert N. Foerstel, *Surveillance in the Stacks: The FBI's Library Awareness Program* (New York : Greenwood Press, 1991).

ARE WE SO PROGRESSIVE?
THE VALUE OF
PROFESSIONAL CHILDREN'S LIBRARIANSHIP

Diana Brawley Sussman

The December 1995 *American Libraries* article "12 Ways Libraries are Good for the Country" proclaims that "Democracy and libraries have a symbiotic relationship. It would be impossible to have one without the other." That relationship is contingent on the fact that "Libraries make knowledge and ideas available to all regardless of age, race, creed, gender, or wealth." Oh, the equality! Yet, can one be certain that this same institution upon which democracy itself depends, this institution which actively promotes equality of knowledge, actually offers equal pay for equal work?

Consider this: "the increasing feminization of the workforce has by no means erased barriers to opportunity whether in the guise of blatant discrimination or disparate impact. Women earn 69 cents on the dollar compared to men and more than half of all women in the nation's workforce are employed in female-dominated job titles. Even in prestigious or highly technical professions that were once the exclusive domain of men — engineering, architecture, law — women generally make less than men."[1]

It's easy to say that the median income for women in mathematics and computer science should be more than 87.1 percent of that earned by males in the same field.[2] My question is tougher: why are those "female-dominated" jobs not more valued? Daycare providers and teachers do not make less than acceptable wages because they do less important work than mathematicians and computer scientists. Nor do they make so little because this is an evil malevolent society. Women held jobs in these typically feminine professions back when men were more often than not the sole or primary breadwinners in American households. This, however, is no longer the case and 23 percent of wives in dual-income families manage to make more money than their husbands.[3]

While it is easy to show the discrepancy of a female lawyer earning thirty percent less than a male lawyer,[4] it is quite another thing to place a grade school teacher between the two and say that all three of them ought to be earning the same amount. Yet they ought to be, because as Mary R. Somerville says, "Early literacy fosters crime prevention."[5] The defense lawyer and grade school teacher share a common goal of keeping people out of jail. In this sense, they work in the same field and ought to be paid comparable salaries. While we are handing out sweeping controversial pay increases lets include the ultimate champions of early literacy, children's librarians.

This argument about women's earnings is so applicable to children's librarianship because "while the term the 'feminized profession' has, in the past, been used to refer to the profession as a whole, the youth services area of librarianship has indeed been notably influenced by the feminine presence."[6] Will Manley tells us just how much children's librarians are devalued when he admits that "children's librarians are the only librarians who are equated with their clientele. There is a strong feeling in the library profession that some entry-level positions such as technical services and computer services are the best way to get ahead in your career and that children's services are a ticket to oblivion."[7]

Do children's librarians make less than adult reference librarians do? Yes. In fact, many children's librarians are not even given the title of librarian. As one of these under-titled librarians myself, I went into classrooms in library schools in two different states and asked my fellow children's librarians about their job titles. We were all apparently "library assistants." This discrepancy allowed the libraries we worked for to staff children's reference positions with underpaid and under-qualified people. This system, which might work as a method of training new librarians, is gravely flawed in that once a new librarian receives a master's degree in library science, she will usually maintain the library assistant job title unless she promotes out of her current position. The status of the position then, is not dependent upon the qualifications of the person who holds it. It is, quite simply, a librarian position under the guise of a library assistant position. According to the Bureau of Labor Statistics, library assistants "register patrons so they can borrow materials from the library. They record the borrower's name and address from an application and then issue a library card. Assistants sort books, periodicals, and other items and return them to their designated shelves." Do those sound more like shelving or circulation duties? There is nothing there about collection development, outreach, reference or programming. That's what I did as a children's librarian. I was no one's assistant.

Mary R. Somerville looked at barriers to recruiting and keeping children's librarians. Many of the libraries she looked at are attempting to create a "career ladder" for children's librarians. In each case this "step up" involved giving children's librarians managerial duties. After all, it is the managerial role that often separates the adult reference librarian or "branch manager" from the children's librarian. I'm certain that children's librarians do make excellent managers. As Will Manley points out, "If you can manage kids, you can manage anything." However, I would contend that children's librarians should not have to become managers in order to get better status and pay. Children's programming takes at least as much time, expertise, and talent, as a whole heap of managerial duties. The idea that management is several rungs up on the success ladder from story time is a leftover from that single-income, male-centered household we left behind years ago.

Let me emphasize this: children are good for business! "Emphasize children's services and your adult business will increase even more than your children's. No one is more persuasive than the 4-year-old who demands to be taken to story hour."[8] "Circulation of juvenile materials in public libraries is up by 54% in the last 10 years. Almost three-fourths of all children ages 3–8 visit a public library every year. From story hours for preschoolers to career planning for high schoolers, children's librarians make a difference because they care about the unique developmental needs of every individual who comes to them for help."[9] I cannot believe that the effort it takes to meet those developmental needs is worth less than the effort it takes to manage employees.

As library schools and library literature dive into the issues of technological progress will social progress be forgotten? It would certainly be the normal, status quo thing to do. People are more intelligent than moral. Fossil fuel technology progresses in spite of its effect on the environment. The atomic bomb was invented and dropped before there had been any widespread discourse on what it would mean to burn the skin off of people. How small it seems, the plight of the children's librarian, if she is even allowed to call herself that. Yet the "12 Ways Libraries are Good for the Country" article says that "Libraries offer alternatives to the manipulations of commercialism, from the excellence of public-television productions to the free-thinking of renegade publishers and the vision of poets and artists outside the mainstream business of art and literature." Outside the mainstream. Progressiveness. Equality. Ahem.

Notes

1. *A Matter of Fact: Statements Containing Statistics on Current Social, Economic and Political Issues.* (Ann Arbor, MI: Pierian Press, 2000): 438.
2. *Ibid.*
3. Anne E. Winkler. "Earnings of Husbands and Wives in Dual-Earner Families." *Monthly Labor Review Online* 121, no. 4, April 1998. <http://www.bls.gov/opub/mlr/1998/04/art4full.pdf>.
4. *Matter of Fact*, 438.
5. Mary R. Somerville. "Facing the Shortage of Children's Librarians: Updating the Challenges." *American Libraries*, October 1998, 50–54.
6. Karen P. Smith. "Imagination and Scholarship: The Contribution of Women to American Youth Services and Literature." *Library Trends* 44, no.4 (Spring 1996): 679.
7. Will Manley. "Theories on the Disappearance of Children's Librarians." *American Libraries*, March 1998, 128.
8. *Ibid.*
9. "12 Ways Libraries Are Good for the Country." *American Libraries*, December 1995, 113-19.

I WAS A TEENAGE ANARCHO-TERRORIST

Piers Denton

The world has seen many changes since the fall of the Berlin Wall, the collapse of the Internationale and the emergence of the unipolar world. My story is but one.

From a very early age, courtesy of radical '60s parents, I have been a fellow traveler. I received my own copy of Mao's *Little Red Book* whilst still young enough to think it wise, and for schooling I had the *Little Red School Book* straight out of Denmark. What real education I received was from the study of the history, politics and military strategy of every liberation or anti-colonial movement around the world. This being the early 1970s, my innocent fantasies revolved around such stars of the international terrorism scene as Leila Khaled and Gudrun Ensslin. So much so, that I sought but failed to join them in a little military training in North Yemen with what remained of the Japanese Red Army after their airport adventures. My heroes were Durutti, Makhno, Che and Carlos. Like them, I sought the dual goals of freedom via anonymity and, at the same time, revolutionary celebrity. In imitation of them, I developed certain skills that have no current application. I also learnt how to move about as an unknown, to build and discard identities at will, and, of course, to survive. Whilst in Britain, my youthful enthusiasm was given meaning by the 1979 election of Margaret Thatcher as British Prime Minister. The destruction of almost the entirety of the industrial base of Britain caused a political upheaval which led to race and youth riots across the nation in 1981, the fantastically exciting "Stop the City" massed anarchist attacks on London's financial center from 1983–5, the doomed miners' strike, and culminated with the successful Poll Tax Riots. Caught up in all this activity in the early 1980s, revolutionary armed struggle seemed a legitimate means to an end.

Yet, nearly two decades later, I sit at a desk in a library on the other side of the world. How I got here instead of being holed up in a tenement block in Syria revolves around a simple idea. Some time ago in Belgium, some revolutionaries considered, "We are too hot; the police watch us and everyone we know. How are we going to do anything constructive to defeat the system?" The answer they came to was to re-enter normal society, start afresh, get jobs, learn skills, make contacts, and wait till they were in positions of security and respectability. This they did, whilst also managing to keep their revolutionary fervor intact. A number of years later they re-emerged, as the Cellules Communistes Combattantes, and carried out, for a time, the armed struggle. In the end they still got caught, but they were still an inspiration. In mid-1980s London after a year of constant police surveillance, I remember having the same conversation with my anarcho-syndicalist comrades as the CCC had before. "We will re-emerge," we said, "stronger, better and where they failed we will succeed." So underground or, in fact, overground, we duly went. At first it was hard keeping work, taking orders, and having to always resist the urge to leave an incendiary device in the workplace overnight. My training and skills became surplus to requirements. I hated having to have the most boring banal conversations with people who had no idea of conversing on a "need to know basis." But the worst part was the lack of excitement, the lack of the thrill of destruction. After a few years, however, normal became normal. After another few years, I made the first tentative steps towards re-establishing contact. Unlike the CCC, however, we did not re-emerge as the people's vanguard, but seemingly had gotten caught in a drift instead. Some had not given up the old anarcho-punk lifestyle and were still involved in activity which made them unclean, and therefore too much of a risk. Others had adapted wonderfully to a new lifestyle and had lost their conviction and desire to destroy the society that was now making them rich, whilst others still had just passed by.

Which left me. I continued on even through the events of 1989 and 1990, which changed everything. I continued to do indifferent jobs, and for some reason I still kept waiting. As the eighties turned into the nineties I started a family, bought a house, and did all of the normal things. Slowly but surely, things and people began to cling around me and depend upon me. I kept the secret knowledge that at some point I could strip it all away, and lose myself once again in the struggle. With something akin to horror, though, it slowly dawned on me that the life I was living was indeed my life and would continue to be. This fact was far more terrifying to me than the consequences of pursuing the armed struggle. I had distanced myself from all political activity, cut myself off from everyone I knew, and now had to realize that it had been in vain. At first I considered going it alone as a one-man cell. But even lone terrorists need an information network, a support group, and supplies. I considered joining a group, but who? The French Action Directe were no longer in action, the Red Brigades were in prison, and the only active groups of note were either purely nationalistic like ETA or Islamic fundamentalist. The only two real alternatives were the November 17 organization in Greece (who were impossible to contact), or a Palestinian faction (who unfortunately no longer encourage non–Arab volunteers, as they seemed invariably to be unstable, Nazis, or both).

But then instead and by some chance I became a librarian. As a worker I still find it difficult to take orders from paper tigers, but I persevere, as it is rare work that enhances rather than oppresses society. Whilst *la lotta continua*, the political motive of opposing the machinery of the state remains the same. The aim of the armed revolutionary is to show to the populace that the personal is political. That their situation in society, their poverty or poverty of opportunity, their pointless jobs, and their lack of control over their lives is dependent on a clearly devised political manipulation. That their lives are controlled and mediated by political forces solely in support of economic objectives. In pursuing the armed struggle the anarcho-terrorist's aim was to rip away the facade of liberalism that Western capitalism displays, to make the state appear as it really is: violent, remorseless and not admitting of any real dissent. Violence alone, against the state and its structures, forces the state to show its true face and so allows people to see themselves within that system and to understand that through their decadence, people elsewhere die. I now see that, though it may seem trite, libraries can also confront people with the hideous truth. Where else is information freely imparted? Where else is there a repository of information to some extent unmediated by the market place? Where else are there people who are trained to find and freely deliver information to you? Where else but in the world's books is there access to the world of ideas, from W. H. Auden to Ken Saro-Wiwa, reflecting life, love and expectation from every field of human experience?

Libraries remain important because they represent one of the last vestiges of the potlatch, or gift economy. As Andrew Carnegie once wisely said, libraries "give nothing for nothing." Libraries, if they are truly used, require the active participation of readers to inform themselves and others. A reader is the essential and equal partner to the library, which makes the current library management trend of turning readers into customers such a menace. Customers merely consume and are powerless and dependent; readers read, an activity that is both productive and cooperative. And, with luck, the motivated library reader may also become the writer and so continue in the provision of free thought.

Whilst libraries remain free at the point of access, they will be part of the arsenal of liberation, and it remains my pleasure to be at my reference desk handing out books. I may not live out the dream of fighting with the P.O.U.M at the barricades in Barcelona, handing out Molotov cocktails, but I am still hopefully fermenting dissent. From urban guerrilla to public librarian may seem a large leap, but if knowledge is power and access to that power brings freedom, then libraries too are revolutionary, and librarians can be counted amongst the workers political vanguard. Books, like bombs, change lives and governments, and are, of course, easier to handle. However, I still understand that an armalite rifle will always cause less damage than a ballot box.

IV. CREATIVELY REVOLTING SELF-EXPRESSION

buried in haiku
too much to say in few words—
questions, not answers

storytime by day
clubbing at night, my five cats
like my purple hair

Clark Kent could not beat
mild-mannered librarian
at phone booth changes

—KATHLEEN KERN

THE GROWING WEB OF CATASTROPHE: THE STORY OF A MAD LIBRARIAN

Keith Buckley

Just as Jane had predicted, the savings account ran dry before Paul could finish his semi-autobiographical novel, *Ravished Standards*, let alone find an agent or publisher. They made the mortgage on their shambling farmhouse thanks to his father's pension, but the monthly checks from TIAA-CREF and Jane's salary as a paralegal weren't enough to cover utility bills or the groceries.

Paul spent his first day of poverty gnashing his teeth and broke the stems of three different pipes. Once he'd gotten over the migraine from his aching molars, he climbed up to the attic to search for the only suit that fit him anymore. Next, he drove into town and paid the outrageous sum of $45 to have his wildly frizzy, shoulder-length hair deforested. Finally, he trudged across his muddy backyard to the barn. There in the loft, half-buried in rotting hay and five years' worth of bird-droppings, he found his dad's army-issue footlocker. In the bottom of the footlocker lay an M.L.S. diploma issued by Indiana University on Saturday, May 3rd, 1980, to one Paul A. DeMusa.

Paul read the diploma for the first time in almost twenty years. He needed to make sure he had the correct date before cobbling together a résumé.

"You've also got a degree in English," Jane nervously reminded him when he returned from the barn. "Why not apply for this copy editor thing at the newspaper?" She'd been reading the want ads ever since Paul had announced his decision to go after the new reference position at the local public library. She'd been reading the want ads very, very carefully ever since that ancient tic reappeared, tugging at the left corner of her husband's mouth.

"I've already talked with Belinda, the head of Readers' Services," Paul said. "She was a big fan of the band."

"And there's always McDonald's! Didn't you tell me you worked there for two years? I bet you'd be a manager in no time!"

Paul tucked the résumé into a battered leather briefcase. He played with the knot in his tie for a moment. "Jane, the reference gig means health insurance. A retirement plan. Benefits. Remember what those are?"

"But librarianship? Working that close with the public?" she asked. Jane could barely stand to look at his gaunt, quivering face. It reminded her of a glacier calving icebergs into the ocean at spring. "Please don't go to this interview, Paul. You get hives just talking to the mailman!"

He stood up, closed his briefcase, and gave her a perfunctory kiss on the forehead. "I keep telling you, I'm allergic to his cologne," he muttered. "With any luck, I won't get patrons who wear Eternity For Men."

Paul knew the reference spot was his for the asking. When he first discussed the opening with Belinda Harris, she erupted into bubbly little giggles. Harris told him she owned every Raging Whippets album and bootlegged concert tape, taking care to emphasize how much she adored Paul's keyboard solos.

What could be a better fit, DeMusa asked himself as he pulled into the parking lot of the Concord County Public Library. He'd fallen in love with the tidy, Carnegie-funded building the moment he saw it, at the tender age of seven, a few months after his family had moved to Winston. How he adored those Bedford limestone columns, the brick facade, its complete set of "Boxcar Children" books. And then there was the holy of holies—a copy of Jules Verne's *The Mysterious Island*, illustrated by N.C. Wyeth. Why, he was so enamored of the library that he'd taken his first girlfriend up to the deserted Oversize Collection for an impassioned make-out session.

The distraction of regular employment, he'd decided, would be the perfect spur to see him through those difficult final chapters of the novel. He'd convinced himself that high-profile public services work would actually be therapeutic, ridding him of the anti-social tendencies he'd developed ever since arthritis had forced him to leave the band.

Yes, a perfect fit! He wanted to sing to the world as he waltzed back to his truck three hours later. Twelve long years ago, he'd given up his last day job, slogging away with a band that was going nowhere. Now, he'd finally rejoined the ranks of the gainfully employed!

The experiment, needless to say, failed disastrously on all counts. Two months after his first day, he got into a screaming match with Jane when he heard her sighing under her breath, "I told you so."

You see, Paul hated the stillness of the library. All that untapped and generally useless information gasping at him. All those mindless questions. All the grumbling geriatrics who couldn't fathom the online catalog and kept demanding to see "those drawers with the cards in 'em." All the twits who asked, "Where'd you hide the restroom?" when there were huge blue and white pictures of commodes posted everywhere!

He often sat drumming his swollen fingers on the desk of something called "The Info-matrix Center." He started wondering where The Raging Whippets were playing next. Why he'd surrendered his plum job behind the grand piano and his precious Hammond B-3 organ. And why, oh why, was everyone he talked to such a blithering idiot?

Frustration and a frenzy of bored terror soon had DeMusa dreaming up blatantly criminal acts of vandalism.

The day after he learned the band had signed a contract with Geffen, Paul unleashed his reign of chaos on an unsuspecting public and his colleagues.

Some of his exploits went unnoticed for years.

He began his campaign innocently enough. He made up facts and dates. He handed out non-existent call numbers. He misshelved books. He misled the library's patrons with cunning and impossible responses. He hid standard reference works that would prove each of his fabricated answers untrue. He sabotaged the subject authority file with dead-end "see also" notes. He poured book-binding paste between the pages of recent bestsellers. When the local high school seniors were assigned a term paper on substance abuse, every book with the words "marijuana" or "alcohol" in its bibliographic description was sent off on interlibrary loan to the University of Almaty in Kazakhstan. He recalled materials that had been checked out only the day before. He pulled from the spines little red tags that said "Info-matrix Center" on heavily-used directories and encyclopedias, consigning the volumes to the stacks.

With the wrong call numbers, of course.

As he became intimately familiar with the library's policies and procedures, DeMusa hit upon even more insidious schemes against the order of things. He directed fragile old ladies from the Winston First Baptist Church to the most salacious, bodice-busting romances. He disabled the security system when well-known book thieves entered the building. He stole the office copy-card and xeroxed dozens of books he couldn't find at Dalton's. Having penetrated the new computerized acquisition profile, he entered subscriptions for foreign periodicals no one in the community could read. He filled all the electric pencils sharpeners with Liquid Stormwindow, put sugar in the Bookmobile's gas tank, ran audio cassettes and videos through a bulk tape demagnetizer, and spent countless hours in his basement, resplicing the Blackhawk collection of classic silent films with scenes from "Caligula" and Frank Zappa's "Uncle Meat." He searched the Internet for new email viruses and anonymously forwarded them to Automation's main server — each in the director's name.

Paul's ultimate outrage?

Deep in the dust-enshrouded bowels of the library's basement, he stumbled upon a book called *Show Me.* This one had been banned in 1979 by the board of trustees. This one offended even his vaguely defined sense of boundaries. This one he left casually lying open in the Children's Room when members of the Concord County Family Values Committee arrived for an inspection.

The resulting uproar made headlines on CBS, NBC, ABC, the Fox Network, and the *Concord Gazette,* not to mention the American Library Association's *Newsletter on Intellectual Freedom.*

Throughout DeMusa's entire year-long tenure, however, nobody ever traced the growing web of catastrophe back to him. Like *Kung Fu*'s David Carradine, Paul could walk across a scroll of rice paper without leaving so much as a footprint.

The day after the Concord County Library's director was institutionalized, a certain reference librarian discovered his arthritis had been miraculously cured. He immediately resigned.

Six months later, *Ravished Standards* and The Raging Whippets' new album (with Paul DeMusa back on keyboards) got rave reviews. Paul's hair was wildly frizzy and shoulder-length once more. His facial tic, along with *Kelly's Bluebook,* Automation's operating system, and an illustrated copy of a Jules Verne novel, had mysteriously disappeared.

YOUNG SOMALI WOMEN IN THE LIBRARY

Diana Brawley Sussman

When they see me
behind the desk their eyebrows
         float   up
and something as daunting
as ten written pages in their third
or fourth language
on the history of
         a natural element becomes something
   they can slide through...
         ah... say their eyes
   ...that one
                  she will help me.
         Kin chooses silicon over oxygen
      although nothing about her is as fake or as easy
   as what comes to mind when hearing
the word silicon. She says,
      you are nice. What's your
name, and this
         is her sister beside her, Hani, which sounds
            like Honey,
      who would rather be Hannah, because Hani is just

                                             something sweet
But Hani is draped in pink. It is the teenage girls
   who tie their scarves in bright crowns,
      wearing their dreams on their head.
But Hani
   is small
      and unknotted
         and pink, and cannot choose *not*
            to be Hani
               yet.
                  Another young woman chooses
                  helium
                     Her face is
                        a nut colored moon
                  and like me
                     she likes anything
                           that makes things...
                     anything...
                              even eyebrows
         float   up

PERSONAS NON GRATAS; OR, AN ARCHIVIST'S CLASSIFICATION OF PROBLEM PATRONS

Katharine Salzmann

THE MUTILATOR
rip, snip, crumple, tear
what is your weapon of choice?
spill, crush, highlight, bend

THE PROCRASTINATOR
paper due, no clue
i need to choose a topic
what do you have here?

THE ABUSER
defensive, angry
accusations, no excuse
temper tantrum, tears

THE MANIPULATOR
special privileges
i was allowed yesterday
why can't i today?

THE COMPLAINER
no pens? no scanner?
too hot, too noisy, too cold
no change, no patience

[Any resemblance to actual persons, living or dead, is entirely coincidental.]

ANOTHER DAY IN THE LIFE OF...
REFERENCE LIBRARIAN

Cathy and Jennifer Camper

WEATHER REPORT: HALE AND DRIVEL (OR MATT HALE VISITS MY LIBRARY)

Biblio l'Teca

Matt Hale is the Pontifex Maximus (or Gluteus Maximus, as I like to think of him) of the World Church of the Creator, a high profile white supremacy group that is known for scheduling meetings in libraries and other publicly funded venues, invoking his First Amendment rights when denied use of public space. His visits are usually three-ring-circuses, creating an unholy assemblage of Hale's goons, local peacenik hippies, out-of-town, anti-fascist punk agitators, the Jewish Defense League (who have been known to disperse the crowd with a bomb threat), cops in riot gear, a handful of dead-eyed supporters, and unsuspecting/angry/fearful library patrons. In 2001, a visit to Peoria (IL) Public Library resulted in a melee with several bloodied noses and over $5000 in damages to the library's community room.

Benjamin Smith, the young man who went on a racial killing spree a few years back (in Indiana and Illinois), belonged to this group. Hale has his law degree, but can't get anyone to grant him a license. Even Montana, white supremacy haven that it is, said no to Hale's request for a license. Hale, an intelligent, musically gifted 30-something sociopath, runs the "church" from the house he shares with his father in Peoria, IL. Hale has been to my library three times, and has planned a return visit for July 2002. It's always a mixed bag for me when he comes. I love the spectacle and passion that come with his visits, but I also know that the "church" is as visible as it is, solely because of the media attention that comes from the spectacle. I'd love to keep Hale and his sorry-ass, pitiable, disenfranchised goons out of our library, but they've got a right to be here, loathsome as their rhetoric is. The following poem-like thing came pouring out on the morning of Hale's second visit last year.

Heil Hale?
Oh, hell.

I might as well
stay by my coat,
be prepared to bolt,
should the JDL
call in and threaten to bomb
us into oblivion.
(nudge nudge, wink wink)

That pencil-neck geek,
he comes here to speak
again and again and again.

He's surrounded by goons,
and white trash buffoons
who eat whole, from his hand,
rotten nuggets of ill-logic,
enough to choke a rational person,
but easily swallowed
by the True Members of the Master Race.
Shit in, shit out.
No digestion required.

My blood boils and I argue,
          politely,
with the indignant ones:
     How can you let them in here?
     I pay taxes.
     This is wrong.

The cops shift back and forth
     from heavy-shoed foot to heavy-shoed foot.
I think they hate the barefoot bearded guy
wearing a smart cocktail dress
who waves a sign that says
     "Free Your Mind and Your Ass Will Follow"
more than the slack-jawed, eye-blackened standard bearer
     at the front of the front of the room.

All in a day's work.

A LIBRARIAN'S SUICIDE NOTE

C. M. Stupegia

This treatise is dedicated to all of those who work in libraries, do their best and are taken for granted every day. Yes, you know who you are. You are the ones who stay late to get the job done. You are the ones who stay to help a patron as they do research for a term paper, then you get yelled at by your boss because you are 5 minutes late to work the next morning. You are the ones who, with a shrinking staff, make access a reality by making sure thousands of resources are cataloged. You are the ones who write the policies and procedures that reflect the true-to-life situations and your boss takes all the credit.

You are the ones who teach BI sessions to students who are hung over and couldn't care less. You are true unsung heroes.

To whoever will listen:

Yes, I have decided to end it all. To walk away from the people, the books, the indices, the information, the dot matrix, and to go to a much better place ... I hope! Of course, if I do go to hell, I will be doomed to catalog children's picture books using Sears subject headings for all eternity. But why should I go to hell? I have served my profession well — at least, that's what I used to think until I entered the 4th year of my "professional" career. With all the internal and external pressures facing young librarians and librarianship in general, I question whether it is all worth it, whether ours is still a noble profession that matches people with information or if the saying, "You can find *everything* using the Internet!" is really true.

From the ripe old age of 6, I had such passion for libraries. I was introduced to such historical characters as Martha Washington, Amelia Earhart, Rosa Luxemburg, and Emma Goldman at the library. Living on the farm, it was a big event when we traveled 15 miles to visit our township library. Later, my family moved to a small town with a library I visited every chance I had. The town had converted an old house into a library. Upstairs was the adult section and downstairs were all the children's books. This library was not automated and the patrons were given a hand-written library card with a number on it. All the records were kept in a spiral notebook. I will never forget my library card number as long as I live — it was the number 4! I won my first contest at the library when I guessed the number of jelly-beans in the jar during the summer reading program. Whenever I had a paper assigned at school, the first place I went was the library: for the knowledge, the solitude, and just to be among all of those books.

My enthusiasm and regular visits to the library began to pay off when I was asked to work as a substitute for the adult services librarian. This was my big break! I was only 14, but the librarian in the adult section needed someone to watch the library when she had a day off. I was put in charge of the library for a day or two every other month. I thought I was hot stuff. I got to see everyone's library number in that spiral notebook. I got to shelve books and shelf-read at the same time. I got to unpack the bag on Thursday when the interlibrary loan van made a delivery. I got to give change out for the copying machine. I even got first dibs on the bestsellers. Yes, I was in my glory and I was paid $3.50 an hour to work at a place where I would have worked for free. The library was a privilege and housed all human knowledge — or, at least as much knowledge as a town of 1100 people could handle. What I wouldn't give to smell those books and open that spiral notebook once again!

Yes, libraries have been very good to me. They have employed me not only as a teenager, but also as a student assistant and a graduate assistant during college. The people and resources found in libraries taught me things that I would never have imagined. The library as a place has offered me solitude and refuge in some very difficult times in my life. It was the library and the people who worked in them that made me believe that I could do anything, that I wasn't a "hick chick," but could be a "hip chick." They may not have had all the answers immediately, but they always put me on the right track to finding the answers to my questions. It was like the librarians knew everything. Without their help, I would never have been able to receive two master's degrees by the age of 27. I owed so much to these time-honored institutes and to the all-powerful individuals who worked in them. I loved them so much that I wanted desperately and with everything that I had (trust me, I have the student loans to show for it) to be among their ranks.

I entered library school with all this love and admiration for the profession. Of course, looking back now, there were signs leading to my road of discontent and the beginning of my burnout. I studied hard in library school and spent countless hours answering all of the questions for the reference treasure hunts, even those questions that the instructor threw in because the answer was that there was no answer. I killed many trees in my quest to prove that there is more than one way to answer a reference question. I drove my fellow classmates nuts when they would come up with an answer and I would make them explain in 500 words or less how they arrived at that answer. I became obsessed with learning every aspect of librarianship. Even though I had to glue my eyes open, I read every word of the AACR2. During my online searching class, I did so many Dialog searches that three years of my current salary could not pay the fee. I would travel anywhere to talk to a professional librarian to learn more about what they did and how they did it. I was like a wild animal; I didn't sleep my entire last semester of library school and drove myself nuts. I believed that everything — and I do mean everything — that I learned in library school was gospel.

Boy, did I have a rude awakening at the beginning of my first professional job. That library administration class taught me that the key to a successfully and harmonious work environment was training and communication, so I listened eagerly to every bit of training that I received ... which only lasted half the morning. I was always under the impression from my administration class that I would be allowed to ease into a new job. Instead, on my first day I found myself checking out books, answering reference questions, and describing the virtues of large public libraries to a group of paraprofessional trainees. These reference questions weren't easy either. They were questions like, "I have a blue crystal bowl with a flower design on it. Is it worth anything?" From that day on, I began to see everything that they didn't teach in library school. I began to see the dark side. For instance, I had to answer such questions as: "Can somebody tell me what exactly E-Rate is?" "What is a LSTA grant?" "What is the difference between a library district and a city library?" If this wasn't bad enough, no one ever taught me what was involved in being a supervisor and handling personnel issues. What you do when you find out that the person that you hired lied on their application and they turn out to be a convicted felon? What if you suspect that the person you are supervising is sleeping on the job because you can see the indentation of the desk on their face? These types of things are not supposed to happen in a library, right? Libraries are virtuous and virtuous people work in libraries, right?

I began to become a bit suspicious of the training that I received in library school, but I continued to hone my craft and celebrate the essence that is libraries. I worked every waking moment finding answers to reference questions; even if they seemed a bit unusual on the surface, I knew they meant something to the patron. Questions like, "My uncle Fred read a poem as a child, it was in a blue book and it started something like this.... Can you help me find it?" Or "We are doing a project with tanks and we need to find out more about pig slurry." Or the one a fellow colleague had to answer: "My cat died 3 weeks ago and has been buried out in the back yard. I would like to know how to perform an autopsy on the cat."

Yes, we looked and looked again, never questioning why, never laughing in the person's face, all because we care.

Today I ask myself, WHY SHOULD I CARE?

Where did the passion go? Where did the enthusiasm go? Where did my life go?

I keep asking myself these questions. I just feel that what I am doing is never enough. Working 12-hour days, teaching anywhere from 3 to 5 classes per week, going to committee meetings, preparing for classes, and — if you're one of the fortunate few who gets to be a tenure-track academic librarian — publishing is never enough. Yeah, we librarians really have copious free time to publish. Staff shortages and fish-bowl offices provide quite a conducive environment for reflection and true scholarship.

While I am not against scholarship and the sharing of ideas, I am torn between publishing and providing the best quality service to the community that I serve. I actually enjoy doing research and growing as a writer, but is that the true calling of a librarian? Tell me how you would handle this situation: two out of four members of the staff have suffered physical injury, it is final paper time for your students, and you have just been told during your annual job review that you're not publishing enough. In fact, your lack of publishing is due to your being a little "chatty." It is perfectly acceptable to be pulled from your writing project to chat, teach, guide, and actually *help* a patron for an unscheduled hour every other day, but it is totally unacceptable to chat with your colleagues from other parts of the building about issues that affect your working environment. How am I to balance on this tightrope? What is really important here? Can anyone do it all? Can anyone have it all?

Whenever I have a few moments (once every six months or so), I ask myself these questions and I am transported back to my days as a graduate student in history, studying the Russian Revolution. I believe that Lenin would see this as a plot by the ruling class to suppress the workers and prohibiting them from organizing. This whole idea of divide and conqueror and keeping a "good man [or woman, as the case may be] down" seems to be preposterous in a library where good, kind-hearted people work and the answers are seemingly at the librarian's fingertips. Why does this happen? If there is a lack of trust and too much meddling from those who are considered trustees or administrators, even libraries become cesspools and perfect candidates for revolution. Why can't librarians unite and fight the bureaucracy that is keeping them down and subjugating them to second-class citizenry? It is pathetic how human greed, lust for power, and overall ego get in the way of some very good work. It really makes me sad and depressed. It has led me to the decision that I will execute shortly.

Before I go, I beg you to listen to me for one more minute. Although I have raved like a lunatic, I have witnessed the dark side of librarianship that will result in its ultimate death. Our profession is at a crisis point in its history. People are out there saying, "We don't need you." "I can find it on the Internet, why do we need libraries?" "What does a librarian actually *do*?" We have no one to blame for this situation but ourselves. We have not valued ourselves. We have lead people to believe that libraries are "free" and that it is "free" labor and "free donations" that make a library run. When there is a budget crisis, our automatic response is to try and do more with less. We pile more and more work on our shrinking staffs with no regard to their personal well-being. Instead, we should be shouting from the rooftops, "Libraries aren't free! It costs money — real money!— to subscribe to a full-text database! At $10 per article, you couldn't afford to buy articles on your own, Mr./Ms. Patron! You would not be able to write your school reports, buy a car, make major managerial decisions, or search your family histories without a library and unless you cough up some real dough, you are going to have to settle for *less*!" When are we going to be proud of who we are? Why do we accept inferior status in our communities? For crying out loud, we are in the midst of an information revolution. We just stand on the sidelines, waiting and wondering when we might be asked to partake.

DAMN IT, PEOPLE — THIS IS WAR! We need to showcase our talents, abilities, and greatness so our communities don't forget us. We need to shine our brilliance and attract new people to the profession. Statisticians have predicted fifty percent of librarians will retire in the next five to ten years. They have not predicted if this is confined only to administration, middle management, or the front lines. Even worse, students receiving their MLS aren't becoming school, academic, public, or special librarians. They're going where the money is, and who can blame them for wanting to make a buck and keep their self-respect?

While this grim picture breaks my heart, what sickens me and what brings me to my current state of mind (or lack thereof) is how those bright, energized, new librarians are being treated like crap. Listen up, administrators: these people need to be treated like gold. They need to be nurtured, and they need to be guided. They need you to listen to their needs, their wants, and their fears. They are the future. They are the ones that will keep librarianship alive. Using the current managerial methods, we will perish ... much like me. Librarianship has never faced extinction! I hear library administrators discussing how they can't understand the new librarians of today. The administrators don't understand why new librarians don't want to work 12 hours a day, 7 days a week. I just love the party attitude: "We had to do it, so should they!" Please don't break their spirits. Allow them to explore. Make sure they have appropriate workloads. Tell them when they do something wrong, and also applaud them when they do something right. Don't let them go home at the end of day wondering, "Is being a librarian worth it?"

Another piece of advice to all of you sitting in seats of power — get rid of the

"We've always done it this way and we're not going to change" attitude. The circumstances and the stakes are different today then they were five years ago. Change takes place not over years, but milliseconds, and it keeps speeding up. We need to be working together, not tearing each other apart. Our mission statements should include a line about creating "whole" people both within the library and for our communities. We need to encourage, and not discourage. We need to celebrate our accomplishments.

With all the change that is going on around us, it is time that we decided to change and reinvent ourselves. It is time that the world knew exactly how much goes into acquiring, cataloging, shelving, and finding one book. It is time we joined the party and started teaching people how to be good information consumers and expose the truth about the World Wide Web. People need to know that the Internet is a tool, not the keeper of all human knowledge.

Well, the day is growing late and I need to pack my desk. Tomorrow, I hope to finally get some rest and start rebuilding my spirit. I know that I sound like a jilted lover, but I feel broken and do not know if I can go on. While I plan on saying goodbye to my career as a librarian, I hear that Wal-Mart greeters have no threat of becoming extinct any time soon. They help people, make them feel welcome, and tell them that dog food is in aisle 4. They are imparting knowledge and service with a smile. Maybe my heart can heal and I will find peace in the world. Wasn't that the storyline of an Oprah book?

Song of the Reference Librarian

Erica Olsen

By the light of the public access terminal
The librarian makes his stand.
Boldly wielding a Cutter chart
He raises up his hand:

"Courteous Patrons, Eager Staff, Library Friends,
Stop your information seeking for a moment and attend,
As I tell you the story
(Call number 027.6251)
Of library professionals, and how I became one."

A hush fell over the stacks,
Children crowded near,

Even the cranky genealogist
Leaned forward to hear.

"It began in my childhood,"
He spoke as through a fog,
"When other boys learned how to swim,
I learned to catalog."

"I went on to high school,"
He said with a smile,
"And dazzled the teachers
With my homemade vertical file."

"During the war, I was in trouble
With the local constabulary,
For organizing protests
Supporting controlled vocabulary."

"In my college library,
Giddy with scholarly freedom,
I learned that serials disappear
Only as you need them."

"I met a woman in graduate school,
With gray eyes like the sea.
We gave birth to a son named MARC.
Our daughter's named LC."

"I love my job, dear patrons,
The reference questions that I face,
I love community information,
And searching the database."

"But one thing dims my ardor,
An error tugs my soul,
A single misconception
That I must address in whole."

He raised his eyes to their faces,
Taking in their solemn looks.
"Ladies and gentlemen, you must understand,
I DO NOT JUST STAMP BOOKS!"

V. Our Revolting Issues

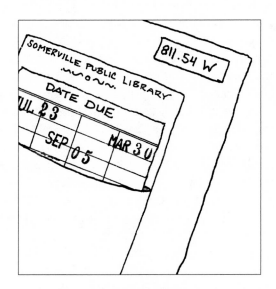

my revolting job
politics in triplicate —
patience like a stone
—Kathleen Kern

RADICALS DEFENDING TRADITION: AN APPEAL TO THE BABY BOOM GENERATION

Rory Litwin

This article was written just before the financial scandals and stock market crash of 2002.

The contributors to the original *Revolting Librarians* may or may not admit to being embarrassed by the groovy poetic explosion of their 1972 rebellion against the library establishment, but embarrassment is the only explanation I can come up with for the thorough reversal of direction and backward charge in which baby boomers are presently leading society. (Note: throughout this article I speak about baby boomers and Generation Xers in very general terms, as a group. There are significant minorities in all cases who do not think or behave according to my observations.) The few baby boomers who do stand up at American Library Association Council meetings in defense of the longstanding traditional values of librarianship — equity of access, information as a public good, intellectual freedom, or personal privacy — are accused of being "stuck in the '60s." If Gen Xers — who differ from their 1972 counterparts primarily in feeling burdened by a past that is full of lessons, leaders, and relevance — stand up to defend the same traditional values, our concerns are dismissed as the radicalism of youth (never mind that most Gen X librarians are in their thirties), as though, like the preponderance of the baby boom generation, we will ten years from now feel embarrassed and reverse our course.

I realize that most readers will, at first glance, consider this a false picture. Surely the mainstream of ALA is generally liberal and deeply supports what are still called "library values." Surely these values don't need to be defended from the mainstream. But look at what the library profession and ALA have decided to do in the last ten years. We've outsourced materials selection and other functions to corporations who don't know our patrons. We recently formed an immediate consensus to cooperate with the FBI in their requests for patron records as provided for in the USA PATRIOT Act. We celebrated predatory vendors as "library champions." We have missed important opportunities to articulate to the public the library perspective on the copyright battle and the information commons. We have begun renting out bestsellers, on the model of video stores. We failed, as an association, to come to Sanford Berman's defense in 1999 in his fight for free speech rights at work, instead preferring to support the interests of the HCL administration. Most egregiously, we have begun experimenting with "two-tiered," fee-based services.

Admittedly, some of these seem to be unconnected events, but they do indicate trends in overall library thinking. This thinking says, "There is no alternative." It says, "The world is changing; we must change with it" (as a rationalization for making ALA more like a for-profit corporation or library systems more like businesses). This thinking is a way of making our own decisions seem like the only decisions possible, as though in making these decisions we are merely conforming with "what is happening," and as though "what is happening" is not the result of individuals, like us, making decisions, but something inexorable, like the hand of God. In specific terms, most of these decisions against our fundamental beliefs are explained as compromises with economic necessity. But isn't it odd that these "difficult compromises" have corresponded in time precisely to our country's greatest period of "prosperity" since the post–WWII boom, and in all cases were decided against a vocal opposition which argued for alternatives? Isn't it also odd that the economic bind in which has caught library administrators and others during this era hasn't been met with an appropriate political analysis and response, but rather with an affirmation of the era's neoliberal movement, with its attendant privatization and "fiscal discipline"?

Having been through these experiences and having seen where these trends are leading us, we should take stock of our position as a profession relative to the political economic currents of society and develop a response. To do this will require some serious myth busting, however. Mainstream liberals, who make up the majority of the profession, tended to support Bill Clinton in his advocacy of "free trade" and corporate globalization, in which a major strategy of the neoliberal movement is hidden. The hidden strategy is to create, through a process free from the meddling of representatives of civic and popular groups or democratic constituencies, a body of international agreements that will allow secretive arbitration panels to override domestic laws which have been designed to benefit the public interest. This includes laws that protect our quality of life in areas ranging from food safety to labor standards to environmental protection to laws guaranteeing free library service. Generally speaking, mainstream liberals have supported "trade liberalization" policies, fooled by a propagandizing news media and influenced by their loyalty to a newly money-driven Democratic Party.

The particular manifestation of this corporate globalization strategy that has implications for libraries at the present time is the General Agreement on Trade in Services (GATS), whose negotiation continues to go through iterations at meetings of the World Trade Organization. Under this agreement, governments which subsidize information services (e.g. libraries) could be financially penalized for "unfairly" competing with foreign corporations (e.g. fee-based digital libraries). This would represent a legal enforcement of the commodification of information — information as a commodity being exactly the thing to which libraries offer an alternative.

Much has been written on the implications of the GATS for libraries in recent years, but trying to get mainstream liberals on ALA Council to read a little bit about the issue is like trying to get their parents to drop acid. The resistance to this and other "big picture" library issues is what I consider the major threat from within in librarianship. It is related to that sense among the majority of liberal baby boomers that "there is no alternative" (to disencumbering capitalism from public interest concerns); that the supposed alternatives, in the form of progressive social policies, have been tried and failed. But what failed during this period of the baby boomers' maturation were not progressive policies. What failed was merely an exuberant moment enjoyed by a generation which thought that everything it envisioned was new, when in fact everything it envisioned was part of a long, well established progressive tradition.

Typical baby boomers (though certainly not all of them), recalling the '60s and '70s, sometimes seem confused about exactly what it was that has collapsed, as though they regard everything they wanted then as a dream from which they have now been awakened to the harshness of reality. But now that it is members of this generation who are in charge, the harshness of the present day free-market capitalist movement must be understood as a creation of their own free decisions. Ironically, the conservative policies to which they have now turned, in apparent repentance for their dreams of social justice (or shame at having rejected the authority of their elders), threaten to bring a world of capitalism that truly would be new. In this new world, positive and longstanding aspects of the social order, distributing opportunity and risk throughout communities, could be undone, tearing the social fabric in favor of a capitalist ideology that, measured against the stability of existing, established communitarian values (manifested in such things as public libraries), and the now-outmoded traditional societies, is as radical as any utopian ideal.

We stand at an awkward moment. A popular trope of politicians who want to project an image of originality and new ideas is to say that we have "moved beyond the tired definitions of Left and Right." Nothing could be further from the truth; the definitions of Left and Right have never been more applicable to real politics than they are today. On the other hand, "conservative" and "liberal" are definitely showing their age as labels. The original meaning of "liberal," which is still used in Europe and by economists and political scientists, referring to a philosophy of limited government and trust in the benevolence of human nature, is becoming more common in the U.S. as more people become aware of the neo-liberal direction of government policies of the past twenty years, creating an uncertainty about what is meant when the word is used. At the same time, "conservative" has begun to seem an inappropriate label to apply to the Right wing, which is often anything but cautious and concerned with preserving established values.

We on the Left, therefore, should recognize and embrace the conservative aspect of our present-day concerns. At the same time, we should not lose sight of the fact that our philosophy is based on the belief that we can create a better world according to those humanistic values that are now so derided by "conservatives" populist anti-intellectuals.

The place of libraries on this shifting scene is absolutely central. While libraries have a classical-liberal aspect in the core value of intellectual freedom and personal privacy, these social aspects of liberalism are presently losing ground (unlike the classical liberalism of free-market economics). While libraries have a communitarian aspect in their public nature, this is the economic aspect of communitarianism, which is also presently losing ground (unlike the communitarian drive to protect children from pornography, for example). Finally, while libraries have a conservative aspect in representing the preservation of culture and ideas, this is the conservatism of educated humanists, which is also losing ground (unlike the conservatism of the protection of the powerful and the intolerance for difference, both gaining ground). These tendencies are all contributing to the decline of libraries and the decline of society — all apart, it should be noted, from the impact of the Internet. And all during the period of the baby boom generation's rise to power.

The paradox is that most baby boom librarians don't believe that they have lost their ideals or that they are different people than they once were. Nor do they seem to realize what has become of librarianship and the world since the days they tried to change it. Tell them about the corporatization of libraries or about the WTO and what it means, and their response is to ask why Generation X isn't unified behind these political causes the way boomers were in their youth. The message, in other words, is "Social change is the responsibility of the young." When they were young this is certainly what they believed.

A major part of the problem we face now is that baby boomers see themselves as having moved to the other side of the generation gap that so defined their worldview, and therefore past the ethical responsibility of social action and criticism. This generation gap that was (and is) so idiosyncratic to the baby boom generation is now having a ripple effect. The role of Generation X, who never felt that such a major generation gap existed between themselves and their elders, should now be to remind baby boomers of both their continuing social responsibilities and their new, unfamiliar power to actually affect the course of history.

While boomers correctly realized, sometime in the '70s, that they did not in fact have the power to create the land of milk and honey in a short time, this feeling of ineffectiveness or futility (and the concomitant loss of ideals for some) is out of place now that boomers are in their years of power and entering into leadership positions in institutions and government.

Boomer librarians now have a real power that is dangerous if it is not self-conscious and held to critical standards (as we are seeing) but promising if it is intelligently used. Generation Xers, in my opinion, have a little acknowledged need for boomers to help set a truly ethical example, to cure us of our early-developed cynicism. Thus, the political dimension of the future of librarianship depends upon the baby boom generation coming to terms with its past and newly appreciating what it has repressed.

Things aren't looking groovy right now, but with effort and action, we don't have to be in for a completely bad trip either.

OLD MAIDS AND FAIRIES: THE IMAGE PROBLEM

Polly Thistlethwaite

"As for the old maid librarians, they still exist, to be sure, but you really have to look around for them, for their places are rapidly being taken by pretty career girls and smart young matrons."
— Ernestine Rose, *The Public Library in American Life* (Columbia University Press, 1954), 4–5

"Sometime in the late sixties or early seventies, a group of dissatisfied librarians, disgusted at the way the desiccated little old ladies and waspish closet queens of the American Library Association (ALA) were doing nothing more than playing empty parliamentary games with themselves, established the Social Responsibilities Round Table...."
— Harleigh Kyson, Jr., "Library Service & Gays," *Gay Sunshine*, October-November 1971

Librarians are preoccupied with an Image Problem. The Image: female librarians = pinched old maids; male librarians = fastidious, limp-wristed aesthetes. The Problem: this is unflattering and unfair! Librarians are REALLY NOT like this at all. Really. There are too many "negative images" out there like this, and for no good reason. We need more "positive images" librarians in movies and books, images more in line with how we REALLY ARE. We need more heroic, gorgeous, witty, clever, actively heterosexual, and smartly dressed librarians. Fantasy should reflect reality because — it hurts to be Miss Understood. It's bad for our self-esteem and bad for our salaries. Librarians would climb in cultural and economic value if Tom Cruise and Meryl Streep clamored to play exciting, complex librarians having love affairs and promoting information literacy in major cinematic roles. The Image Problem is killing us. Hollywood functions to discourage young people from becoming librarians. Our rep is undeservedly uncool. "My son the librarian..." — when have you *ever* heard that? How are we to reproduce, recruit, replicate under these conditions? We are doomed, at least until the culture industry WAKES UP and lionizes us.

STOP WHINING.

Some librarians say, "Just shrug and laugh it off." Ha, ha, ha. Loosen up, brush it back. Not a Big Deal. If you've got a Problem with the Image it must be, uh, that you've got an Image Problem of your own, a deep down, personal, a problem with Yourself. You're not Really Like That, are you? Laugh now, or else you're insecure and you don't have a sense of humor. Other librarians say, Don't Talk About It; that just makes it worse. Serious. Shut Up. Speculation on this topic is dumb and frivolous.

Write about what librarians Really Do, discuss the profession's social service, its demo-cratic indispensability, its cataloging statistics. Work is reality, and that's all that matters.

WHAT'S REALLY REEL?

Cut through all the fuss about the old maid and the aesthete stereotypes and you find that Western popular culture offers a surprising variety of librarian characters, yet there are several recurring subtexts producing this variety. Librarian characters are often drawn around tensions between order and disorder, the known and the unknown, the sacred and the profane, the sexual and the asexual. These subtexts and tensions are sufficiently abstract to produce an exciting and complex array of characters. There are librarian heroes and librarian villains, wild librarians and tame librarians, rule-bound librarians and rule-breaking librarians, beautiful librarians and ugly librarians. Often a librarian character experiences movement and transformation along these dramatic axes. With this variety of representations, why do librarians have knickers in a twist tighter than, say, other classes of people with an arguable mass mediated Image Problem like, say, engineers, New Yorkers, cops, or Latinas over 50?

WHY SO HOT 'N' BOTHERED?

I'll Tell You Why. Though there are thousands of fantasy librarians extant in our cultural milieu, the librarian character types most firmly embedded in our collective cultural bosom are the Old Maid and the Aesthete, *and* these stereotypes read QUEER with a Capital Q. Their Queerness is what makes them offensive. In academic translation: Librarianship's Image Problem is generated by a heteronormativity which functions discursively to identify and marginalize Queerness. In other words, Librarians' concern with Image reflects the tremendous uneasiness Straight and Gay and Lesbian librarians alike experience while negotiating the "label" Queer and its undesirable associated characteristics, including asexuality, hypersexuality, sexual perversion, political correctness, pretentious snobbery, and strangeness. Such unflattering attributes are commonly packed into baggage carried by the stereotypical Old Maid and the stereotypical Bitchy Queen.

In the movie *It's a Wonderful Life* Jimmy Stewart sees what the world would have been like if he'd never lived. He calls out from his window beyond to Donna Reed his now-librarian wife looking frumpy, unhappy, unfucked, and practically dressed. She lets rip a hysterical scream. Had Jimmy Stewart never lived, might Donna Reed have been ... a lesbian, I mean a librarian? Horror. Could sensible shoes alone warrant such distress? Might there be not only fashion anxiety, but also sexual anxiety motivating Miss Reed's blood curdling shriek? I would say so.

Jim Carmichael's 1992 survey of male librarians indicated the most common stereotypes articulated by male librarians are "effeminate, probably gay," "powerless, socially inept," and "unambitious."[1] Morrisey and Case's 1988 research indicated that despite the "positive" non-stereotypical image the non-librarian public has of male librarians, the masculine bibliophiles themselves were haunted by concerns about their perceived "negative" image.[2] Were these fellas surveyed just humble and self-depreciating? Or were they performing their hypersensitivity to the Question of Queerness? Methinks the latter.

All this professionally internalized homophobia blooms fully, despite of *and* because of the presence and influence of Queer librarians in the ranks, politics, and history of librarianship. What professions were available to unmarried women around the turn of the century? Nursing, teaching, librarianship, and prostitution. I suspect that librarianship in its earlier years attracted an inordinate number of "spinsters" secretly, or even openly, attracted to other women. These days, folks openly speculate about the unannounced sexual preferences of unmarried and unattached library colleagues. In bygone days, such speculation might not have been so glibly articulated, but it circled in the more submerged conversational currents around the water cooler. Despite the substantial closet doors in a profession clamoring for legitimacy, the American Library Association happily became the first professional organization to sponsor a Gay and Lesbian subdivision: the Task Force on Gay Liberation formed in 1970. This fact alone was a selling point when I was a dyke pup considering career choices in the early 1980s.

Librarians share a preoccupation with "positive" and "negative" images with other classes of frequently maligned folk, not the least of which are Gays and Lesbians. Funny, that. The Gay and Lesbian Alliance Against Defamation (GLAAD), one of the country's leading GLBT political organizations, tackles media stereotypes gravitating towards serial killers, pedophiles, cowards, predators, and suicidal alcoholics. Concerned librarians take heart! It could be worse.

Stop Whining, Postscript.

GLAAD's positive images campaigns seek "positive" media role models for queer youth and adults deprived of "healthy, constructive, inspirational" self-representations. Critics charge GLAAD's campaigns with excessive political correctness (the moralistic Shhh! of Etiquette Queens smacks to some of censorship), a focus on fantasy confused with reality, and an underdeveloped sense of humor and self-confidence. Similar arguments appear in librarians' discussion of the matter.

Notes

1. James Carmichael. "The Male Librarian and the Feminine Image: a Survey of Stereotype, Status, and Gender Perceptions." *Library & Information Science Research* 14 (1992): 411–446.
2. Locke Morrisey and Donald Case. "There Goes My Image: the Perception of Male Librarians by Colleague, Student, Self." *College & Research Libraries* 49 (1988): 453–464.

LIBRARY ETHICS AND THE PROBLEM WITH PATRIOTISM

Emily-Jane Dawson

The powerful have seized an opportunity. They have maximized America's fear in the wake of the hijackings of September 11th and are using it to justify restrictions on our freedoms, our civil rights, and our free access to information. Law enforcement is finding justification for more latitude in conducting surveillance and performing searches. The Justice Department has gained new powers to detain immigrants indefinitely. Federal agencies are acting to classify previously accessible information. The Attorney General has advised federal agencies to ignore the Freedom of Information Act. If you're not worried for the users in your library, you should be worried for your own sake.

After September 11th, the Congress moved quickly to restrict personal freedom and political rights with the cleverly titled USA-PATRIOT Act (the acronym stands for "Uniting and Strengthening America by Providing Appropriate Tools Required to Intercept and Obstruct Terrorism Act of 2001"). The Patriot Act gives federal law enforcement many new powers in the areas of surveillance, secret searches, and detention of immigrants.[1]

It also expands the Foreign Intelligence Surveillance Act (FISA), allowing the FBI to obtain court orders requiring any person or business to hand over books, papers, and similar materials. This order is granted by a secret court, and is subject to almost none of the restrictions applied to standard criminal search warrants— basically, the FBI says to the judge, "We want a FISA warrant because some of the records we're seeking are relevant to a foreign intelligence investigation." The FBI does not have to offer affidavits or any other proof, as it would with a criminal search warrant. To make matters worse, the person or business named in the FISA warrant is prohibited from telling anyone besides an attorney about the warrant.[2]

Both the American Booksellers Foundation for Free Expression and the ALA's Office for Intellectual Freedom have advised their constituencies to contact them saying they need legal advice as soon as they receive notice of a court order under FISA — but there is some doubt as to how much good this will do library workers or libraries. It is not likely to protect the privacy of library users.

While the FBI is trying its best to get at confidential patron information in your library, the rest of the government is making it harder for you to access government information. In October, U.S. Attorney General John Ashcroft issued a memo gently reminding heads of all federal agencies that Freedom of Information Act (FOIA) requests can be refused on the grounds that disclosure would violate commercial, institutional, or personal privacy. Ashcroft's memo assured federal administrators that their refusal to disclose records under FOIA would be supported by the Justice Department.[3]

Also in October, the Government Printing Office (GPO), which runs the Federal Depository Library System, asked member libraries to destroy a copy of a CD-ROM in the libraries' depository collections. The GPO asks libraries to destroy or return items from time to time; if, for example, the information in a database is superceded, or it is discovered that a report contains inaccurate information or was printed incorrectly. But documents librarians interviewed by the *Chronicle of Higher Education* reported that they had never before been asked to return a depository item for security reasons.[4] In addition to this, the Environmental Protection Agency, the Federal Aviation Administration, and the Nuclear Regulatory Commission have all deleted "sensitive material" from their web pages.[5]

Local libraries are not immune. Florida librarian Kathleen Hensman went straight to the police when she recognized the name of a library patron on the FBI website in September 2001. She told the cops that a man who had used the name Molad Alshehi had used the computers at the Delray Beach Public Library where she works, and could be the Molad Alshehi the FBI lists as one of the men who participated in the hijacking of four airplanes that were later flown into the World Trade Center in New York, the Pentagon in Washington, DC, and into the ground in Pennsylvania.[6]

Hensman didn't just happen to notice the name while watching television or reading the paper — she sought it out on the FBI's website. And she didn't trust her memory that the man she saw in the library had the same name she saw on the FBI list — a *Sun-Sentinel* article reported "Hensman said she is still searching library records to see whether any of the suspects' names match the sign-in sheets used as a waiting list for computer users."[7]

Most states have laws protecting the privacy of public library patrons in situations just like this. Florida's law makes library registration and circulation records confidential and exempt from public records disclosure laws, and makes it illegal for a person to reveal information within these records without a judicial order.[8] But Kathleen Hensman is not being prosecuted under Florida law. She can still be found working at the Delray Beach Public Library, with the full support of the library's administration and board. And even librarians seem to think she acted reasonably. Judith Krug, director of the ALA Office for Intellectual Freedom, said, "I suspect most people faced with the same situation would have done what she did."[9] Mary Wegner, Iowa's chief librarian, said that the more she thought about it, the more she agreed with what Hensman did.[10]

What is really going on here, anyway? The information Hensman gave the police in Delray Beach may have been vital in helping the government to hunt down the people who are responsible for the tragedy of September 11th. Hensman didn't tell the police what her patrons were reading, or what websites they were visiting. She just told them who had been in the library. Hensman acted like a good citizen, right?

Wrong. Even if we set aside the climate of paranoia and increased racism[11] that has enveloped the country since September 11th, Hensman acted unethically and illegally. It's clear that she went to the police because she knew that otherwise they would have no inkling that terrorists had been in the Delray Beach library. If they didn't have this information, they wouldn't know to get search warrants and seize library computers.[12] Hensman didn't tell the police what websites the suspects visited — instead she told the police to look for this information themselves. But then she started looking through the library's records to see if she recognized more names from the FBI list.[13] Hensman ignored the principles of intellectual freedom and patron privacy because they were inconvenient to her desire to aid the authorities in apprehending criminals.

Jonnie Hargis, a library assistant at the University of California–Los Angeles, was suspended for one week without pay in late September 2001, after he responded to a patriotic mass email sent by Michelle Torre, a co-worker at the Young Research Library. Torre's email quoted Gordon Sinclair's "America: The Good Neighbor," a speech defending the United States' international policies; Hargis argued that the United States' bombing campaign in Iraq and its support of Israel's violence against Palestinians makes it a bad neighbor, and asked "…so, who are the terrorists anyway?"[14]

Library administrators justified the suspension with a policy banning political, religious, or patriotic email messages. The policy was created the day Hargis was informed of his suspension, *after* the email exchange in question took place. Torre was not disciplined.[15] Hargis' suspension was later rescinded by UCLA administration, but only after he filed a grievance through his union.[16]

Kathy Hoeth, director of the Florida Gulf Coast University Library, also made the news in the last few months of 2001. In the end of September it was reported in local newspapers that Hoeth had prohibited library employees from wearing "Proud to be an American" stickers, fearing that they would create a climate in which the university's 239 international students would feel uncomfortable. The university administration found that Hoeth's actions were in violation of "general Academic Freedom statements," and suspended Hoeth for a month without pay. She later wrote a formal apology.[17]

Why was Hoeth disciplined for limiting freedom of speech, and Hargis for exercising it, while Hensman (who not only violated professional ethics, but also broke the law) has not been reprimanded, disciplined, or prosecuted for her violation of patron confidentiality? The simple answer is that Hensman acted in a way that the government, the media, and the ruling class are encouraging us all to act — like a snitch!

One imagines Hensman assessed her situation and decided that the FBI's search for criminals was more important than the privacy of library patrons, despite her training and Florida law. Her bosses categorized her actions as patriotic and honorable, so she has not been reprimanded. In contrast, Hoeth and Hargis both acted in ways their supervisors saw as unpatriotic. Hoeth restricted her employees' freedom of expression in a way that her bosses did not support, so she was disciplined. Hargis exercised his own freedom of expression in a way his bosses did not support, so he was disciplined. It is easy to imagine that Hoeth and Hargis would have found institutional support easily, as Hensman did, if only their actions had been "patriotic."

At the Multnomah County public library in Portland, Oregon (where I work as a library assistant), two of the staff in my branch began wearing U.S. flag pins shortly after September 11. While this was not in violation of Oregon law or library policy, I—like Hoeth—was concerned that it would have a negative effect on some of our library patrons. I imagined several unhappy possibilities: an Arab-American patron might worry that the staff were making note of what he was reading; a pacifist patron might hesitate before asking for help finding an anti-war website; a teenager might think twice before checking out *Johnny Got His Gun*. Because I work in a small library with a fairly close-knit staff, I was able to sit down with each of the two staff members with the flag pins and talk with them about my concerns. I explained my perspective, and reminded them that their ideas of what the flag represents might not be the same as our patrons'. I asked them each to consider not wearing the pins. One continued to wear a flag, the other did not. The supervisor of my branch remained neutral on the issue. In October, the library announced to staff that U.S. flags would be installed in each branch. At that point it was unclear who had made the decision, or why it had been made. Flags had been ordered and were on their way.

I was worried. I have lived in Portland for most of my life and don't remember ever seeing a flag in the library. What message would their sudden appearance send to the public? How much worse would it be for the patrons I imagined feeling uncomfortable with a staff member's patriotic lapel pin?

I talked with my co-workers about my worries, and wrote a memo of concern to the library's Intellectual Freedom Committee. Together with a few other library workers, I circulated a letter among staff members, asking the administration not to install flags. Twenty-one of them signed it,[18] and two of us presented it to Janet Kinney (director of community services) and members of the Intellectual Freedom Committee at a meeting in mid–November.

It was a tense meeting. My coworker and I explained our position and presented our letter of petition. We presented the basic ideas that the meaning and significance of the American flag is interpreted differently by each person, and that many people have good reason to interpret it negatively in our current social and political climate, and that this would hinder some patrons' intellectual freedom. I also asserted that the timing of the planned installation of flags would aggravate this problem.

Kinney explained that a request to install flags in neighborhood libraries came from a patron who used a particular branch. Apparently, the patron came into the library shortly after September 11th and was horrified to realize that there was no flag there. She talked with the branch supervisor, and left unsatisfied. She lobbied the County Commission, Kinney, and other members of the library administration to have U.S. flags installed in all the libraries. Eventually, Kinney decided that she would do so.

Kinney indicated that she would consider our concerns and planned to discuss them with the library director. She implied that the matter was not firmly decided, although she had presented the library's plans as finalized earlier in the conversation. A few weeks later, flags arrived in the neighborhood libraries as planned.

The funny thing about this whole series of events is that the flags delivered were the wrong size for the flagpoles that came with them. The flags dragged forlornly on the ground, and had to be returned. That was in December 2001, and at this writing I haven't seen replacements, or heard that they were coming. The administration seems to have taken the opportunity to drop the matter quietly, no doubt hoping for the least amount of friction from pro- and anti-flag patrons and staff alike.

What is the mechanism that makes all this possible? Americans are afraid because after a lifetime of believing that we alone in the world are safe, we have seen people die by the thousands in one of our own cities. And we're encouraged to respond to this by displaying flags on our houses, our cars, and on our clothes. We're asked to remember our country's welfare, to put our country before our humanity, and to trust the president to win the war on terrorism. We are asked to be mindless patriots.

Patriotism is a set of values that every American is supposed to uphold, and is treated as politically neutral by the dominant culture. But progressives need to critique patriotism in the same way we do other programs of the state. Radical librarians have an additional responsibility to look at the effects patriotism has on intellectual freedom, the rights of library workers, and even narrower issues like the acquisition and cataloging of library materials.

It's easy to defend patron privacy, or any principle of professional ethics, when the stakes are not high — but we have a code of ethics[19] precisely so that we will have a guide when things get tough. Our ethical guidelines are written to protect the rights of library users. We cannot abandon them when basic rights of personal privacy, access to public information, and freedom of expression are being curtailed in other arenas.

Notes

1. American Civil Liberties Union. "ACLU Calls New Senate Terrorism Bill Significantly Worse; Says Long-Term Impact on Freedom Cannot Be Justified" [press release], 5 October 2001.

2. Christopher Dreher. "He Knows What You've Been Checking Out," *Salon.com*, 6 March 2002, <http://www.salon.com/news/feature/2002/03/06/libraries>. See also: Nat Hentoff. "Eyeing What You Read: FBI in Libraries and Bookstores," *Village Voice*, 14 February 2002, <http://www.villagevoice.com/issues/0208/hentoff.php>; and Nat Hentoff. "Big John Wants Your Reading List: Has the Attorney General Been Reading Franz Kafka?," *Village Voice*, 22 February 2002, <http://www.villagevoice.com/issues/0209/hentoff.php>.

3. John Ashcroft. "Memorandum for Heads of All Federal Departments and Agencies," U.S. Department of Justice, Washington DC, 12 October 2001, <http://www.usdoj.gov/04foia/011012.htm>.

4. Alex P. Kellogg. "An Order to Destroy a CD-ROM Raises Concern Among University Librarians," *Chronicle of Higher Education*, 8 March 2002: A34. Database online. Available from *EBSCOhost Academic Search Elite*.

5. Margaret Kriz. "Vanishing Web Pages," *National Journal*, 20 October 2001: 3268. Database online. Available from *EBSCOhost MasterFile Premiere*.

6. Amanda Riddle. "FBI Searching Delray Beach Apartment of Two Hijackers," *Sun-Sentinel*, 16 September 2001, <http://www.sunsentinel.com/news/local/southflorida/sfl-worldtrade-917 delraysearch.story>.

7. John Holland, Jennifer Peltz, and Robin Benedick. "Investigators Look Into How Library Computers May Have Linked Terrorists," *Sun-Sentinel*, 16 September 2001, <http://www.sunsentinel.com/news/local/southflorida/sfl-culprits16.story>.

8. Florida Statutes 257 § 261 (2001).

9. David E. Rosenbaum. "A Nation Challenged: Questions of Confidentiality; Competing Principles Leave Some Professionals Debating Responsibility to Government," *New York Times*, 23 November 2001: 7. Database online. Available from *Dialog File 471:New York Times Fulltext-90 Day*.

10. Ibid.

11. See, for example: Christian Leonard. "Suspect Called Himself a 'Patriot' After Killing Immigrant, Authorities Say," *Arizona Republic*, 17 September 2001.

12. Hensman uses this reasoning herself; see Rosenbaum 2001.

13. John Holland, Jennifer Peltz, and Robin Benedick. "Investigators Look Into How Library Computers May Have Linked Terrorists," *Sun-Sentinel*, 16 September 2001,
<http://www.sunsentinel.com/news/local/southflorida/sfl-culprits16.story>.

14. Sarah Schmidt. "UCLA Suspends Librarian for 'Electronic Harassment': Politically Charged Email Sparks Lawsuit, Free Speech Debate," *National Post*, 19 October 2001,
<http://www.nationalpost.com/news/world/story.html?f=/stories/20011019/743789.html>.

15. "Freedom of Speech Under Attack at UCLA Library," *Daily Bruin* [University of California-Los Angeles], 5 October 2001. Database online. Available from *Electric Library*. Also: Robert Salonga, "Union Representing UCLA Library Assistant Takes Action One Step Further," *Daily Bruin*, 24 October 2001. Database online. Available from *Electric Library*.

16. Stephanie Armour. "War of Words: Free Speech Vexes Employers," *USA Today*, 7 December 2001. Database online. Available from *Electric Library*.

17. Marci Elliot. "FGCU Library Director Suspended Over Badge Flap Returns to Work," *Bonita Daily News*, 30 October 2001, <http://www.naplesnews.com/01/10/bonita/d693661a.htm>. See also: Marci Elliot. "FGCU Library Director Is Suspended for Banning U.S. Pride Badges," *Naples Daily News*, 26 September 2001, *NewsBank Public Library Collection*; and Marci Elliot. "FGCU Library Director Reprimanded for Stance on Patriotic Stickers," *Naples Daily News*, 20 September 2001, <http://www.naplesnews.com/01/09/naples/d684319a.htm>.

18. I talked to a large number of staff who seemed to generally agree with the letter but felt uncomfortable signing it, because they feared it might make them appear negatively to their managers and co-workers.

19. As just about anyone likely to read this essay knows, library workers are taught ethics in library school and in on-the-job trainings. Most libraries have a formalized list of principles, or a mission statement that expresses their particular institution's interpretation of the ethics of librarianship. The Council of the ALA adopted a *Code of Ethics* in 1995, which can be found at <http://www.ala.org/alaorg/oif/ethics.html>.

IN THE STACKS AND IN THE SACK: AN UNDERCOVER LOOK AT LIBRARIANS AND EROTICA

Cindy Indiana

Librarians are exposed to erotica through the nature of our work. Since the first dirty picture or nasty words were put on paper, erotica had the potential to be collected, cataloged, stored, protected, defended, and even found on shelves for the discriminating library user. *Library of Congress Subject Headings* includes more than 100 subject headings beginning with "erotic" or "erotica," as well as narrower terms, including "Women and erotica" (but not men), "Sex in the theater" (in the back row, perhaps?), "Hair—Erotic aspects" (unfortunately, no "see also" reference for "buns"). In the eleven years since a collection of essays entitled *Libraries, Erotica, and Pornography* was edited by Martha Cornog and published by Oryx Press, the Internet has made it much easier — and more entertaining—for librarians to find information about erotica or about the relationship between librarians and the erotic. Indeed, it is now much easier for anyone to find erotica or even spicier material that is true, false, fictional, or fraudulent. Cornog asks in her introduction entitled "For Sex, See Librarian," "How many libraries set up a [vertical] file in the mid-1980s on a phenomenon variously called *gerbiling* or *gerbilization*...?"[1] Not only do librarians no longer need vertical files to keep track of hot topics, but the public doesn't need them either. Web surfers can find 95 references to *gerbiling* on Yahoo and 207 on Google, but many reference librarians would pick up enough clues on the topic to do a search in the AFU (alt.folklore.urban) archive and the Urban Legends References Pages, where they would find 20 items about *gerbiling*.

Advertisers, writers, and the media identify librarians themselves with the erotic and risqué, probably because the media sees an opportunity for humor in suggesting that even a librarian might enjoy sex. As Antony Brewerton points out, "the tense sexual atmosphere of the quiet library and the repressed sexuality of library workers are well-established elements of the image" and, as a result, "the sexual side of the image is given much attention on the Web ... naked librarians abound."[2] A cartoon in the collection of the Kinsey Institute for Sex Research takes advantage of the humor inherent in the idea of a bespectacled bookworm enjoying sex — she actually reads while engaged in the act![3] As preoccupied as librarians are with their image, advertisers seems to enjoy making their point (and their sale) by emphasizing what the librarian's image is not. An advertisement for Candida Royalle's Natural Contours vibrators suggests, "After a long day at the library, the last thing Margaret needed to unwind with was a good book."[4] Margaret is perky, obviously anticipating what awaits her at the end of the day, wears lipstick and nail polish, but also sports eyeglasses the thickness of which has not been seen since the invention of ultralight lenses. In a Bacardi advertisement, a voluptuous woman in a barely-there gold mesh top and skirt reveals a Bacardi bat logo tattooed on her lower back, accompanied by the legend, "Librarian by day; Bacardi by night."[5] Obviously, she isn't a librarian anymore if she looks and dresses like this—and has a tattoo.

Beyond the merely erotic, a website entitled "The Image of Librarians in Pornography," has been compiled by Dan Lester, who presented a paper on the topic at a meeting of the Popular Culture Association in 1990. The website lists 49 hardcore pornographic novels published between 1978 and 1988 and invites suggestions or contributions of additional material in order to expand his collection. Lester notes that the librarians in the books on his list are usually women and that 90 percent of the text or more is "explicit description of all types of sexual activities." Lester also notes "Some library descriptions seem to have been written by librarians or by regular library users, as they're quite realistic; other authors have apparently never even been in a library."[6] Many titles include or begin with the words "horny" or "hot" (*Hot to Trot Librarian, Horny Peeping Librarian*) or both (*Horny Hot Librarian*). Some titles have links to Lester's lengthy annotations, including *Chained, Whipped Librarians* and *Bang the Librarian Hard*. Some betray an at least rudimentary knowledge of library terminology, such as *Sex Behind the Stacks* and *First Rear Entry*—but most don't. Candi Strecker, a librarian, zine publisher and self-described "observer and cataloguer of oddball popular cultural phenomena" also created an annotated list entitled "Sex in the Stacks: Librarian Porn Novel Reviews," with fewer titles but more annotations than Lester's. Strecker's theory about librarians and porn is that "writers often base sexual fantasies on women in the workplace and their uniforms: you'll find bushels of porn about nurses, teachers, nuns. Part of the arousal factor seems to based on the paradox that a woman might be brainy and slutty" and that "exploring the urges of the body in the temple of the mind may be a sacrilege, but it's also a giggly dare." Unlike Lester's comprehensive list, Strecker's is more selective, discarding books "so badly written that they defied arousal." A couple of the horny and hots make the Strecker's cut, including *The Hottest Librarian*, by Gary F. Woods, published by Oakmore Enterprises in 1985. Although Woods' librarian, Gussie Fennimore "loses her cherry, she keeps her bun," and "Along the way, she encounters a bewildering range of penis shapes: stumpy, crooked, pencil-thin and the ever-popular Enormous."[7]

Contrary to what many librarians believe about our image, sexy librarians are no strangers to film either. Martin Raish's excellent and up-to-the-minute filmography, "Librarians in the Movies," includes references to what Raish called "low key erotic" librarians, such as the fashionable, sexy, and efficient librarians in the research department of a television network in "Desk Set" (1957) and Gloria Grahame as a librarian in "The Man Who Never Was,"(1956) who "is a bit of a wild one and goes out with a lot of RAF officers," and "Bliss," (1997) in which a "middle-aged, sexy but sane" librarian, played by Lois Chiles, helps a husband with his research in search of sexual compatibility. Raish's list also includes "Tomcats" (2001), in which "a meek, bun- and spectacles-wearing librarian transmogrifies into a leather-clad, whip-cracking S&M aficionado" in the bedroom, and "Debbie Does Dallas," which includes scenes of sex in the stacks, filmed at the Pratt Institute in Brooklyn.[8]

For keeping up with the erotica in librariana, one of the best sources is librarian.net, a weblog created by Jessamyn West, about whom Library Juice wrote, "Jessamyn likes anarchism and sex, and anything relating to the image of librarians."[9] librarian.net includes a links to hard-to-find web-published stories, stories posted on newsgroups, literature about sex in the library, stories about real sex in libraries (such as the couple caught having sex in the British Library), link to an article about a librarian who quit her job and became a sex worker specializing in "low-risk fantasy" so that she could make more money and finally take a vacation. Interestingly, this former librarian "gets to do librarian fantasies at work at $300–$500/hr. clear."[10]

Erotic Resources for the Librarian:

> West, Jessamyn. *Librarian.net.*
> <http://www.librarian.net>

If something involving librarians and sex has happened in the world today, Jessamyn West will write about it in her weblog.

> AFU Archive
> <http://www.urbanlegends.com>

> Urban Legends Reference Pages
> <http://www.snopes2.com>

Think someone may be making up that story about the gerbil or the guy who got his penis chopped by a vacuum cleaner? Check it out at the Urban Legends website. Both urban legend websites have categories for "sex," so you don't even need to guess at what the stories might be.

> Raish, Martin. Librarians in the Movies.
> <http://www.lib.byu.edu/dept/libsci/films/introduction.html>

Describes librarians in film, both stereotypical and spicy.

> Lester, Dan. Image of Librarians in Pornography.
> <http://www.riverofdata.com/librariana/porn/>

A list of hard-core pornographic books with library staff members as characters. Read books on Lester's list or send him your own contributions.

> Strecker, Candi. "Sex in the Stacks: Librarian Porn Novel Reviews."
>   ChipRowe.com
> <http://www.chiprowe.com/articles/library2.html>

Candi Strecker is a little more discriminating than Dan Lester.

Notes

1. Martha Cornog, "For Sex, See Librarian: An Introduction," in *Libraries, Erotica, and Pornography*, ed. Martha Cornog (Phoenix: Oryx, 1991), 2.
2. Antony Brewerton, "Wear Lipstick, Have a Tattoo, Belly-Dance, Then Get Naked: The Making of a Virtual Librarian," *Impact: Journal of the Career Development Group* 2:10 (November-December 1999), (9 September 2002).
   <http://www.careerdevelopmentgroup.org.uk/impact/archives/abrewerton.htm>
3. Catherine Johnson, Betsy Stirratt, and John Bancroft, eds., *Sex and Humor: Selections from the Kinsey Institute* (Bloomington: Indiana University, 2002).
4. Photocopy of advertisement from *Bust* magazine; in author's collection.
5. Photocopy of advertisement from *Rolling Stone* magazine; in author's collection.
6. Dan Lester, *Image of Librarians in Pornography*, 8 August 2000, (9 September 2002). <http://www.riverofdata.com/librariana/porn/>
7. Candi Strecker, "Sex in the Stacks: Librarian Porn Novel Reviews," *ChipRowe.com*, (9 September 2002). <http://www.chiprowe.com/articles/library2.html>

8. Martin Raish, *Librarians in the Movies: An Annotated Filmography*, 21 May 2002, (9 September 2002). <http://www.lib.byu.edu/dept/libsci/films/introduction.html>

9. *Library Juice* 3:20, 24 May 2000, (9 September 2002). <http://www.libr.org/Juice/issues/vol3/LJ_3.20.html>

10. Patricia Holt, "Dear Pat," *SfGate.com*, (9 September 2002). <http://www.sfgate.com/eguide/word/holt-dworkin.shtml>

LIBRARIANS!
INTO THE WORKERS' CORNER!

Bruce Jensen

Dylan Thomas joked about Yanks and Brits "up against the barrier of a common language." Ho ho ho. Want to meet people up against real language barriers? Check into industries that employ a lot of low-priced immigrant workers. Maybe even *you* have benefited from *their* services. Ever sleep in a motel? Eat in a restaurant? Use a public restroom?

> *I began to study English in order to defend myself*
> *From an American bastard where I was working.*

Language is an instrument of power — economic, political, informational ... without mastery of the dominant language, you're wide open for exploitation in the workplace.

> *They jerked me around like a puppet*
> *Just because I didn't speak that damned English.*

And another good place to see language barriers in action is @ your library. While the retail store across the street hires multilingual staff, installs vernacular signage, and crafts polyglot PR to attract a diverse clientele — because, at the end of the day, a brown person's money is as green than anyone else's — the library lets those things slide but pats itself on the back for flimsy overtures toward local linguistic and cultural minorities.

Minorities? Is that the word? Consider a city like Santa Ana, California, where the 2000 census found a 76% "Hispanic," primarily Spanish-speaking population, and whose 2002 downtown library looks like it was put together by Pete Wilson. Remember how Generalísimo Francisco Franco called Catalan the "language of the dogs" and outlawed its use? He would've been right at home behind a library administrator's office desk.

The American told me, in English and all pissed off,
"You wetback, you don't understand what you are supposed to do..."
— Los Jornaleros del Norte, "La Frasesita"[1]

Libraries are crucial in helping people *understand what they are supposed to do* when they want to fix their cars, succeed in school, get better jobs, raise their kids, pay their taxes, cook their meals, know their rights, enjoy their lives more fully.

Which people? That's for the library to decide. Consider immigrant day laborers. They present an increasingly prominent public face all around the country, and yet they are flatly ignored by libraries. It's hard to imagine a more information-impoverished constituency. For a number of economic, linguistic, legal, and cultural reasons, the *jornaleros* who gather on sidewalks and the parking lots of hardware stores each morning to scramble for job offers are effectively shut out from essential services and information sources that most of us take for granted.

Public libraries are in an ideal position to address many of their needs. There is a solid library tradition of doing just that for other labor groups, and the accelerating development of day laborer organizations nationwide offers enticing opportunities for collaboration involving librarians.

WHO ARE DAY LABORERS?

Despite regional variation, some broad generalizations hold true: the typical *jornalero* or *esquinero* (labels derived from Spanish words for "workday" and "street corner") is a young to middle-aged Spanish-speaking male. About half are single guys and the other half are married with families to help support.

Their first important demographic portrait was painted by UCLA professor Abel Valenzuela's Day Labor Survey of 481 *jornaleros* at 87 Los Angeles and Orange County, CA hiring sites in early 1999. He found that nearly 30% had been in the US less than a year, and two-thirds were under 37 years of age. While more than half had six years or less of formal education, more than one-third had gone to high school or beyond. All but ten of Valenzuela's 481 interviews were conducted in Spanish.

Nearly 60% of his informants hit the streets four or more days per week, and their mean estimated yearly earnings from day labor amounted to about $8,500. Lynn Svensson's Day Labor Research Institute found that only one in eight of L.A. day laborers owned a vehicle, and she estimated that perhaps as few as ten percent of those seeking work on a given day are hired.

Valenzuela emphasizes that Los Angeles day laborers are men, almost without exception. At some organized hiring locations, such as the Central American Refugee Center in Houston, TX, women are explicitly barred (Byars).

Some 85% of the workers in Valenzuela's survey lacked legal immigration documents. Unlike others in the culture of "temps" (affectionately labeled "*disposable employees*" in corporate HR jargon), a mammoth sector where Manpower, Inc. claimed 2.7 million employees and $12.4 billion worth of business in 2000, and where companies often get away with denying proper benefits), *jornaleros* avoid the middleman, so need not show legal residence papers. This seeming perquisite exposes them to severe abuses.

WHAT DO THEY DO?

Jornaleros are important participants in labor markets where fluctuating workloads encourage employers to minimize commitments to permanent staff. Their jobs are, often, literally here-today-gone-tomorrow arrangements. In L.A.'s garment district, one hiring site mainly furnishes hands to load or unload clothing shipments. Day laborers are often used in agriculture, where crop patterns and weather conditions dictate a heavy short-term demand for workers followed by long intervals when the employer cannot afford to keep them around. The civil-service or corporate cultures in which most librarians operate may make it difficult for some to appreciate the level of occupational instability faced by day laborers, and the flexibility that this requires of them.

Perhaps most familiar to most librarians are those urban *jornaleros* who gather at places such as hardware stores and truck rental lots to offer their services to construction contractors and homeowners for short-term projects. Day laborers at any hiring site may bring a formidable range of specialized trade skills and expertise. The requests are most commonly for manual labor; the fields the *jornalero* might be called upon to work in may well include plumbing, painting, masonry, welding, mechanics, landscaping, concrete finishing, tile-setting....

As much as their vocations differ, most frontline librarians should strongly identify with day laborers in at least one respect: the gaps between what *jornaleros* know and are capable of doing, and what they actually *do* all day long, are frequently enormous.

The biggest part of their working lives? A lot of standing around. One factor here is the fierce competition at hiring sites where there might be ten workers for every available job. *Jornaleros* must be alert and quick in order to find work — they vigilantly focus upon slowing motorists who might hire them, and they swarm vehicles relentlessly. Not to do so would jeopardize their chances to make money. Inevitably, this means that a large part of the typical *jornalero*'s day is, at non-organized hiring sites, spent watching for and accosting trucks and cars. To the uninitiated, it seems a colossal, tragic waste of time.

A growing number of experienced day laborers who resent that dead time have taken action to make better use of it. The educational and organizing work going on at structured hiring sites presents librarians with their best chances for community-building and humane support of day laborers.

ORGANIZED HIRING SITES

Formally regulated job centers have been established in many US cities. With July 2000's first national day laborers' conference in Northridge, CA, which brought together 18 organizations as the National Day Laborer Organizing Network, the work at local centers has become a coordinated national movement.

The Coalition for Humane Immigrant Rights of Los Angeles (CHIRLA) was founded in 1986 and has been dedicated to this kind of organizing a long time with its Day Labor Project. Working alongside local governments and an affiliate educational organization, IDEPSCA (Instituto de Educación Popular del Sur de California), the project has succeeded in applying principles of Freireian popular education to enhance the opportunities available to *jornaleros* and bring more dignity to their working lives.

A key component, simple yet essential, is the use of a lottery system to distribute jobs. Employers pick the names of laborers, classified according to vocational specialties, out of a hat. The workers are thus freed from competition and so can use their down time constructively, without missing chances to earn money.

CHIRLA's job centers commonly offer classes and training sessions, and it is not unusual to see *jornaleros* playing games or music while waiting to be called for a job. The band whose song opens this chapter, in fact — the Jornaleros del Norte, who have performed from coast to coast, have been featured several times on national radio, and appear in the Ken Loach film *Bread and Roses*—came together at one of these sites, and several of the group's members continue to work as day laborers.

Thus the guiding philosophy of organized hiring sites, usually municipally funded and supervised by community-based organizations with close ties to Latino immigrant groups, involves not only the cooperative maintenance of comfortable and humane surroundings, but also the provision of educational and recreational opportunities. Job centers typically host English classes or literacy instruction, and some provide training in occupational skills and safety.

In addition, job centers often help with filing wage claims for *jornaleros* who have been stiffed. Employers have been known to exploit day laborers by withholding pay and threatening to report workers to the INS if they complain. It is a fearsome threat if the laborer is unaware of his rights, but organized hiring sites have had a good record of winning justice in such cases. Lawyers working with a job center in Silver Spring, MD reported retrieval of $300,000 in unpaid *jornalero* wages in a 12-month period (Harrington).

So why aren't all day laborers flocking to job centers? David Bacon and others have described resistance among workers who favor non-organized sites (Reza and Casillas), but most media reports focus on exemplary regulated hiring sites such as that of Austin, TX (Zen Zhen), a refugee center in Houston, TX (Byars), and the L.A.-area sites operated by CHIRLA and other organizations (Voices); on calls to establish, fund, and maintain better day laborers' facilities, as in Seattle, WA (McOmber) and Atlanta, GA — where, unlike L.A., a good many day laborers are African-American (Bixler); or on measures taken by many municipalities to restrict or systematically harass day laborers (Cleeland).

In such instances, where local outcry and sometimes even violence — as in the case of the 1999 beatings of two Mexican *jornaleros* in New York (Baker) — spurs calls for "solutions" to the day laborer "problem," well-informed librarians can help facilitate positive community action instead of anti-immigrant outrage. And where organized sites have already been established, libraries have a golden opportunity to collaboratively support and help enhance the services of these job centers.

WHAT LIBRARIES *COULD* DO FOR DAY LABORERS

Get this straight: without a clear, practical plan based on study of the local situation, library outreach to non-organized hiring sites could easily be more intrusive than helpful. Gustavo Arellano, a journalist who has done ethnographic research among day laborers, maintains that on "corners that are not organized, offering library services will be fruitless because, although the men might stand around all day, they are standing around for a reason: they are looking for work." Librarians who do consider extending services to such locations must do so very carefully, staying conscious of the *jornaleros*' purpose for gathering there. First, do no harm: your services should not be an intrusive distraction that impedes the men from earning a living.

This is not to suggest that your library should ignore non-organized workers. They share most of the compelling information needs and barriers as those who frequent organized job centers. Although non-organized workers will be more difficult to reach, a carefully tuned approach—keyed to local attitudes and desires—could bring great benefit to them and their families.

Librarians shouldn't underestimate the real information deficits of hardworking laborers with little formal education living in a place where they don't understand the dominant language. I dropped by an organized job center where a pickup soccer game had been going on and one of the men had severely twisted an ankle. When I asked his companions tending to him if there was any ice around; they wondered sincerely what the hell good a cold drink could possibly do for a guy's ankle. Not until the site director seconded my opinion did the men accept the unheard-of idea that applying a cold compress would inhibit swelling.

Manual laborers have more reason than most of us to know basic first aid, but *jornaleros* ordinarily work in settings where such information is not posted and training is not provided. Health and safety information leads the following list of information that a library could help provide; this however is merely a general guide. It should go without saying that service providers must consult with local workers and site directors when formulating strategies and approaches. In any case, *jornaleros* could certainly use language-appropriate, comprehensible information about:

- First aid
- Chemical safety (in industrial and construction situations, solvents, paints, cleaners, etc.; in agricultural settings, pesticides)
- Personal protective equipment
- Local health clinics, emergency rooms, and procedures for summoning aid
- Medical issues, including diabetes
- Back care and lifting techniques

- State and local labor laws, including regulations about minimum wages and mandated breaks
- Filing wage claims
- Accessing available services and benefits for workers
- Trade skills (the finer points of their own fields, and how to pick up the basics of other crafts)
- Local job opportunities
- English language study, particularly vocational English
- Job-seeking skills (while it shouldn't be assumed that they all aspire to move out of day labor, some *jornaleros* do)
- Vocational training classes and programs
- Immigration laws, news, and legal assistance
- General news relevant to the site's users

Ideally, the library would furnish materials in a variety of appropriate print and non-print media. In addition, there are also recreational interests that ought not be ignored; insofar as it's possible, librarians should strive to satisfy desires for music, sports periodicals, fiction, and other topics and genres that emerge in their scans of local tastes.

Library services need to be inviting and unambiguously accessible in order to attract users who have good reason to fear government agencies. Serving *jornaleros* is likely to entail some compromises in patron identification. Some organized job centers issue photo IDs to their regulars; the library that honors such a card goes a long way toward gaining the trust and goodwill of day laborers.

WHAT LIBRARIES *HAVE* DONE FOR DAY LABORERS

In a word, almost nothing. If services for *jornalero* groups do exist, they are the best-kept secret in libraryland, absent from the literature and not reported in response to repeated queries in the two major discussion for a dealing with library services to Spanish speakers, REFORMANet and SOL.[2] This is one of the most significant missed opportunities in current librarianship. If libraries truly seek to be a relevant force in community advocacy, it's hard to understand how they can disregard the resonance between their own mission statements and the explicitly educational and informational aims of groups such as CHIRLA.

At best, one hears of programs that peripherally serve *jornaleros*, but precious few library-like projects have been designed with them in mind. Granted, day laborers could scarcely be more different from public libraries' typical user base of well-off middle-aged Caucasian women. Many have relatively low levels of education. Although this begs a common question — what can a library do for people who can't *read?*— a bit of analysis exposes the absurdity of such doubts. Not only is the promotion of literacy supposed to be one of the time-honored missions of US libraries, but it is also true that public libraries offer much more than just books. Videotapes and recorded music are important, high-circulation parts of any library's collection. Furthermore, "literacy" is not an either-or condition, but a continuous variable that occupies a variety of skill levels.

Ana Álvarez, Seattle Public Library's Spanish-language computer instructor, offers classes well used by *jornaleros*, thanks largely to orchestrated promotion and the library's proximity to the organized job center operated by a group called CASA Latina. Raul Añorve of CHIRLA mentions that his organization's North Hollywood hiring site had a small independent lending library that was popular among the laborers there.

A modest project at the Hollywood Job Center (HJC), another organized site in L.A., can serve as a template for one way of approaching design and implementation of library services for *jornaleros*.

My work began with several visits to the HJC and a nearby non-organized hiring site. Conversations with workers and site overseers gave me a rudimentary feel for some of the information needs of the people at the sites, and their attitudes toward libraries.

At the same time I explored potential resources—nearby libraries and community volunteers—trying to conceive a project that would be both practical and useful. Consultation with librarians at L.A. Public Library and with Sergio Ruiz, HJC site director, suggested that the workers might be well served by a small deposit or donated library including materials related to trade skills, a special concern of Ruiz.

The introduction of Sergio to the manager of the Hollywood Branch of LAPL (fairly described by L.A. social historian Mike Davis as, architecturally, "the most menacing library ever built" [239]) prompted the Spanish-speaking librarian, through selective weeding and other means, to assemble a small starter collection composed largely of practical DIY materials in Spanish. Ruiz was pleased to receive the books and install them at the job center. His ongoing contact with LAPL librarians holds promise for more ambitious development of this small library.

LAPL's reluctance to install a deposit collection is no surprise. It would be risky, initially anyway, to assure a manager in a library bureaucracy that materials left at a job center would be absolutely safe from damage or loss. But here, too, is an opportunity for symbiotic collaboration: site organizers emphasize the role played by day laborers in the upkeep and improvement of their job centers, and this acknowledged responsibility is important if library materials are to be supplied and made available there.

USEFUL RESOURCES

Librarians curious about *jornaleros* and ways to serve them might want to spend time exploring the resources assembled on "Library Service to Day Laborers" at <http://www.sol-plus.net/jornaleros.htm>. There can be found contact information for many of the groups mentioned here, magazine stories discussing day labor from several points of view, materials on adult education and library service to Spanish speakers, and websites offering Spanish-language content of possible utility to *jornaleros*.

Those seeking precedents for inspired collaboration between libraries and labor could do a lot worse than to track down the work of A.S. Meyers, the great Robert Croneberger, and, in this volume's trenchant forerunner, Jana Varlejs and Martha Williams.

Conclusion

Strong and capable men don't enjoy being pitied. Library service to day laborers should not spring from compassion but rather a frank acknowledgment that these vital participants in the local economy are especially hungry for the information and resources that libraries *can* do such a good job of providing, and they are as deserving of such services as anyone else. Librarians would do well to follow the lead of enlightened organizers within the day laborer movement, recognizing that their programs will operate best as fluid, collective collaborations flowing from the needs and interests of the *jornaleros* themselves. This tenet of true, undomesticated Freireian popular education can be difficult to grasp for those of us schooled and raised under different circumstances, yet is among the ideals given faint lip service in the library profession.

If we pay attention to the information needs not only of day laborers themselves, but also those of organizers who work with them and of government officials who sometimes work against them, librarians can play a supportive and maybe even forceful advocacy role in promoting social justice for a hardworking, underserved segment of our communities.

Notes

1. The song's lyrics are in Spanish — please feel free to adjust my translation however you see fit: Me puse a estudiar inglés / Porque me sentí obligado / Para poderme defender de un gabacho condenado / Allí donde trabajaba me querían mandonear / Nomás por el pinche inglés que no sabía yo hablar / El gabacho me decía, en inglés y enojado / "You wetback, don't understand [sic] / What you are supposed to do."

2. REFORMAnet, <http://lmri.ucsb.edu/mailman/listinfo/reformanet> and SOL <http://skipper.gseis.ucla.edu/students/bjensen/html/sol.htm>

Works Cited

Álvarez, Ana. Personal communication. 30 November 2001, 15 March 2002.

Añorve, Raul. Personal communication. 18 May 2001.

Arellano, Gustavo. Personal communication. 26 November 2001.

Bacon, David. "Paolo Freire Hits L.A.'s Mean Streets." *Z Magazine*, March 2001, 23–27.

Baker, Al. "Suffolk Day-Labor Center Appears Doomed as Veto Draws Support." *New York Times*, 24 April 2001, Late Edition — Final, Section B, 8.

Bixler, Mark. "Roswell Day Labor Center Planned." *Atlanta Constitution*, 2 October 2000, 1B.

Byars, Carlos. "Day Labor Site Cheers Its 3rd Year; Center Throws Workers a Party." *The Houston Chronicle*, 25 August 1996, A44.

Cleeland, Nancy. "Many Day Laborers Prefer Their Work to Regular Jobs." *Los Angeles Times*, 19 June 1999, Part A, 1. Reprinted at <http://www.sscnet.ucla.edu/chavez/daylaborer.html>.

Croneberger, Robert Jr., and Carolyn Luck. "Defining Information and Referral Service" in *Social Responsibilities and Libraries*, edited by Patricia Glass Schuman, 194–199. New York: R.R. Bowker, 1976.

Davis, Mike. *City of Quartz*. New York: Verso, 1990.

Day Labor Research Institute. "The Demographics of Day Labor: A Survey of 500 Los Angeles Area Day Laborers." <http://www.daylabor.org/research/resrch1/resrch1.htm>

Harrington, Caitlin. "What's In a Day's Work." *U.S. News & World Report*, 3 September 2001, 40.

Jornaleros del Norte. "La Frasesita." *Cruzando Fronteras*. JDN 001–2.

Manpower, Inc. "Manpower Inc. Facts." <http://www.manpower.com/en/story.asp>

McOmber, J. Martin. "Center for Workers Under Budget's Gun." *The Seattle Times*, 11 November 1999, B4.

Meyers, A.S. "Building a Partnership: Library Service to Labor." *American Libraries*, August 1999, 52–55.

Mora, Raul. "Day Laborers Gather to Focus on Unity, Improved Conditions," 2001. <http://www.globalexchange.org/education/california/news2001/ap072901.html>

Reza, H.G. and Ofelia Casillas. "Workers to Go: City Hiring Centers Are Popular, But Many Day Laborers Still Gather on Street Corners." *Los Angeles Times*, 26 February 2001, B1.

Thomas, Dylan. "A Visit to America." *Dylan Thomas Reading, Volume Four*. Caedmon Records TC 1061.

Valenzuela, Abel Jr. *Working on the Margins: Immigrant Day Labor Characteristics and Prospects for Employment*. Working Paper 22, Center for Comparative Immigration Studies, University of California, San Diego, 2000. <http://www.ccis-ucsd.org/PUBLICATIONS/wrkg22.PDF>

Varlejs, Jana. "Continuing It?" in *Revolting Librarians*, edited by Celeste West and Elizabeth Katz, 67–68. San Francisco: Booklegger Press, 1972.

Voices Desk. "Southern California Voices: A Conversation With Day Labor Activist Pablo Alvarado." *Los Angeles Times*, 7 September 1996, B7.

West, Celeste and Elizabeth Katz, eds. *Revolting Librarians*. San Francisco: Booklegger Press, 1972.

Williams, Martha. "Doing It: Migrant Workers' Library" in *Revolting Librarians*, edited by Celeste West and Elizabeth Katz, 63–67. San Francisco: Booklegger Press, 1972.

Zen Zheng, Chunhua. "Day-Labor Site in Gulfton to Get Added City Funding." *The Houston Chronicle*, 22 November 2000, "This Week," 1.

MY LIFE AS A LIBRARIAN EXPOSED! PERSONAL WEBSITES AND THE LIBRARIAN STEREOTYPES

Chris Zammarelli

Clairol's Herbal Essences made a commercial in which a librarian tells a female patron, "I urge you to be quiet!" At the sound of the word "urge," the patron launches into an elaborate hair washing fantasy, complete with three or four studly hairdressers singing and carrying shampoo. As she reaches orgasm, the ad cuts to a close-up of the shocked librarian just as soap suds splash all over her face in a suggestive manner.

The librarian, of course, is a picture perfect example of the librarian stereotype:

an overzealous school marm[1] with ugly glasses and her hair tightly pulled back. She's rude to the patron and, at least in the commercial's subtext, sexually frustrated.

At her website "Library Chicks of the World Unite,"[2] Megan Palasciano declares that librarians are not "a porn fantasy." The advertising industry, however, seems to be run by librarian fetishists. One print ad describes a Honda Accord as "the automotive equivalent of a really hot librarian."[3] Another has a picture of the back of a woman in a skimpy outfit holding a drink with the caption, "Librarian by day. Bacardi by night."[4]

In addition to being viewed as both sexual objects and uptight bitches, librarians are also seen as nefarious corruptors of youth. After all, where do kids go to read about sexuality, evolution, and Harry Potter? Oh, and to surf the Web for porn? The public library. Any parent can tell you that. Any politician could, too.

Underlying all this is the perception that librarianship is a doomed profession because of the Internet. All the information we'll ever need is online, so print is dead, and if print is dead, then what do we need libraries for, and if we don't need libraries, then why do we need librarians?[5]

Ironically, librarians have become arguably the most Web-savvy professionals. Having a research-oriented job tends to make one adept at finding information in any form, whether it's a website or just a plain old antiquated book.

It stands to reason that if we're spending a lot of time online, then librarians are going to have a strong web presence. This turns out to be true. As Owen Massey[6] points out at his website, "a peculiar online library culture was quick to grow up ... and nearly every adjectival librarian has their own library weblog."

It also stands to reason that if we have issues with our self-image, then librarians are going to use our personal home pages to try and tear up the stereotype. Well, the negative aspects of it, anyway. There is something infinitely badass about being perceived as a bad influence on children.

Anyway, peppered around our websites one can find statements on what we are and what we aren't. Eris Weaver's "The Bellydancing Librarian,"[7] for example, states, "We do not spend our days shushing people and dusting books! Public librarians toil to provide free information access to all citizens in the most democratic of institutions."

Palasciano's website offers a point by point description[8] of what librarians are and are not. "Library chicks are ... Smart, funny and unwilling to take bullshit from anyone," while "Library chicks are NOT ... Any sort of person that you can easily pigeonhole."

Massey blows the stereotype off by calling it "nothing more than cartoonists' shorthand, like depicting Frenchmen as cyclists in berets, striped jerseys and necklaces of onions."[9]

He also raises the issue that the public perception of librarians matter more to us than to everyone else. Citing an article[10] by Deirdre Dupré in NewBreed Librarian,[11] he writes, "the true responsibility for perpetuating any poor image lies with librarians ourselves."

It is true that librarians tend to be a bit overly touchy about how we're regarded by others. Take the uproar that occurred when Sony Barari's column that poked fun of library science made its way around various librarian-oriented email lists. We completely overreacted, flooding his inbox with irate emails and throwing our two cents everywhere we could.[12]

But, all that said, the fact is librarians are still frequently underpaid. Tami Sutcliffe[13] notes, in a section of her website called "librariansRgeeks2,"[14] that the average librarian made $31,915 in 1998, and Salary.com[15] shows that the average went up to $40,399 in four years.

And while it may be more a myth than a reality that librarians aren't valued,[16] sometimes issues such as library outsourcing[17] can do a lot of damage to a librarian's self-esteem.

But, all *that* said, by letting this bother us so much (and it does bother many of us a lot), we're only just putting ourselves down instead of raising ourselves up. Therefore, we're self-propagating the stereotype.[18]

Perhaps, then, the best way to fight the image is to simply be ourselves, and to not worry about how we're being perceived.

For example, Kristina Spurgin[19] and Jessamyn West[20] both have home pages that are essentially websites by people who happen to be librarians, as opposed to being librarian websites. The distinction lies in the fact that they don't necessarily use their profession as the basis of their respective home pages.

On the other hand, Katia Roberto's website[21] branches off from librarianship. She includes two personal essays about why she became a librarian and why she became a cataloger, as well as a list of reasons why one should get one's MLS. The aforementioned websites by Massey and Palasciano are also good examples of using the profession as an informational base for a home page.

The mainstays of almost every personal site are links. All the personal sites I've mentioned have them, and something seemingly so basic or innocuous can actually go a long way to outline the site owner's personality. For example, Palasciano and Spurgin both use links to provide more information on their various interests. Roberto scatters links around her autobiographical essays as a means to fill them out.

Related to a links page is a resource page, which is more focused on providing general information that isn't necessarily internet-based about a particular subject matter. For example, Roberto's "A Topical Guide to Queer Resources in the Social Sciences"[22] is divided into areas of study, then subdivided into print and online resources.

A less formally structured resource site is Dan Cherubin's Second Generation page.[23] Providing information for gay children of gay parents, Cherubin states, "Second Generation was formed out of my own needs and what I presumed were the needs of others."

One of the drawbacks of the Internet is that it only has the information that people provide for it. The reason why all the information one will ever need isn't online is because someone has to put it there first. That was Cherubin's motivation for the creation of Second Generation page, and it seems to be the motivation for many of the pages Rory Litwin hosts at Libr.org.[24]

After all, how else would you find information about Cuban libraries, globalization's effects on librarianship, or anti-war librarians?[25] There's not a lot of personal information at Litwin's home page, other than a résumé and some photo galleries,[26] but his sites collectively offer a good glimpse into his character. Speaking of character,[27] another style of librarian personal home page is the _____ Librarian site. The site owner takes one aspect of their interests or personality and either elaborates on it or uses it as a starting point for a website.

I mentioned earlier a perfect example of this type of page. Eris Weaver's "The Bellydancing Librarian" consists of two pages. One is autobiographical, discussing briefly her work and her interest in bellydancing. The other features pictures of, bios of and links to other bellydancing librarians.

Weaver was one of the first people to use the Web as a way for librarians to redefine their self-image and public perception, so the number of people who list it as an influence is fairly sizable.[28]

Another influential site, Dan Cherubin's "The Ska Librarian"[29] uses his music interest and profession as a starting point to build upon. As he points out, "[The Ska Librarian] was an enigmatic name, now it's called a poseur name. By next year, it'll be just another pick-up line."

Despite that, the name does offer a unique hook to lure in readers. Like "The Bellydancing Librarian," it plays off the stereotype and introduces site visitors to aspects of librarian culture they may not have encountered before.

A good way to summarize all this is by mentioning Jonny Neutron's "Rockabilly Librarian."[30] The unique name draws people in, and while he opines briefly on shaking up the image of librarians, he isn't self-conscious in going about it. In addition, while his profession is at the base of the site, his website isn't necessarily about his profession.

It's probably inevitable that a librarian's website is going to touch upon the librarian stereotype at some point, but it's also increasingly unnecessary. As the online librarian community grows and develops, it's likely going to be less defined by cool librarians and more defined by cool people who happen to be librarians.[31] It's a small distinction, but it's a good distinction to make.

Notes

1. A description used by Sony Barari in his now-infamous UCLA Daily Bruin column "Library Science Degree: File That Under 'Stupid.'" <http://www.dailybruin.ucla.edu/db/articles.asp?ID=18860> I'll be coming back to this later.
2. <http://www.librarychick.com>
3. <http://www.queerest.org/honda.jpg>
4. <http://www.newbreedlibrarian.org/news/bacardi.html>
5. Of course, and you may sense some personal experience here, an attorney who declares as he gives a client a tour of his firm's library that "someday this all will be online" is the first person who gets annoyed when a librarian tells him that the information he's looking for is available online.

6. <http://owen.massey.net>

7. <http://www.sonic.net/~erisw/bdlib.html>

8. <http://www.librarychick.com/whatis.html>

9. <http://owen.massey.net/libraries/index.html.>

10. "The Perception of Image and Status in the Library Profession" <http://www.newbreed-librarian.org/archives/01.04.aug2001/feature1.html> was instrumental in helping me establishing the tone of this piece. Also of help was a similarly-themed article from 1999 by Antony Brewerton called, "Wear Lipstick, Have a Tattoo, Belly-Dance, Then Get Naked: The Making of a Virtual Librarian." <http://www.careerdevelopmentgroup.org.uk/impact/archives/abrewerton.htm>

11. <http://www.newbreedlibrarian.org/index.html>

12. I stress the word "we" here, because I sent him an annoyed email. After all the controversy, I felt bad and apologized for contributing to the uproar. Anyway, a good overview of the situation can be read at LISNews: <http://www.lisnews.com/article.php3?sid=20020308125444>

13. <http://homepages.waymark.net/~bikechic>

14. <http://homepages.waymark.net/~bikechic/manifesto.html>

15. <http://www.salary.com>

16. Again, referring to "The Perception of Image and Status in the Library Profession."

17. <http://www.llrx.com/features/outsourcing.htm> This is a topic that is near and dear to my heart in that I was at Pillsbury Madison & Sutro when they outsourced their library. It took a lot of might for me not to go into painful detail about the story. Maybe in *Revolting Librarians Neoredux*?

18. If you haven't already, you really ought to read "The Perception of Image and Status in the Library Profession."

19. <http://www.le-champignon.net>

20. <http://www.jessamyn.com>

21. <http://www.dangpow.com/~katia/home.htm>, and I realize that I could be perceived as kissing up to my editors by including sites by both Jessamyn and Katia in this essay. However, both home pages have been very influential to me, so I'll be damned if I'm going to ignore them.

22. <http://www.dangpow.com/~katia/queer/index.html> The site was created as part of a project for a class she took in grad school, but it is still updated with some regularity.

23. <http://www.geocities.com/WestHollywood/Village/3497/sg.html>

24. <http://libr.org>

25. <http://libr.org/CLSG>, <http://libr.org/GATS>, and <http://libr.org/peace>, respectively.

26. All of which can be found at <http://libr.org/rory>.

27. How's that for a segue?

28. She told me in an email that she was inspired to put up her site by *The Lipstick Librarian*, <http://www.lipsticklibrarian.com>. I didn't include that page in this survey because it didn't feature any personal content, but its influence on the development of librarian Web culture casts far and wide.

29. <http://www.geocities.com/WestHollywood/Village/3497>

30. <http://www.rockabillylibrarian.com>

31. Either way, you can find a whole bunch of librarians' home pages at *Open Directory*, <http://dmoz.org/Reference/Libraries/Library_and_Information_Science/Librarians/>.

REVOLTING VOCABULARY: MENTAL HEALTH AND LANGUAGE IN *REVOLTING LIBRARIANS*

Karen Antell

For Savannah

Revolting librarians are sensitive to bias in language, especially language used for referring to people. This is why so many articles in the original *Revolting Librarians*[1] rightly express outrage at subject headings still current in the 1970s—"Mammies," "Yellow Peril," "Jewish Question," "Women as Physicians"[2]— not to mention the fact that "Homosexuality," according to subject heading hierarchies, was still a form of "Sexual Deviation."[3]

Revolting librarians care about bias in subject headings because language *matters*. We cannot expect to end prejudice against, say, Africans, if our controlled vocabulary—the terms we *choose* and *authorize*—institutionalizes racism in the form of subject headings like "Primitives" or "Native Peoples."[4] Joan Marshall probably expresses it best: "The entry of works under FILTHY BOOKS or NIGGERS would be castigated by the profession, which would recognize that such an obviously biased *approach* to the material also biased the *material*, whatever its content."[5]

So I was surprised when reading the original *Revolting Librarians* to find so many biased and insensitive references to mental illness, usually as an attempt at humor that the authors never would have made at the expense of people with physical illnesses or, for that matter, ethnic or minority status. Among the statements they never would have made are the following:

- "if it turns out some [students] are really too *quadriplegic* to function, we can flunk them out on their comprehensives."[6]
- "the library literature doesn't pertain, and I have a *bisexual* sensation that … it should."[7]
- "we are not advocating that librarians have only leftist books, periodicals, and newspapers in their libraries. That is *retarded*."[8]

I feel certain that none of the revolting contributors would ever have been insensitive enough to make any of the preceding remarks. To do so would have been to propagate bias against people with illness, disability, or other minority status. In the 1970s, making fun of people with disabilities might have been more acceptable than it is now, but the revolting types with their raised consciousnesses would not have done so.

Except that when it comes to mental disabilities, they did. The book is riddled with language that demeans the suffering and belittles the victories of people with mental illness: those whose potential—intellectual, emotional, interpersonal—is utterly destroyed by terrifying diseases such as severe schizophrenia, as well as those who fight and triumph over their illnesses and might even like to share their wisdom with others, if only the rest of the world didn't find mental illness quite so worthy of ridicule.

- "When in disgrace with fortune and men's eyes, when old zeitgeist gets me down, I turn to silence. Give me silence or give me librium!"[9] Librium is a psychoactive drug used to treat debilitating anxiety—not your garden-variety "blues." (Imagine inserting "chemotherapy" here instead!)

- "Not even a peep of thanks from a computer, which we love/hate as much as the next schizoid librarian."[10] Yes, "schizoid" and "schizophrenic" have long been used—until quite recently erroneously—as synonyms for "ambivalent," thanks to the word's Greek roots, which literally translate to something like "split brain." This doesn't make it a correct use of the word, at least not in the 1970s (you're probably a librarian, look it up in a 1970-era dictionary if you don't believe me)—much less a sensitive or unbiased use.[11]

- "No wonder Shirley's library recruiter is so schizophrenic."[12] See discussion of "schizoid," above. The library recruiter carries on an inner dialogue disagreeing with the speech he delivers out loud. I suppose arguing with oneself is enough like being severely psychotic to be considered funny?

- "I found the work and the salary pointless, and I began to feel my sanity ebbing."[13] That will do it every time: an unpleasant job usually leads to psychiatric hospitalization, right?

- "give me a dewey decimal system, / make it for my mind. / fix me a dewey decimal system, / madness is so unkind. / classify my strong emotions, / rectify my silly notions. /… / sanity's hard to find. / … / catalogue my fears and sorrows / shelve them away until tomorrow / …."[14] It seems cheap and somehow unfair to bring library poetry into this, especially since this poem does not explicitly poke fun at mental illness as so many of the other references to insanity and schizophrenia do. But, well, contrary to this poem's plaintive plea, insanity is not the same as having "strong emotions … fears and sorrows." Everyone has these, and they can be powerful, but claiming that they constitute "madness" is just adolescent. It is grossly out of proportion, like Art Plotnik's outrageously tasteless claim that "quiet" rules at libraries "can be one great big fat concentration camp of a drag."[15] (But that's another story.)

- "Library School Lunacy" is the title of Harleigh Kyson's article about the absurdities of our professional training. Apparently not content to equate incompetence and low intellectual standards with mental disability (lunacy), he also impugns the physically disabled, referring to library school students as "human vegetables."[16]

- "Besides, library work in itself is vital and dealing with the public can be a crazy, funny, detective-story trip."[17] Crazy is funny. Need I say more?

Ironically, Sanford Berman's contribution wins the prize for the most demeaning use of language referring to people with mental disorders. Summing up his discussion of bias in subject headings, he says, "If this sort of embedded racism, Western chauvinism, prudery, and senility rubs anyone the wrong way, let librarians know about it. Urge them to humanize their own card catalogues."[18] Excuse me, did I read this right?—in the same breath, Berman equates senility, a devastating brain disease, with "racism, Western chauvinism, [and] prudery" *and* calls for librarians to "humanize" their catalogues?

Lest anyone take my comments the wrong way, let me make clear that I have a great deal of respect for Sanford Berman's work over the past 30 years. And I think that the emphasis on sensitivity to language in the first *Revolting Librarians* is one of the great strengths of the work. The contributors to the first edition did not make bias-promoting references to mental illness because they were insensitive jerks. They did it because mental illness was not yet an issue about which people's consciousness had been raised—not even revolting types' consciousness.

And this leads me to wonder whom we—always so careful to avoid linguistic bias—are inadvertently offending, demeaning, belittling, or making fun of today. What uses of language that we currently employ will revolt us 30 years down the road?

Notes

1. All subsequent notes refer to essays and poems in Celeste West and Elizabeth Katz, eds., *Revolting Librarians* (San Francisco: Booklegger Press, 1972).
2. Sanford Berman, "Libraries to the People," 56; Joan Marshall, "LC Labeling: An Indictment," 47.
3. Steve Wolf, "Sex and the Single Cataloger," 39.
4. Berman, 56.
5. Marshall, 46.
6. Paraphrase of Shirley Olofson, "The Recruiter Speaks," 26: "if it turns out some are really too insane to function...."
7. Reva Landy, "Reflections of a Head Librarian," 111: "the library literature doesn't pertain, and I have a schizophrenic sensation that ... it should."
8. Linda Katz and Julie Babcock, "The Liberated Librarians Newsletter," 131.
9. Art Plotnik, "The Liberation of Sweet Library Lips," 6.
10. Ibid., 9.
11. I have learned that the "ambivalence" meaning of "schizophrenia" has recently entered the dictionaries, no doubt thanks to the revolting librarians and others who have published books and articles using the term for humorous effect and thus popularized this meaning of the word. The 2001 edition of Random House Webster's Unabridged Dictionary's second definition of schizophrenia is "a state characterized by the coexistence of contradictory or incompatible elements." However, earlier unabridged dictionaries, such as the 1979 edition of Webster's Unabridged, include only the "mental illness" meaning of schizophrenia—so in 1972, when the first *Revolting Librarians* was published, the "ambivalence" meaning of schizophrenia was still erroneous.

12. Celeste West and Elizabeth Katz, introduction to "The Officious Orthodoxy," 22.
13. Melinda Schroeder, "I Never Wanted to Be a Librarian," 115.
14. Tod Hawks, "A Dewey Decimal Mind," 71.
15. Plotnik, 7.
16. Harleigh Kyson, "Library School Lunacy," 29, 31.
17. Judy Hadley, "Trials of a Paraprofessional," 79.
18. Berman, 57.

Silencing Sandy: The Censoring of Libraries' Foremost Activist[1,2]

Naomi Eichenlaub

Sanford Berman is perhaps the most legendary library persona of the second half of the 20th century. He is also, perhaps, the most highly praised and highly esteemed librarian of our time. In parallel, some also regard him as the noisiest and most irritating of librarians. Just who is this guy? The question, sadly, must be rephrased as who was this guy, for he was somewhat recently (June 1999) forced to take early retirement from a job he held for over a quarter of a century as the radical, renegade head cataloger of Hennepin County Library (HCL) in Minnetonka, Minnesota. In his work at HCL, Sandy was first and foremost a cataloger. But he was a cataloger with a conscience, an activist working to ensure that cataloging fulfilled its primary goal, that of access. Berman can be attributed with creating awareness for the need for socially responsible librarians. Furthermore, he is responsible for demonstrating that for a librarian to truly fulfill their professional duties, they must be socially responsible. Sandy worked zealously in an effort to preserve free speech, to ensure access to information, and to promote an uncensored press (Gilyard 1999). It is indeed ironic, therefore, that it was in exercising his own right to free speech, in a profession which bases its mandate on the premise of the promotion of free speech, that he was censored, reprimanded, and forced to retire.

Sandy's ranting is his greatest contribution to librarianship. It is this ranting that has landed him the position of the library world's leading activist for social responsibility. He his credited with having influenced "an entire generation of librarians" by setting an example that "activism and librarianship can co-exist" (Roberto 1999). With a festschrift in his honour, and more recently, an e-zine entitled *Kiss My Filing Indicators: the Sandy Berman Rocks My Socks Issue*, the praise offered up in his name by his supporters knows no bounds. Debra Stevens, in an article on social responsibility and librarianship, quotes Patricia Schuman's 1976 assertion that "silence has been recorded throughout history as affirmation" (Stevens 1989). With a publishing record that is beyond impressive, as his 1988 select bibliography in *Worth Noting: Editorials, Letters, Essays, an Interview, and Bibliography* illustrates (and that was fifteen years ago!), Sandy has done his best to ensure that silence is not mistaken as affirmation.

Always at the core of Sanford Berman's writings has been social responsibility in librarianship. In his contribution to a 1972 collection of essays entitled *Revolting Librarians*, Berman wrote a lament entitled "Libraries to the People" in which he described the collections of most public libraries in the U.S. at that time as "stodgy preserves of the elite" (Gilyard 1999). Berman reminds readers that the Bill of Rights, long ago adopted by the library profession, explicitly states that libraries should carry materials that cover all possible political viewpoints (West and Katz 1972). Berman points out the complete absence of radical, underground publications in the collections of public libraries. He warns that this "denies [the] very vitality, conflict, and color that help to make this country unique" (Berman 1981). He laments this oversight in "Libraries to the People":

> How in hell can the pothead groove on *Business Week* and Norman Vincent Peale? A feminist get excited over *Cosmopolitan* and the *Ladies' Home Journal?* Or an acid-rock fancier find any goodies in the *Reader's Digest?* It ain't easy. Still, longhaired freaks and madassed revolutionaries are as much members of the community as Big Money Makers and hard-hat "straights" [West and Katz 1972].

Other works to Sandy's credit include the 1971 *Prejudices and Antipathies: A Tract on the LC Subject Heads Concerning People*, in which he exposed the Library of Congress Subject Headings (LCSH) as being Eurocentric and androcentric, among other biases. Sandy is perhaps best known for his criticisms of, and work to improve, the user-friendliness of LCSH. In 1993, Sandy gave a speech at the Library of Congress where he condemned what he called "bibliocide by cataloguing," the process whereby works are made inaccessible "through LC's misleading and biased subject headings" (Dodge and DeSirey 1995). The catalogers in his cataloging department have come to be known as *Sandynistas*, after the Nicaraguan *Sandinistas*, (leftist revolutionaries headed by Augusto Sandino during the Nicaraguan Sandinista Revolution of 1979), as they worked with Sandy to establish HCL's own subject headings and other pioneering work such as assigning subject headings to works of fiction. In fact, Sandy is so well known for his hounding of the LC to change and expand their subject headings that a librarian at the Library of Congress, known only as Fred,[3] is quoted as saying:

> Sandy Berman is a major pain in the ass. He runs a horse-and-buggy cataloging operation in Minnesota and he thinks he can tell us how to do our jobs. He's an insufferable, self-righteous, unrealistic, naive, head-in-the-clouds idealist who knows nothing about the real world of grind-it-out bibliographic data [Dodge and DeSirey 1995].

Sandy also wrote the 1981 *Joy of Cataloging: Essays, Letters, Reviews, and Other Explosions* which features in one of its sections a sample sex index, entitled "If There Were A Sex Index...." According to Berman, "libraries' skittishness around sexual topics is a disservice to patrons" (Gilyard 1999). Patrons need to be able to find what they are looking for, and if they are too shy to ask a reference librarian, Berman argues the library catalog should accurately represent the materials that a library has in its collection (Gilyard 1999). In fact, Berman has even received an award for his work toward promoting access to sexual information. In 1997 he was recognized by Factor Press in Alabama with the Golden Phallus Award for "body- and sex-positive contributions to society" (Gilyard 1999). The award honours Sandy's "lifetime commitment to promoting the availability of unpopular, ignored, and even condemned literature ... on all aspects of sexuality" (Dodge 1998).

Sandy's other contributions to socially responsible librarianship include founding the ALA Social Responsibilities Round Table on Hunger, Homelessness and Poverty, being a charter member of the Progressive Librarians Guild (PLG) and co-editing the biennial anthology *Alternative Library Literature (ALL). ALL* collocates critical and alternative perspectives on all facets of the library world. With articles on cataloguing, collection development and social responsibility, Elaine Harger, a PLG cofounder, urges that the latest edition of *ALL* should be a required text at library schools (Dodge and DeSirey 1995).

Sanford Berman has a history of voicing his opinion about issues that he deems socially irresponsible. A self-professed purveyor of information, it was also (and still is) his habit of circulating information to all those he feels would benefit from it. He is quoted in numerous places (Dodge and DeSirey 1995; Gilyard 1999) as saying "I can't have information I know would be of interest to someone and not share it." Unfortunately, his policy usually clashed with that of the HCL administrators. Chris Dodge, friend, former co-worker of Berman, and co-editor with Jan DeSirey of the 1995 festschrift *Everything You Always Wanted to Know About Sandy Berman But Were Afraid to Ask*, points out in his contribution entitled "Troubled Waters," that Sandy's work at HCL "has been perhaps more tumultuous than idyllic" (Dodge and DeSirey 1995). The following paragraphs detail examples of occasions where Berman, in his work to provide socially responsible librarianship, has been censored from and reprimanded for expressing concerns that relate directly to his profession and area of expertise.

An incident occurred in 1990 whereby Berman came across a book published by Life Tapestry Press which contained statements such as "'AIDS is a form of self-punishment' and 'maybe a cry of the belief system of many that homosexuality is unnatural or wrong'" (Dodge and DeSirey 1995). Sandy responded by sending a letter to the publisher on HCL stationary in which he urged the publisher, who was also the author, to recall all copies of the book, make appropriate deletions and corrections, and "issue an apology to the gay community and all persons with AIDS" (Dodge and DeSirey 1995). Berman sent copies of this letter to a number of gay, lesbian and AIDS-related bookstores, organizations and periodicals. The publisher, angry, threatened legal action against HCL. In response, Sandy suggested that the publisher send a written response to his letter, which he would then forward to everyone who received his letter. HCL directors, however, did not approve of Berman's idea and instead Sandy received a formal reprimand.

A second example dates to 1996, when HCL administration announced a plan to raise $100,000 a year of revenue by doubling late fines on children's materials. Berman points out that "the purpose, let me assure you, was not to get books back on the shelf quicker, or to instill greater responsibility in youthful borrowers" (Berman 1998). Instead, the sole purpose was to increase the library's financial self-sufficiency by raising non-tax, that is, non-publicly funded money in order to impress the County Board of Commissioners (Berman 1998, 2002). Sandy, aware that none of HCL's two dozen children's librarians had been consulted on this proposal, circulated a petition, "asking simply that the fine policy be withdrawn" (Berman 1998). In addition, he, by his own admission, spoke with someone in the media at an alternative news weekly in Minnesota, which in turn ran an article entitled "Library Pinches Nickels, Kids" (Berman 1998).

Not surprisingly, HCL administrators were about to take action against Berman again, this time for "testifying publicly and starting a petition" (Berman 1998). Sandy, about to be reprimanded, decided to hire labour lawyers who advised HCL that free speech issues might be involved. Administration backed off and did not file the formal reprimand. However, in a very poignantly worded question, Berman asks, "How many librarians can afford the 500 bucks to buy their first-amendment rights?" (Berman 1998).

A further incident occurred in 1998, when HCL decided to implement the "Bestseller Express," a program that would allow patrons, for a three dollar fee, to rent new-release, high demand titles. "Bestseller Express" was proposed as a means of reducing long waiting lists, but Berman was quick to bill it as an "elite, discriminatory service based entirely on a person's ability to pay" (Gilyard 1999). Despite Berman and others' opposition, the program was implemented. When Berman restated his concerns in a short email memo sent to all HCL staff, Director Charles Brown branded Berman's email as "unnecessary and inappropriate," further requesting that Berman "please refrain from utilizing this important library communications tool to broadcast [his] personal perceptions and views" (Gilyard 1999).

On January 18th, 1999, in an act that Berman saw merely as contributing his professional opinion, he responded to a memo from Bill DeJohn and Carla Dewey of MINITEX, the Minnesota library network that was overseeing a new move at HCL to join OCLC. Berman was responding to a statement in the memo that extolled strict adherence to AACR2 standards (Berman 2002), a practice that, under Berman, had not been in strict adherence by HCL catalogers.[4] Furthermore, HCL was in the process of re-examining their AACR2 modifications and the continued modification of them in the future. What was supposed to be a participative process was not, and the decision was made arbitrarily and in secret, with no discussion permitted (Berman 2002).

Berman began his response by affirming that "he was convinced that the Hennepin County Library and AACR2 could collaborate on the transition to an expanded cataloging system" (Gilyard 1999). Berman did, however, express his concern that "School, public, and community library users, in particular, were not well served by the AACR2 drafters" (Litwin 2: 17). He closed the memo by inviting DeJohn, Dewey, and MINITEX "to join me in a nearly 3-decade-long campaign to genuinely make library catalogs more user-friendly & much less elitist and mystifying" (Litwin 2: 17). Signing off "with warmest regards," Berman copied the email to HCL administration (including Director Brown and Elizabeth Feinberg, his immediate boss) and HCL cataloguing staff.

The recipients at MINITEX did not find the memo contentious. According to DeJohn, he saw the memo as "a friendly response to my note" (Gilyard 1999). Dewey added that "I received it as just a statement of [Berman's] position, some of his concerns about the widely accepted standards" (Gilyard 1999). HCL administration, however, reacted much differently. Berman was censored from expressing his concerns regarding cataloguing matters, something that as head cataloger, he should have been encouraged to do. Instead, Brown and Feinberg charged that

> Your active support of these changes is required. At this time, your "three-decade-long campaign" is extremely counterproductive to the cataloging reengineering process, causes divisiveness throughout the organization and presents an extremely poor image to colleagues who are working with HCL [Gilyard 1999].

Berman sought to have the formal reprimand "rescinded and removed from his file" (Litwin 2: 17), emphasizing that he supported the decision to join OCLC. When Brown refused to withdraw the reprimand, Berman went public about the reprimand he received, publicizing the issue in an attempt to raise support from colleagues and friends in the library world (Litwin 2: 17). As a result, Brown's office was flooded with angry letters and petitions in support of Sandy and his right to voice his professional opinion without fear of being reprimanded. In an email dated February 27, 1999 and sent to both the ALA Council List and the SRRT Action Council, Sandy highlighted the irony of the situation by creating a mock-tabloid headline to describe his own situation: "Much-Honored Minnesota Cataloger Disciplined For Talking About Cataloging! Free Speech a "NO GO" Inside Nation's 5th-Ranked Public Library" (Litwin 2: 9). In his appeal, Sandy demanded that his reprimand be withdrawn and that "an apology for false accusation and wrongful discipline — plus firm guarantees that staff can freely address professional and policy issues without fear of reprisal" (Litwin 2: 9) be issued. Director Brown and Elizabeth Feinberg were later awarded "The Staff Morale & Unity Award" in the April Fool's edition of Library Journal, for their written reprimand to Sandy (*LJ* 1999).

Further censorship was at issue when OCLC was preparing to announce HCL's OCLC membership in its newsletter. A copy of the article was sent to Sandy for his approval and in order that he make any corrections he deemed necessary (Litwin 2: 17). Sandy submitted "a number of corrections & additions, solely to the passages dealing with [him] and cataloging, in order to make the report fuller and more accurate" (Litwin 2: 9). In what Berman calls a case of "rank & arrogant censorship" (Litwin 2: 9), the recommended changes were, by order of his immediate supervisor, ignored (Litwin 2: 9).

On April 19, 1999, three months after Berman had sent his memo to MINITEX, he arrived at work to discover that he would no longer be serving as head cataloger. With absolutely no prior consultation or notification, Berman was notified in a meeting that very morning that he was to "immediately occupy a remote office ... no longer supervise Hennepin catalogers or perform cataloging" and was informed "that his new project was to create a cataloging manual" (Dodge 1999). Berman viewed the reassignment as retaliation for going public about the reprimand he received for writing the MINITEX memo and, commenting on the lack of respect it showed for him as a colleague and a person, is quoted as saying that the project was a "reassignment to full-time toilet cleaning" (Gilyard 1999).

This was clearly a violation of Berman's right to free speech. Sandy maintains that when he wrote the MINITEX memo regarding the HCL OCLC partnership, he was only attempting to encourage professional discourse on certain aspects that he felt still needed addressing before the merger was completed (Gilyard 1999). Instead of accepting his new job assignment, Berman surrendered and submitted his resignation from HCL for June 10, 1999, going on sick leave effective April 23, 1999 (Gilyard 1999). HCL administration had finally succeeded in permanently censoring Sanford Berman — at least as one of their employees. His words in a final email message to HCL staff echo this surrender: "I refuse to submit to any further muzzling, punishment, and humiliation" (Gilyard 1999).

Berman may no longer be at work at HCL, but he has far from abandoned his attention to the incident. Since he received the reprimand for writing the MINITEX memo, he has been photocopying and mailing documentation of the events to colleagues and library presses around the world, in an attempt to seek support for his right "to freely address professional and policy issues without fear of reprisal" (Litwin 2: 17). In addition, ALA Councillors and supporters of Berman including Mark Rosenzweig and Maurice Freedman asked the ALA Council to consider a resolution which called for the censure of HCL administration for what they describe as "its infringements of Berman's free-speech rights, for its retribution against him, and its overall violations of his professional rights" (*AL* August 1999).

Berman, in his last post as ALA Councillor at the Annual Conference in New Orleans in June of 1999, presented a resolution that called for an amendment to the Library Bill of Rights. It would include the addition of the following sentence: "Libraries should permit and encourage a full and free expression of views by staff on professional and policy matters" (*AL* August 1999). Unfortunately, the motion was defeated and it was suggested that it would perhaps be more appropriate to include the proposed amendment in the ALA Code of Ethics, since the Bill of Rights "addresses the relationship between libraries and their users, not the rights of employees" (*AL* August 1999). In an attempt to rescue his proposed amendment, Berman put forth the argument that "a muzzled or chilled staff is frankly unlikely to render the most effective service to library users" (*AL* August 1999). There was lengthy debate on the issue and the motion was referred to the Ethics Committee of ALA (*AL* August 1999). In a similar situation in Minnesota, the Minnesota Library Association rejected the following resolution in support of employee free speech:

> Whereas: Libraries value the free expression of ideas; Whereas: Library profession-als have a wide range of professional expertise; Whereas: A fair and rigorous debate of ideas will result in the best decision for any organization; Therefore be it resolved: That the Minnesota Library Association encourages the freedom of librarians and other library professionals to freely express their professional opinions as it is related to the responsibility of their job. That the Minnesota Library Association discourages the use of disciplinary action against library employees for expressing their opinion about matters related to their professional responsibilities [Dodge 1999].

Berman's attempt to lobby for the right to free speech for library employees was rejected both by his state library association as well as the ALA. However, as the evidence suggests, Berman is not one to give up without a fight, even if he has been forced to resign from working directly within HCL and the ALA. There are still plenty of other venues, especially within the radical librarian community, which holds Sandy Berman as nothing short of a guru. The Progressive Librarians Guild website has an online petition in support of Sanford Berman in which they demand that HCL management request Sandy's "return to his position in the cataloging department at HCL" <http://libr.org/PLG>. Finally, on the afternoon of Saturday, June 12, 1999, at a celebration being held in honour of the now-retired Berman, his former colleagues awarded him the first annual Sanford Berman Award for Social Responsibility in Library Services (Gilyard 1999). The award was created and presented by HCL's Librarian and Support staff unions (AFSCME locals 2822 and 2864). Since the award's inception, it has been awarded twice to HCL staff who work with immigrant families and at-risk children (Berman 2002).

It may appear, in retrospect, that this story tells a sad tale, but that is only half of the truth. It is indeed a sad tale. Sad for HCL administration and the loss to their library system that they are directly responsible for, sad for Sandy who is now retired and no longer cataloging and hounding LC, sad for the Sandynistas, and sad for the library profession. There is, however and more significantly, a happy tale here as well. If Sandy were not the earth–shaking, trouble-stirring soul that he is there would not even be a story here. And so we must thank Sandy for that. Thank-you Sandy, for your work, impact, inspiration for change, and most of all, your ranting.

"'All I did', [Berman] offers with a sigh, 'was write a letter'" (Gilyard 1999).

When Sandy left HCL, he left behind a legacy of cataloging and authority work unique to our profession. Unfortunately, recent events threaten to destroy both the continued application of, and the existence of this list of user-centered, original subject headings. This list, created by him and his staff over two and a half decades at

Hennepin County Library, will now be replaced in the catalog by straight LC subject headings (Litwin 5: 9 2002). Hennepin was not the only library using this subject authority file. Other libraries, including the database Novelist, have also been benefiting from subject authority work done by Berman and HCL cataloging staff.

As it stands, it is unknown what steps, if any, will be taken to preserve the HCL authority file from the Berman era.

The HCL press release can be read at

<http://web.library.uiuc.edu/ahx/ead/ala/9701040a/berman/biblinks/hclpr.pdf>.

Sandy's response can be read at

<http://web.library.uiuc.edu/ahx/ead/ala/9701040a/berman/biblinks/sresp.pdf>.

For an authoritative source for documentation concerning Sandy's "last stand," including all relevant correspondence, plus petition and various support letters, please see the double issue of *Librarians at Liberty*, December 2001.

See also *The Sanford Berman Website*, created by Madeline Douglas at

<http://web.library.uiuc.edu/ahx/ead/ala/9701040a/berman/sanford.htm>.

Notes

1. The title comes from a letter dated February 26, 1999 and reprinted in *Library Juice* 2: 16, April 21 1999, written by Robert Hauptman, Professor of Learning Resources and Technology Services at St. Cloud State University, Minnesota and Editor of the *Journal of Information Ethics*, in which he calls Sandy Berman "one of librarianship's foremost activists" in response to the HCL press release and staff memo of April 19, 1999, announcing the development of a Cataloguing Practices Manual. <http://www.libr.org/Juice/issues/vol2/LJ_2.16.html>

2. This paper was originally written as a requirement for LIBR 560, Organization of Information, School of Library, Archival and Information Studies, University of British Columbia, December 1999. Some revisions and updating have been done to the original paper.

3. "Fred" is rumoured to be a fictitious character (Berman 2002).

4. According to Berman, he only expressed his sentiments regarding AACR2 to DeJohn and Dewey "because they, by invitation, had contributed a statement extolling strict adherence to standards that was attached — as justification — to an email proclamation to the entire staff that HCL would completely embrace AACR2, abandoning its several departures or deviations from those rules developed over many years" (Berman 2002).

Works Cited

"Absurdity Has Returned to Librarianship." *Library Journal*, 1 April 1999.
   <http://libraryjournal.reviewsnews.com/index.asp?layout=articleArchive&articleid=CA158846>
"ALA Council Biannual Report: Berman Supporters Angry." *American Libraries*, August 1999, 92.
Berman, Sanford. Personal correspondence, 23 March 2002.
Berman, Sanford. "Sandy Berman's Valedictory." *Street Librarian*, 1999.
   <http://www.geocities.com/SoHo/Cafe/7423/sandy.html>.
Berman, Sanford. *Talking the Talk and Walking the Walk: What Libraries Say They Do but Frequently Don't*, 1998. <http://www.library.uiuc.edu/colloquium/berman.html>
Berman, Sanford. "Access to Alternatives." *The Joy of Cataloging*. Phoenix, AZ: Oryx Press, 1981.
"Cataloger Demands Reprimand Be Rescinded." *American Libraries*, April 1999, 20, 22.
Dodge, Chris. "Activist Librarian Resigns." *MSRRT Newsletter* 12, no. 2, Summer 1999.
   <http://www.cs.unca.edu/~edmiston/msrrt/1999/summer99.html>

Dodge, Chris. "MSRRT Briefs." *MSRRT Newsletter* 11, no. 2, March/April 1998.
    <http://www.cs.unca.edu/~edmiston/msrrt/1998/mar98.html>
Dodge, Chris and Jan DeSirey, eds. *Everything You Always Wanted to Know About Sandy Berman But Were Afraid to Ask.* Jefferson, NC: McFarland, 1995.
Gilyard, Burl. "Sandy Berman's Last Stand." *City Pages: Minneapolis/St. Paul* 20, no. 971, 1999.
    <http://citypages.com/databank/20/971/article7781.asp>
Litwin, Rory, ed. "Sanford Berman." *Library Juice* 2:17 Supplement, 28 April 1999.
    <http://www.libr.org/Juice/issues/vol2/LJ_2.17.s.html>
Litwin, Rory, ed. "Sanford Berman's Appeal to Colleagues, Some Background." *Library Juice* 2: 9, 3 March 1999. <http://www.libr.org/Juice/issues/vol2/LJ_2.9.html>
Litwin, Rory, ed. "Mitch Freedman's Appeal to Colleagues for Sanford Berman." *Library Juice* 2: 9, 3 March 1999. <http://www.libr.org/Juice/issues/vol2/LJ_2.9.html>
Litwin, Rory, ed. "Sanford Berman Has Been Removed From His Job." *Library Juice* 2: 16, 21 April 1999. <http://www.libr.org/Juice/issues/vol2/LJ_2.16.html>
Litwin, Rory, ed. "HCL's Rosy Press Release." *Library Juice* 2: 16, 21 April 1999.
    <http://www.libr.org/Juice/issues/vol2/LJ_2.16.html>
Roberto, Katia et al. "The Sandy Berman Rocks My Socks Issue." *Kiss My Filing Indicators* 1, 16 June 1999. <http://www.sarcastra.net/sandy/>
Rogers, Michael and Norman Oder. "Hennepin County Rebukes Berman: Legendary Cataloger Fighting Reprimand; Wants Assurances for Staff." *Library Journal* 126, no. 6 (1999): 13–15.
West, Celeste and Elizabeth Katz, eds. *Revolting Librarians.* San Francisco: Booklegger Press, 1972.

LIBRARIES TO THE PEOPLE, REDUX

Chris Dodge

The word "DISCARDED" is stamped on the title page of my copy of *Revolting Librarians*. It stands for something larger than the edition's removal from the Lincoln Public Library in Lincoln, Illinois. All across North America other libraries seem to have done away with the very principles on which the book is based and abandoned practices for which it passionately advocates (if in fact they adopted them in the first place).

Take Sandy Berman's contribution, "Libraries to the People," which describes a lack of diversity in the Los Angeles Public Library collection circa 1972. Great for bankers and investors, crappy for workers. Full of orthodox literature, but almost devoid of local and ethnic publications, radical papers, gay and lesbian literature, and anti-war titles. "The closest it comes to any rag dealing with Third World revolutionary struggles is the *African Violet Review*," Berman quipped.

Public libraries belong to everyone — or do they? Alison Parker's book *Purifying America* (University of Illinois Press, 1997) contains an interesting chapter on the American Library Association's historical role as "guardians of public morals." Fiction itself used to be considered of dubious propriety in public libraries. When I was a child, librarians evidently discriminated against low-brow popular materials. My hometown library excluded Hardy Boys and Nancy Drew mysteries, just for one category. Sure, it had a recorded music collection, but that was entirely classical. And comic books? You've gotta be kidding. The closest I could find were a few musty collections of cartoons from *The New Yorker.*

We've come a long way since then. Popular materials flood libraries, from graphic novels, comics, and mass market paperback series, to feature films on video. Still, something is always excluded, in part due to budgetary constraints. Instead of focusing and specializing — with local history collections being standard practice, say — more public libraries seem to have identical middle of the road materials. Everything You Know About Your Public Library Can be Learned by Reading the Daily Papers and Watching "Oprah," it sometimes seems.

Librarians have been proud of their gatekeeper role. It behooves us, though, to notice what (and who) these gates keep out. Ask teenagers about libraries — elicit their frank opinions. Do they expect to find recordings by The Weakerthans or Fugazi? Subscriptions to *Maximumrocknroll* and *Punk Planet*? Ask recent immigrants — Can they find *fotonovelas* , the latest *bandas* CDs, or newspapers from their community? Public libraries sometimes "allow" local publications to be distributed in their foyers, but how many of those ethnic papers (to name one example) are cataloged and retained within the library?

Public libraries I've used have large collections of materials catering to investors, business managers, and international travelers — upper middle class folks — but far fewer how-to items for the large percentage of people who are poor. Just fourteen institutions own copies *of The 99 Cents a Meal Cookbook* (Port Townsend, WA: Loompanics, 1996), to name one title. Where are the street newspapers and books about squatting? Just three OCLC libraries hold the excellent monthly *Street Spirit*, and none own *Not for Rent* (Williams, OR: Evil Twin Publications, 1995). People's preconceptions about what may be found in libraries are often accurate. And it's not insignificant that a Gallup poll commissioned by ALA in 1998 found that income correlates with library card ownership. Classism pervades library materials selection.

At a 1992 Library Information Technology Association session, novelist Bruce Sterling quoted librarian James Angell who trumpeted at the beginning of the twentieth century: "I think it must be confessed that a great deal of the fiction which is deluging the market is the veriest trash, or worse than trash. Much of it is positively bad in its influence. It awakens morbid passions. It deals in the most exaggerated representations of life. It is vicious in style."

A dissenting non-librarian voice from Angell's era, Voltairine de Cleyre, wrote, "I include in literature ... not only standard novels, stories, sketches, travels, and magazine essays of all sorts, but the poorest, paltriest dime novel, detective story, daily newspaper report, baseball game account, and splash advertisement. O, what a charming picture of ourselves we see therein! And a faithful one, mind you! Think what a speaking likeness of ourselves was the report of national, international, racial importance — the Jeffries-Johnson fight! Nay, I am not laughing. The people of the future are going to look back at the record a thousand years from now and say, 'This is what interested men in the year 1910.'"

Ninety-five years later, the large public library system where I worked owned over 1200 copies of the latest "standard novel" by John Grisham, but just one of Ben Bagdikian's *Media Monopoly*, a book in its 5th edition. What twisted kind of classism is this?

I once heard my colleague Adela Peskorz describe two kinds of librarians — pointers and walkers. Pointers expect library users to do all the work — "You should find that over there in the Business section." Walkers show people where and how: "Come on over here…" Two other categories of librarians are controllers and sharers. Some librarians don't want their books to leave their shelves, do want to be a necessary intermediary (between library user and what the user is seeking), and believe rules are made to be blindly followed to the letter. In the Department of Put a Lid on the Internet, Fast: I visited an urban public library branch in 1996 which promised Web access. This "access" amounted to a canned list of about twenty links provided by the library's catalog vendor — and the search command (beyond these options) had been disabled. Internet filtering proponents are some of today's controllers.

As for rule-following, I remember that ALA's Cataloging of Children's Materials Committee, on which I once served, has been involved in publishing several editions of *Cataloging Correctly for Kids*. Not only does that title sound sanctimonious, but isn't the whole point of cataloging to be useful? Sandy Berman's suggestion that the book be titled *Cataloging Usefully for Kids* went unheeded.

Berman is the quintessential sharer, acting on his words, "I can't have information I know would be of interest to someone and not share it." Such sharers get things to people in advance of their even requesting it: pertinent articles, citations, magazines, book and film recommendations, and much more. Someone once asked me about "Street Librarian" — the name for both my website and the column I write in *Utne Reader* magazine. I answered that I think of my library as being wherever I am — it's not just a building full of shelves, but a living concept, a verb. A library can be about freely and extemporaneously providing connections, sometimes on a proactive basis. Something like street theater.

The library of the streets is wherever I hang out. Nevertheless people still visit public libraries. They come to libraries because they love to read, because curiosity has not yet been murdered, and because these civic institutions still are usually a safe place to sit and read, protected from the cold or heat, to doze, play checkers, and use a bathroom. People use libraries to help find jobs, to entertain themselves with videos, CDs and novels, to learn — and yet do not know how much they are missing, not realizing that libraries' range of materials could be greatly more broad.

Does your library include Green Party tabloids, socialist & communist weeklies, labor papers, specialized newsletters (e.g., *FAMM-Gram*, publication of Families Against Mandatory Minimums), small press litzines and chapbooks, publications from outside the U.S., magazines by and for Muslims, Hindus, Baha'is, and atheists?

When I write "alternative press," it begs the question "Alternative to *what*?" The answer, first of all, is alternative to corporate magazines and newspapers. *Time* and *Newsweek* are delivery systems designed to sell cars, computers, and "revolutionary" wristwatches. With other increasingly narrowcast mass media — including urban dailies— they pander to fear and greed, presenting story after story which give the false impression that everything is happenstance and out of human control. The frequent result: reader numbness and paralysis. Contrarily, lively alternative media are more likely to inspire and offer avenues for change. Their selling arena revolves around ideas and not products.

If the Sunday *Star Tribune* weighs four pounds, how many ounces of that are news? The corporate media exist to make money for owners and advertisers, but they're also about political control, often presenting neat, over-simplified, condensed packages with false context or no context at all. For future historians, the presence of alternative materials in libraries will provide a fuller picture of what really was happening at a given time, what people were really thinking — not just the words of government officials.

Alternative presses are independent — not part of multinational conglomerates which also own food and beverage brands, say, and recording companies and film studios. (For a look at increasingly narrow media ownership, see the January 7/14, 2002, issue of *The Nation*, "Big Media and What You Can Do About It.") The so-called Association of Alternative Newsweeklies is not so alternative. Many urban weeklies are now chains and not locally owned.

Another way of identifying alternative press is by size and scale. How many copies of a magazine circulate? Millions or hundreds of thousands? Then it's part of the mass media. Three thousand? Three hundred? Thirty? Call it small press or micro press.

What kind of issues are covered and from what points of view? Mainstream publications rarely stray far from the status quo, except to ridicule or point to something as an oddity. Alternative presses tend to be a haven for *real* dissenting views, unpopular ideas that aren't likely to be easily sold, books making a connection between U.S. economic policy and civil wars around the world, for one. Would Time-Warner publish books by or about political prisoners, manuals for union organizers, works documenting indigenous people's rights and sovereignty, or how-to guides about anal sex? Leave it to Loompanics to fill the niche of books about revenge, hacking, establishing a new identity, and hiring a contract killer ("For informational purposes only").

Since the word "alternative" has been co-opted ("alternative rock music" is thoroughly mainstream), it's useful to think and speak specifically of *noncorporate* media, or *independent* publishers, or *small* or *radical* press. The word "media" itself, means "in the middle" and suggests separation. Alternative media tend to be produced by people from the very communities they serve, so the buffering from reality is less.

With a special interest in alternative magazines, I've periodically looked at library holdings for noteworthy titles, many of which I've read for years. I'm happy to say that numbers are slowly sneaking up for some; as of April 2002, five OCLC libraries now hold the long-running, influential zine *Cometbus* (up from two in early 2001) and there are now ten institutional subscribers to award-winning *Clamor* magazine (also up from two in the same period). But it's worth noting to see how few libraries — public, academic, and special — hold some other significant periodicals:

- *Nuclear Resister*, the Tucson-based newspaper covering ploughshares actions and people imprisoned for civil disobedience, is held by just ten OCLC libraries.
- *Punk Planet*, a significant bimonthy magazine of music and politics: ten libraries.
- *Geist*, an excellent and well-established Canadian general interest magazine: seven libraries (up from one in early 2001).
- *h2so4*, the literate zine covering "philosophy, politics, [and] how we live": four libraries.
- *Stay Free* magazine, longtime watchdog of the advertising and public relations industries: four libraries.
- *Loving More*, a magazine discussing "polyamory" and polyfidelity, published since 1995: just three OCLC holdings.
- *Land Rights News*, covering Aboriginal Australian issues: three libraries.
- *Dark Night Field Notes*, a radical political magazine: three libraries.
- *Car Busters*, international magazine promoting alternatives to automobiles: two libraries.
- *East Village Inky*, award-winning zine by the author of *The Big Rumpus* (Seal Press, 2002): two libraries.
- *My Evil Twin Sister*, a handsomely produced and well-written zine: one library
- *Danzine*, a zine for sex industry workers: one library.
- *Hair to Stay*, a magazine for people attracted to hairy women: no libraries

How do you go about collecting alternatives? For starters, you might check out the website of the Independent Press Association <http://www.indypress.org>, New Pages <http://www.newpages.com>, and the Alternative Press Index <http://www.altpress.org>. Alternative press publications tend to be affordable, with subscriptions in the $10–$20 range, not $100–$200.

Even cheaper are zines, a sub-category of alternative press, publications produced not for money but from passion — by and for "girls who like girls who wear glasses," Pez collectors (*Optimistic Pezzimist*), straight edge library school students, aficionados of the French auto racing game Milles Bornes, and — not infrequently — flaming egotists. Sometimes understood as being any low-circulation, non-mainstream magazine or newspaper, zines are self-published periodicals often cobbled together using glue sticks and photocopiers, though sometimes painstakingly created with silkscreen (*Spunk*) or letterpress (*Ker-bloom!*). Regardless of format, all embody A. J. Liebling's dictum: "Freedom of the press is guaranteed only to those who own one."

Admittedly, zines may be a nightmare for acquisitions librarians and catalogers. For starters, most aren't available by subscription. Typically zine publishers direct readers to send "well-concealed cash or stamps" to receive the next edition. Since the average zine lifetime is short, serials specialists may be averse to the idea of adding them to collections. This would be a shame. Zines can be a useful reference tool, providing information about emerging cultural trends and news about protests, consumer action campaigns, and other stories overlooked by the corporate press.

Zines' future research value ought to be considered. In every city someone should be collecting locally and regionally produced publications (often found at independent book stores and record shops). Subject specialists might broaden and deepen their collections by seeking zines. Finally, zines may be used in collection development, as they frequently review items not covered in most mainstream journals, from independently-produced videos, to comic books by up-and-coming artists.

It's true that many longstanding zines appear irregularly and infrequently. "Published 4 times/year" may translate to once a year in practice. Do *not* send claims notices to zine publishers; instead, be patient. For publications not available by subscription, consider using petty cash accounts. Some zine editors will be happy to contribute copies, if you take the time to solicit them. Make expeditions to comic shops, independent record stores, or booksellers who offer zines, and utilize distributors such as Pander Zine Distro <http://www.panderzinedistro.com> and Frida Loves Diego <http://www.geocities.com/oddviolet28/mailorder.html>. Public librarians: consider treating zines as many institutions already handle comic books, as "one-shots" placed with teenagers' materials, for example.

I advised someone recently who asked about the task of collecting zines: "Start small, alphabetize, keep your eyes open, stay curious, pick up publications everywhere you go, read widely, send for things you read about which you've never seen. Share generously — or squirrel away *everything*. Document. Start a review publication — or a catalog — or both. Grow. Find more space. Publicize. Keep going." I might add: travel to zine shows and conferences, anarchist book fairs, and comics conventions. Ask friends who travel to send you their finds. (Reimburse them or reciprocate.) Jim Danky suggests: make a deal with someone at a newsstand or bookstore to procure the samples they receive from distributors.

Zines are primarily reviewed in other zines, but a few good review publications exist:

- *The Free Press Death Ship* (P.O. Box 55336, Hayward, CA 94545; donation).
- *A Reader's Guide to the Underground Press* (P.O. Box 330156, Murfreesboro, TN 37133-0156; cash only: $4/issue, $14/4; <http://www.undergroundpress.org>).
- *Xerography Debt* (P.O. Box 963, Havre de Grace, MD 21078; cash only: $2/issue; <http://www.leekinginc.com>)

I'm fortunate to feel part of a community of free-spirited, critical thinking, open-minded librarians. As the administrator of a one-person special library at *Utne Reader* magazine, this sense of collegiality is important. I'm glad to put mutual aid into action with librarians down the block from me at the Minneapolis Community and Technical College. (Check out their web page and notice the alternative press presence: <http://www.mctc.mnscu.edu/Library>.)

Librarians are often disconnected it seems, divided by type (school librarian, public, corporate), by geographic location, and by rank (directors, managers, and front-line staffers). One good way to dispel alienation is to attend library conferences, not so much for the programs and meetings as for the coming together and hanging out with friends and allies who live far away. Internet discussion groups are also good for coalescing solidarity—from *Anarchist Librarians* (send an email message to lists@tao.ca with a blank subject line and the message "subscribe librarians [your email address]") to *Radical Catalogers* (send an email message to majordomo@dangpow.com and put "subscribe radcat" in the message body).

Speaking of solidarity, how about organizing a union? (Librarians at Hennepin County did so in 1997; contact someone at AFSCME Local 2864 to find out more.)

Even simpler: Revolting librarians social events, anyone? Whatever the occasion, here's a toast to energetic, evolving, laughing, wondering, contrarian librarians.

- Revolting librarians have opinions.
- Revolting librarians are unafraid of dissent.
- Revolting librarians think independently — and rely on networks of friends.
- Revolting librarians organize review slams. (Thanks, Brenda Mitchell-Powell.)
- Revolting librarians frequent independent bookstores and infoshops.
- Revolting librarians refute the notion that "everything is on the Internet."
- Revolting librarians are multilingual — and fluent in dialects besides standard written English.
- Revolting librarians question authority and — as Sandy Berman says—"managerial prerogatives."
- Revolting librarians resist special fees in public libraries and tiered levels of service based on payment.
- Revolting librarians aren't afraid of collecting periodicals whose titles change with each issue.
- Revolting librarians are interested in materials not reviewed in *Publishers Weekly*: local and regional publications, fan club newsletters, items found on the ground, items with no ISBNs.
- Revolting librarians read ghetto pulp fiction, neighborhood newspapers, 19th century journals, and publications with staples, smeary ink, crooked margins, and tiny print.
- Revolting librarians foster connections with everyone in the community —

including prisoners, children, homeless people, publishers, authors, journalists, and activists.

- Revolting librarians are willing to leave the comfort of their offices and reference desks to go treasure hunting in their communities.
- Revolting librarians are concerned that new technology is largely controlled by those who profit from it, and so don't wish to rely on it.
- Revolting librarians use appropriate, sustainable, and multiple technology, from the Internet to pamphlets on city buses, graffiti, radical magazines, stickers, mail art, cable TV, and community radio.
- Revolting librarians encourage library users by asking questions and listening respectfully.
- Revolting librarians have not given up hope for the future of libraries.
- Revolting librarians believe in justice, freedom, poetry, joy, and resistance.

In the first issue of *NewBreed Librarian,* I responded to the question, "What makes librarianship exciting to you?" Here again, with a slight revision, is what I answered:

- Sharing books, magazines, videos, zines, CDs, and information that people want (and need) to know about, if only they had a clue.
- Making connections fortuitously in the cause of a happier, more joyful world.
- Imparting passion about poetry, truth, beauty, freedom, ornithology.
- Teaching people to do it themselves.
- Linking those who quest for knowledge, those who love learning, with the tools and resources necessary for them to learn and to grow.
- Promoting alternatives to mass media that offer a respite from cynicism and foster the idea that committed individuals and groups can make a difference.
- Saving the past from being forgotten. (Viva Voltairine de Cleyre!)
- Keeping hope alive for the future.
- Ensuring real diversity in library materials.
- Imparting curiosity.
- Working to make public libraries free for all.
- Countering consumerism and commercialism in publishing.
- Educating library users to stand up for their rights, how to ask for what they want, even though their stereotypes of what sort of things are generally not in libraries (but *ought* to be) is often accurate (say, adult comics, punk music, erotica, small circulation magazines, zines, and street newspapers, to name a few).
- Modeling appropriate technology, from the grassroots: handwritten notes and phone calls, sometimes.

- Showing that a library is not so much about a collection of books on shelves as an attitude that can move wherever the librarian goes.
- To continue to dream and invent the role of activist librarian.

LIBRARIES—IT'S A GOOD THING

Jennifer Young

Who hates libraries? No one ever says that they do, even if "everything is available on the Internet" nowadays. Except for Governor Locke of Washington, hardly any one ever tries to completely abolish a library. Funding may be cut, ballot initiatives defeated, controversial materials removed from shelves, but libraries are generally seen as a Good Thing and are even revered. Why is it then that librarians are often portrayed as uptight middle-aged matrons with a finger and a "Shhh" that can make ice seem hot? Don't forget that once we let our hair out of our buns and take off our glasses we are all sexually insatiable dominatrices. How come so few people see us as the kick-ass information finders that we are? Where's the love? We stand up for libraries, we stand up against censorship, and we stand up for patrons' privacy, but we sell librarians short. Over and over, we always hear about how librarians have an image problem. What have we done, and what could we do, as a profession, to counteract this impression?

In 1988, the art world devised a "Day without Art" in response to intense anger and personal loss due to HIV/AIDS in the arts community. This day, which occurs on December 1, World HIV/AIDS day, helps promote awareness of not only the personal impact of the disease, but also the worldwide impact. What would happen if for one day a year, we closed libraries all over the country as a "Day without Libraries?" Shut down our websites, catalogs, and libraries—would the public notice or care? A whole 24 hours without librarian-assisted access to information—maybe such an action should actually be a week to make more of an impact. Just think: Bar bets would go unanswered; book reports and last-minute essays would not be completed; businesses, doctors, and other researchers would not have information they need; nothing would be cataloged, interlibrary loaned, archived, or bought.

We do a good job of promoting libraries during such events as National Library Week, but what about librarians? If we did a better job of promoting what librarians actually do (other than sitting around all day reading books only managing to look up to shush people, of course) than we have the possibility of not only raising our prestige among the public, but of also attracting new people to the profession.

Librarians often have at least a MLS and more often than not, a second Master's degree or Ph.D. in another field, yet we have low salaries. In this "Information/Knowledge Age/Economy/Zeitgeist" librarians should be seen as the leaders that they are in this arena. Every other library school is dropping the word "Library" and adding "Information Science" or some other variant to try and appeal to more techie-oriented people. Well, I don't know too many librarians that don't deal with technology in some form or another on a daily basis. Whether it's OPAC, database, or just plain ol' Internet searching, librarians routinely use technology to help find information as well as make it available.

Librarians often forget how much power they have. We can impede people's access to information, but more often we help it. We bend over backwards to help patrons find access to the information they are looking for in any format. Perhaps going a day (or longer) without our services will provide a more respectful view of our glorious profession.

Pioneering Progressive Library Discourse

Toni Samek

In a thought piece on library history written for the International Federation of Library Associations and Institutions (IFLA) in the mid-nineties, Paul Schneiders and Pam Richards referred to an "amnesia that threatens to infect the library world."[1] The general purpose of this essay is to begin a process of contributing and documenting a critical perspective on the history of progressive library discourse. To date, little scholarly published work has been produced on the subject in the context of historical and cultural dimensions. Thus, critical perspectives on this discourse are in danger of disappearing from the organizational memory of librarianship.

In a 1990 article titled "Feminist Publishers," Irene Reti of HerBooks is quoted as saying: "I had this sense of lesbian culture being very tenuous, something that had to be built. I had to contribute."[2] This profoundly raw statement of intent reflects what I hope to convey in this brief discussion about the early construction of a new library culture. The story of this culture is perhaps best understood in the narrower context of progressive library discourse, a site of ideological struggle for librarians.

Progressive library discourse, in the western context, is rooted in the 1930s progressive library movement in the United States, when library activists of the 1930s pressured the American Library Association (ALA) to be more responsive to issues put forth by young members involved in such issues as peace, segregation, library unions, and intellectual freedom. In 1931, C. Harvey Brown, director of Iowa State University, Marian Manley of the Business Branch of the Newark Public Library, and Stanley J. Kunitz, poet and editor of the *Wilson Library Bulletin*, formed the Junior Members Round Table (JMRT). Members of the Round Table identified ALA's support for librarians as the central issue on which all the other issues hinged. For example, Philip O. Keeney's dismissal without due process from his position as librarian at the Montana State University in 1937 led to the formation of another library activist group. In 1939, Keeney's appeal was upheld by the Montana Supreme Court. The next year, he took leadership of a new group called the Progressive Librarians' Council in order to provide a united voice for librarians who sought change in the association and to lobby for federal and state aid for libraries.[3]

By the end of its first year, the Progressive Librarians' Council had 235 members. Many were involved with ALA's Staff Organizations Round Table, formed in 1936, and Library Unions Round Table, formed in 1940. In addition, the *Progressive Librarians' Council Bulletin* provided a forum for activities on behalf of freedom of expression. The *Bulletin* printed outspoken opinions "not tolerated" by the traditional communication organs—*Library Journal, Wilson Library Bulletin* and *ALA Bulletin*. Eventually, after ALA's Staff Organizations Round Table and Library Unions Round Table gained momentum and the number of round tables in general increased, the Progressive Librarians' Council disbanded.[4]

Increased ALA responsiveness to its membership was a central issue for activist librarians in the 1930s and again in the 1960s. While comparing radical librarians of the 1930s with the rebels of the 1960s, library educator and scholar Jesse Shera noted that "the actors are different, but the script is much the same."[5] The nature of library activism of the 1930s mirrors the 1960s in a number of ways: (1) activists called for ALA to operate democratically; (2) criticized the homogeneity of the professional discourse; and (3) paid attention to the needs of the librarian, not just of the institution.

Like progressive library discourse, American library rhetoric on intellectual freedom also dates back to the 1930s. Starting in the late 1960s, however, advocates of an alternative library culture based on the concept of library social responsibility, that included the librarian's right to freedom of expression, lobbied the ALA to extend the concept of intellectual freedom to include library practitioners as well as library users. For example, these alternative library culture advocates believed that while, as professionals, librarians have "the responsibility for the development and maintenance of intellectual freedom," as citizens, librarians have the fundamental right to freedom of expression (e.g. library employee freedom of speech in the workplace on professional and policy issues and freedom of the library press).[6]

Progressive library discourse is a site of contestation for various stakeholders in the dominant culture of the profession, because it challenges librarianship to reconceptualize the traditional ethic of intellectual freedom. In the context of contemporary western librarianship, the phrase "intellectual freedom" is widely understood to mean "the right of every individual to both seek and receive information from all points of view without restriction." Intellectual freedom "provides for free access to all expressions of ideas through which any and all sides of a question, cause or movement may be explored" and "encompasses the freedom to hold, receive and disseminate ideas."[7] Traditionally, this interpretation of intellectual freedom has been applied to libraries' public(s).

In the late 1960s and early 1970s, when social protest movements in larger society were mirrored in American librarianship, progressive library discourse flourished against the backdrop of the urgent politics and culture of "Sixties" society. While the nation was divided by deep philosophical debates over the Vietnam War, librarians themselves were arguing over library neutrality, the personal versus the professional, the librarian versus the institution, all in the context of profound social issues such as war and peace, racism, and sexism. The arrival of the social responsibility movement in librarianship, marked by such events as the formation in ALA of a Round Table on the Social Responsibilities of Libraries in 1969 and the Black Caucus of ALA in 1970, signified a new library era. Meanwhile, the very notion of library culture was transforming — and so was the library press.

The 1960s activist librarians became more socially aware through involvement in the causes and issues espoused by the era's alternative press. Some librarians were intrigued by the novelty of the messages in the alternative press, others by the freshness of the medium itself. When, for example, publications like *The Oracle* (San Francisco), *The East Village Other* (New York), *The Fifth Estate* (Detroit), *The Paper* (East Lansing), *The Los Angeles Free Press* (Los Angeles), and *The Berkeley Barb* (Berkeley) began attracting national recognition because they questioned the objectivity of the establishment press in the mid-1960s, a subset of American librarians took note. They began to publish their own alternative library press (in the same vein as the vanguard *Progressive Librarians' Council Bulletin*).

A one-page entry titled "The Library Free Press," published in *Booklegger Magazine* in 1974 noted that "Our profession has finally birthed its own alternative press, with the voice of change publishing ideas, hopes, demands. There at least five totally independent, adventurous library mags. [*Booklegger Magazine, Emergency Librarian, Sipapu, The Unabashed Librarian: A Letter for Innovators,* and *The Young Adult Alternative Newsletter.*] They are not slick with ad money and please-everybody. They are home-grown, in touch, labors of love. Staffs are *paid* in freedom of expression and its warm response."[8]

These new alternative library titles were "a political use"[9] of print culture because they were intended to foster a "universe of discourse."[10] For example, they allowed progressive librarians, "and implicitly, though indirectly," librarianship, "to debate the burning issues of the day," to "define and promote shared meanings," and to encourage freedom of expression.[11] Perhaps the single-most influential print "index" to the new library culture is a book titled *Revolting Librarians*, published by Booklegger Press in 1972.[12]

Edited by Celeste West and Elizabeth Katz, the daring anthology took the field by storm with its diverse collection of library workers' uncensored voices on topics such as the librarians' image, library schools and education, professionalism, mainstream bias and representation in Library of Congress subject headings, undemocratic library work practices, paraprofessional issues, homophobia, alternative libraries and alternative education, young adult services, libraries for migrant workers, and the library press. *Revolting Librarians* "sold 15,000 copies in about three years with virtually no promotion."[13]

Print culture scholar Rudolph J. Vecoli asserted that "rather than simply serving as transmitters of information, communication media" are "forces actively constructing social reality and identity in the minds of their audiences."[14] Based on Antonio Gramsci's concept of ideological hegemony, Vecoli noted that, "communication is viewed as the means whereby the ruling element manufactures and secures consensus to its view of the world among subaltern groups. Since such hegemonic conceptions are subject to challenges by oppositional views, the media become the site of ideological contestation of a struggle over meaning."[15] Contributions to *Revolting Librarians* (e.g., essays, articles, poems, fictional stories, and fables) were aimed at library administrators and managers, not just workers. Indeed, a key purpose of the book was to "oppose the influence of the dominant culture" of librarianship and its publications—"that is, to subvert the hegemony."[16]

The reader response to *Revolting Librarians* reflected the book's political aim. For example, Charles W. Conaway's *Library Resources & Technical Services* review said the book deserved "at least selective reading by all librarians and particularly by administrators and library educators, the groups with whom the revolting librarians have the most difficulty in communicating." Eugene Darling's *Library Union Caucus Newsletter* review said "we have in this book some very vivid and accurate pictures of what's wrong with libraries." Meanwhile, in *Library Journal* editor John Berry wrote, "Get the little red book!"[17] Despite the "underground smash," life above ground was mostly business as usual.[18]

In 1972, ALA was the world's oldest and largest national library association and its complex structure and slow pace presented an impediment to anyone who wanted quick action.[19] Following two quieter decades, however, progressive library discourse gained a new momentum sparked by the many social, cultural, political, legal, economic, and philosophical issues introduced by an emergent digital and global society in the 1990s.

Today, in general, progressive library discourse reflects the divergent voices on the margins of librarianship that question the absolutism of the library ethic of intellectual freedom. These (primarily leftist) voices generally concur that the core value of library neutrality (on which the ethic of intellectual freedom is based) is unrealistic in the context of library practice. In particular, however, these voices have represented a range of viewpoints on a continuum that spans from an anarchist stance to varying degrees of a social responsibility perspective. The Progressive Librarians Guild, for example, defines its purpose as follows:

Progressive Librarians Guild [PLG], an affiliate organization of the Social Responsibilities Round Table o the American Library Association, was formed in January 1990 by a group of librarians concerned with our profession's rapid drift into dubious alliances with business and the information industry, and into complacent acceptance of service to the political, economic and cultural status quo.... Current trends in librarianship assert that the library is merely a neutral mediator in the information marketplace and a facilitator of a value-neutral information society. Members of PLG do not accept this notion of neutrality, and we strongly oppose the commodification of information. We will help to dissect the implications of these powerful trends, and fight their anti-democratic tendency.[20]

Contemporary library publishers, practitioners, web managers, scholars, educators, and students shape progressive library discourse through such communication media as alternative monographs (e.g., *Zoia! Memoirs of Zoia Horn, Battler for the People's Right to Know*), monographic series (e.g., *Alternative Library Literature*), publishers (e.g., CRISES Press), journals (e.g., *Progressive Librarian: A Journal for Critical Studies & Progressive Politics in Librarianship*), websites (e.g., *A Common Ground: Intellectual Freedom and Social Responsibility — A Student Website of the School of Library and Information Studies, University of Alberta*), electronic serials (e.g., *Library Juice*), newsletters (e.g., *Social Responsibilities Round Table of the American Library Association Newsletter*), and mailing lists (e.g., PLGNET-L).

Individuals who participate in progressive library discourse encounter "a radically different definition" of library "reality" and culture than those who do not. Today, thirty years past the publication of *Revolting Librarians*, progressive library discourse both adjusts "our historical focus" of librarianship and continues "to offer alternative visions for the future."[21] To recognize the value of progressive library discourse and progressive library culture is to recognize the value of intellectual freedom for library workers and to counter that amnesia that threatens to rob us of the lessons to be learned from library history — the two surest ways to fuel professional progress.

Author's Note

This essay draws on parts of my 2001 book *Intellectual Freedom and Social Responsibility in American Librarianship, 1967–1974* (Jefferson, NC: McFarland & Company, Inc.)

Notes

1. Paul Schneiders and Pam Richards. "Some Thoughts on the Function of Library History in the Age of the Virtual Library," 1997. Round Table on Library History. International Federation of Library Associations and Institutions. <http://www.ifla.org/VII/rt8/1997/thoughts.htm>

2. Feminist Publishers," *Matrix* (August 1990): 25.

3. Joe W. Kraus, "The Progressive Librarians' Council" *Library Journal* 97, no. 13 (July 1972): 2351–2354. See also Rosalee McReynolds, "Trouble in Big Sky's Ivory Tower: The Montana Tenure Dispute 1937–1939," *Libraries & Culture* 32, no. 2 (Spring 1997): 163–190.

4. Ibid.

5. Jesse H. Shera, "Plus ça Change," *Library Journal* 95, no. 6 (15 March 1970): 985.

6. Canadian Library Association. *Statement on Intellectual Freedom* (Adopted June 27, 1974; Amended November 17, 1983 and November 18, 1985). <http://www.cla.ca/about/intfreed.htm>

7. American Library Association. Office for Intellectual Freedom. *Intellectual Freedom and Censorship Q & A*, 2002. <http://www.ala.org/alaorg/oif/intellectualfreedomandcensorship.html>

8. "The Library Free Press." *Booklegger Magazine* no. 2 (January/February 1974), 24.

9. James P. Danky and Wayne A. Wiegand, eds. *Print Culture in a Diverse America*. Urbana: University of Illinois Press, 1998, 4.

10. Michael Fultz. ""The Morning Cometh": African-American Periodicals, Education, and the Black Middle Class, 1900–1930" in *Print Culture in a Diverse America*, 130–131.

11. Ibid.

12. Violet Johnson. "Pan-Africanism in Print: The *Boston Chronicle* and the Struggle for Black Liberation and Advancement, 1930–50," in *Print Culture in a Diverse America*, 58.

13. "A Conversation with Celeste West," *Technicalities* 2, no. 4 (April 1982): 3–6.

14. Rudolph J. Vecoli. "The Italian Immigrant Press and the Construction of Social Reality, 1850–1920" in *Print Culture in a Diverse America*, 19.

15. Ibid.

16. Ibid., 26.

17. Charles W. Conaway, *Library Resources and Technical Services* 18, no. 3 (Summer 1974): 294–295; Eugene Darling, "Are Librarians Revolting?," *Library Union Caucus Newsletter* 2, no. 1 (January 1973): 5; John Berry, "Little Red Book," *Library Journal* 98, no. 4 (15 February 1973): 515.

18. "A Conversation," 3–6.

19. "The American Library Association," *ALA Bulletin* 61, no. 10 (November 1967): 1155.

20. <http://libr.org/PLG/#statement>

21. Kathleen M. Casey. "Women's Writings that Preserve Voices of the Past." *Cite AB* (March 21, 1994): 1232.

"CHECK OUT THOSE BUNS"; OR, WHAT DO YOU SAY TO A MALE LIBRARIAN?

Owen Massey

This may come as a surprise, but I didn't go to library school to meet girls. As a boy, I would be joining a buyer's market, outnumbered 7 to 1 by female students. Maybe the department only accepted me because of my obvious effeminacy.

In the first *Revolting Librarians* Joan Marshall criticised the LC subject heading WOMEN AS LIBRARIANS (since ameliorated to WOMEN LIBRARIANS), "about which no comment is necessary, except to point out that there is no heading MEN AS LIBRARIANS." If only. It might have made writing this a lot easier.

The figures vary across its subdivisions, but it's indisputable that librarianship remains a dramatically segregated occupation. Nursing, teaching and social work are some of the few professions with a similarly strong female contingent. The makeup at my library school only reflected librarianship's broader composition.

Indeed, you may object, when library school has finished wasting the time and minds of its bright young things, it releases them into the harsh world of employment where the discrimination is reversed. The higher ranks of library administrators are serried with men, in particularly sharp contrast to their scarcity. There is a balance of imbalance.

But this isn't a zero-sum game: one side losing doesn't mean the other side wins. Men who struggle to the top are still rewarded less lucratively than they could be as managers in other sectors. And what about us men keener to refine our craft than to abandon it for administration?

The issue is clearly wider than just a numerical disparity. Remedying the sex divide should be an ethical imperative in itself, but money concentrates the mind wonderfully. Comparing the relative salaries of gendered specialisms like children's librarianship and systems work is instructive.

(Of course, low pay is a spur to radicalism. Revolting librarians might think twice about agitating for the right to be bourgeois.)

But why is librarianship low-paid, as a whole? Harleigh Kyson, another Revolting Librarian, claimed that librarians were in fact overpaid by the standards of clerical work, but this is needlessly provocative. Often we blame our relative low pay on our self-perceived low status, and this in turn on that lazy favourite of a thousand library school essays, the "image problem."

Don't fall for the idea that what's necessary here is a change of name and some glossy marketing. Compare librarians with engineers: both have an out-of-date name (how many engineers work on engines?) that confounds them with their non-qualified counterparts. Both have an image problem: librarians are dowdy, engineers are nerds. Yet engineers are well-remunerated, as are surveyors, and accountants, and other unglamorous professions.

No. The real obstacle to improving our pay, status and image is the shortage of men. Even apologists for the numerical dominance of female librarians admit that the perception of librarianship as a "woman's profession" (and therefore a "feminised" profession) keeps our worth unrecognised, just as it does that of nurses and teachers.

So who's responsible? Originally, Melvil Dewey, whose preference for college-bred women was based on the expectation that they would happily accept a lower salary (and a little personal harassment). The bias is maintained today by the source of so much else of questionable value: library schools.

Vocational courses in areas with powerful sexual stereotype — bricklaying and hairdressing, for instance — suffer from uneven intakes because potential applicants have internalised these stereotypes. Librarianship is, unfortunately, one of these areas, with no campaigns to encourage men to consider it a rewarding career. Thus the pool of employable librarians is automatically skewed by sex. The existence of a bias in favour of men at senior levels is not an excuse for mirroring it with entry-level sexism; neither imbalance justifies the other.

When I spoke to a careers adviser about becoming a librarian, she promised I'd get an easy ride as a man in a female environment. Now, I enjoy working mainly with women, but what she meant, and what she stated explicitly, was that my female peers would dash off to reproduce, freeing me to leapfrog their succession.

I was disgusted. Childrearing is a problem for parents, not women, and to equate those two groups is disingenuous, conservative and insulting to women with the sense to be childfree. It may be that librarians, of either sex, quit only because they are likely to be the lower-paid of any couple. The aging profile of the profession isn't the only reason there's a recruitment crisis.

It was famously observed that information science is no more than a name for librarianship practised by men (or, if that seems too reductive, computer science for those who can't cope with maths). Attempting to attract men by changing the name or content of library qualifications begs the question: in pandering to supposed sexual differences, it reinforces them.

New role models could help. As library users, we see the female frontline staff (qualified or not) and rarely the male managers. Some forceful action from library schools and library associations might even extend the archetypes for male librarians beyond crusty, camp, and cataloguer.

It would be ludicrous to pretend there are any peculiarly male insights into librarianship, though it might be interesting to investigate the effect on collection development of the greater use of public libraries by women. I don't even believe that male librarians have a hard time because of their sex, beyond occasional requests for heavy lifting and late nights.

It's merely that by excluding a large number of potential librarians, of whatever type, library schools are by definition excluding talent. And gods know librarianship could do with more talent. We're winning the battle for diversity in our collections; its natural complement is diversity among ourselves.

STATUS QUO/REVOLUTION: LANGUAGE TO SILENCE DISSENT IN LIBRARIANSHIP

Tara Alcock

Intellectual freedom is currently lauded as librarianship's "core value." Intellectual freedom is thought to be completely equitable and all-inclusive. Yet since intellectual freedom gained ground in the profession, activism and revolt have been systematically knocked, disdained, and frowned upon. I would argue that intellectual freedom, while purporting to "include all," actually feeds on the negation of activism and social responsibility in librarianship. As a result, critiques of the reigning doctrine of intellectual freedom are treated like a crack in the foundation and dealt with accordingly. Dissenting voices and subversive criticisms are too easily brushed aside in this framework. The response has not been to acknowledge dissent but to stop up the cracks and reinforce the walls. It is behind these walls that librarians can hide from their own value systems and how these systems frame all aspects of their professional practice.

If you look closely at the history of intellectual freedom in the profession it becomes clear that intellectual freedom is being defined not by what it *is* per se, but by what it is *not*. Librarians who practice intellectual freedom do *not* censor, are *not* partisan, and do *not* advocate. The history of intellectual freedom in librarianship has rested on this persistent set of oppositions:

intellectual freedom	social responsibility
neutral	activist
professional	personal
librarian	citizen
library issues	non-library issues
democratic	censorious
legitimate social awareness	telescopic philanthropy
professional concerns	micromanagement
normal	special interest
mainstream	marginal
majority	minority
sameness	difference
all	one
institutions	workers
reason	emotion
foundational	relative
objective	subjective
distance	involvement
order	chaos
status quo	**revolution**

This polarization of intellectual freedom and social responsibility has relegated the activism, dissent, and all social considerations to the margins of the profession. Activists are treated as troublemakers indulging in "emotional" pleas. Critics accuse them of allowing their "political" interests as "citizens" to overtake their "professional duties." Their "activism" is seen as a threat to librarianship's "neutrality." This "minority" is disruptive and detracts from "library issues." While the profession is interested in "library" problems, activists loudly "micromanage" pulling in "non-library issues" and thus detracting from the real work of librarians. These arguments regularly turn up in professional publications such as *American Libraries* and they play out daily on a smaller scale in the work lives of librarians.

Ironically, intellectual freedom, while purporting to "include all," is serving to limit the free speech of librarians. Our language is silencing dissent. Yet, as any radical or activist in the profession can attest to, librarianship remains— in the face of decades of criticism — persistently and overwhelmingly white, middle class, mainstream and heterosexual. Librarians have failed to live up to the all-inclusive jargon of intellectual freedom. Instead intellectual freedom and the persistent set of oppositions listed above are regularly used shield our conservative profession from fundamental criticisms. We use it to maintain the status quo.

In my opinion it is the activists, dissenters, radicals, and revolting librarians that are producing the most challenging and interesting insights into the profession. But for this potential to be realized the intellectual freedom/social responsibility dichotomy needs to be revealed as the artificial construct that it is. The terms of the argument need to be radically redefined.

VI. Day to Revolting Day: Our Stories

patrons, council, staff
politics in triplicate —
calm as waterfalls

—Kathleen Kern

What Do Radical Librarians Do? or, Which Way to the Black Bloc?

Chuck Munson

At some point in the middle of answering questions at the info desk of the Anti-Capitalist Convergence Center and juggling cell phone calls from activists and friends who were being detained by the police, I realized that this was one of the strangest places that I had ever plied my librarian skills. The occasion was a weekend of protest against the World Bank and the IMF, which had turned into a protest against capitalism and the new "War on Terrorism" as a result of 9/11. But as any radical librarian will tell you, this kind of volunteer librarianship is not that unusual in our circles.

I had opened up the ACC Welcome Center on the morning of the big marches downtown. The Welcome Center was using rented space in a community center in the Columbia Heights neighborhood of Washington, D.C. The situation I found myself in required both my skills as a radical librarian and as an anarchist organizer. After opening up the building, I parked myself behind the information table and spent the next six hours answering questions with a crew of volunteers. Most of the questions were informational, mainly about where the protests were being held. We gave directions to the nearest Metro subway station and relayed the locations of the protests. In addition to the information desk, all the walls in the entrance foyer where our table was located were covered with sheets of paper with all kinds of information: workshop schedules, notes from people looking for rides, a Metro map and Washington D.C. street map, phone numbers for legal support, and flyers for a variety of activist events. While we didn't have to resort to a reference book collection (though a connection to the Internet would have been helpful), this was like working a regular reference desk in many ways.

Only at most reference desks you don't maintain log book of suspicious police activity in the neighborhood.

This was not my first experience as an anarchist librarian doing library work at a radical event; I had spend some time at the information desk of the Convergence Center during the April 2000 World Bank protests in Washington. This is but one example of what radical librarians do as unconventional professionals. We typically find ourselves balancing work on behalf of our activist causes with work as radicals within the traditional library profession.

Anarchist librarians?

You are probably wondering what an anarchist librarian is. An anarchist librarian is a recent subset of the larger universe of radical librarians. Anarchist librarians are involved in anarchist projects in addition to the traditional activism in which many people engage. You'll find anarchist librarians involved with infoshops, the local Independent Media Center, a special archive, or publishing a zine. Anarchist librarians are more than just professionals who engage in the occasional protest; they live their beliefs and are engaged in long-term struggles for social change. This means that an anarchist librarian who is concerned with media concentration and the stranglehold of intellectual property wouldn't just protest, but would go out and organize alternatives.

Politically, anarchist librarians are pretty similar to the larger network of progressive and radical librarians. What differentiates anarchist librarians from their radical peers is a connection to the anarchist movement and a more deeply held skepticism about authority. You won't find any anarchist librarians who are library directors. Anarchists do not like authority and hierarchy, and they will avoid becoming managers if they can. Anarchist librarians also have lots of skepticism about the whole idea of the library "profession"—that is, the whole system of library schools and artificial distinctions between professionals and paraprofessionals. Contrary to the propaganda often heard in the profession, being a librarian doesn't require the type of specialized knowledge that lawyers and doctors get in their schooling. Who knows how many times a paraprofessional in some technical services department who has been cataloging books for 20 years is suddenly confronted by a new supervisor whose cataloging experience consists of a few cataloging classes in library school?

In addition to being activists on a wide range of issues, anarchist librarians are critical of the entire system of power in libraryland. This plays itself out in ongoing struggles to counteract the interests of corporations in our library associations and libraries. This stance may manifest itself in criticisms of the American Library Association and its cozy relationships with corporate donors, or in raising awareness about the spreading cancer of globalization and privatization in public libraries.

One of the interesting things about the growing number of anarchist librarians is that many of them are people who decided to go to library school after being involved in anarchist projects such as infoshops, bookstores, zine publishing, and Books through Bars. It not unusual to see activist types going to library school. After all, librarianship is a profession with a strong history of support for progressive ideas like freedom of speech and intellectual freedom. The profession is filled with library workers who are interested in intellectual freedom, fighting censorship, diversity in collections, and social responsibilities. As many of us know, librarians don't do this work because they want to make lots of money and fight their way to the top. This appeals to the next generation of radical librarians who are looking for employment in a profession that matches their value systems and political beliefs.

In the Field

Given that the anarchist/radical librarian is also by definition an activist, it's not surprising to find radical librarians using their skills and training at some kind of activist event. I've already detailed my experience working in the welcome center of a national mobilization. Jessamyn West has detailed her experiences working reference at a variety of interesting events, including the annual Burning Man Festival.

Protests are something that is part of the diet of any activist, and radical librarians have organized and participated in numerous protests. One of the more memorable protests at any recent American Library Association conventions took place in New Orleans at ALA's 1999 summer meeting. ALA had decided to make Colin Powell their keynote speaker, which prompted a good amount of controversy in libraryland. A group of radical librarians put together a picket outside of the keynote speech area. The protest was met with a mixture of disbelief, nonchalance, and support from librarians going to the speech. The police finally asked us to leave, but not before the crowd was greeted with signs that read "Books Not Bombs," "Dead Iraqis Can't Use Libraries," "Don't Militarize ALA," and "Down with $70,000 'Volunteers.'"

Earlier in 1999, radical librarians put together a small contingent at the Millions 4 Mumia protest in Philadelphia. In recognition of the fact that the state was preparing to execute Mumia Abu-Jamal, an award-winning journalist, one librarian came with a sign that read "The Death Penalty is the Ultimate Censorship."

Radical librarians have attended many of the recent headline-grabbing anti-globalization protests. These protests came to international attention with the big anti–WTO actions in Seattle in 1999, but that was just the tip of the iceberg. These large "convergences" require a large amount of organization, which takes place on the ground and on the Internet. Typically these convergences will have some kind of welcome center or multi-purpose "convergence center." Activists put together informational guides about what to bring to the protests, where to stay, when meetings and events are happening, and where to eat. These protests also require some amount of promotion and information dissemination on the Internet, in which this author has been involved.

The big protests have also created an opportunity to do some interesting library work on the streets. During the "Battle of Seattle" in 1999, anarchist librarian Jessamyn West took on the role of "street librarian" for part of the protests. She roamed the downtown streets carrying a flag that denoted her role as both an information person and as a "safe space" away from the contentious protests. As a "street librarian" and local activist, Jessamyn was able to provide information and give directions in a rather unique situation.

ON THE JOB

To the extent that being a radical librarian is unconventional, it is pretty rare to find a radical librarian in a job setting that is radical. Many radical librarians are employed in conventional library jobs. They may be able to bring their political activism to work in their day-to-day library tasks, but typically their activism will take place outside of the job.

There are a few radical librarians who work in what can be considered radical library jobs. Julie Herrada is curator of the Labadie Collection at the University of

Michigan. The Labadie Collection is a notable collection of materials from radical social change movements in the United States. It has been described as the "largest holding of social protest literature in the world." If this sounds like an interesting archive, Julie's job as curator has netted her a few headlines in national newspapers, such as the time when she negotiated an agreement to add the papers of Theodore "Ted" Kaczynski, the "Unabomber," to the collection. Her job as curator of this collection also takes her to estate sales, rare book stores, and anarchist book fairs in search of rare and offbeat materials. In addition to doing the usual day-to-day tasks of an archivist, Herrada also does educational talks about the collection, to audiences ranging from high school students to people attending anarchist conferences.

Other radical librarians work regular library jobs, such as the reference desk or in the technical services department. Their activism may come into play when they put together special projects, such as a bibliography or a public display on some subject. While libraries may pride themselves on supporting freedom of speech and intellectual freedom, those principles are curtailed when it comes to library workers exercising them. Libraries are like most workplaces, where freedom of speech ends when one walks through the office door. Thus, radical librarians are usually forced to be activists outside of the workplace, but often in conjunction with their job. One place where radical librarians find more breathing room for activism is in professional activities, such as ALA, or state library associations.

ON THE INTERNET

The Internet and the World Wide Web have had a significant effect on library work in the past ten years. The Internet has changed the very nature of many library jobs, but more significantly it has allowed librarians and library workers the freedom to create their own projects online.

It could be argued that this author manages one of the most typical anarchist librarian projects on the Internet. For over seven years, I've maintained and developed Infoshop.org (formerly the Mid-Atlantic Infoshop). The project got its start after I attended a basic HTML class that was presented by an archivist from the University of Virginia. At the time I was working as a systems librarian in the Information Technology Division of the main library at the University of Maryland-College Park. I had been using the web for several years and was really interested in the do-it-yourself (DIY) aspects of HTML and webpages. The university was providing free web space on its servers for students and staff, so I took the lessons I learned from that class and started coding.

The impetus for starting the Mid-Atlantic Infoshop project came from my involvement at that time with the Beehive infoshop, which was located in the Shaw neighborhood of downtown Washington, DC. I conceived of the web project as complementing the work that the infoshop was doing and I hoped that the web pages would generate some publicity for the infoshop. Eventually the infoshop closed, but

I decided to continue the website and, as projects tend to do, the website grew and took on an identity of its own.

Today, Infoshop.org is one of the most popular websites among activists; many list it as a favorite, along with famous sites such as Indymedia and ZNet. The website averages around 3 million hits per month and is visited by people from almost every country. Infoshop now has sections in six languages. Many people consider it to be one of the best sources for information on the anti-globalization and anti-capitalist movements. Judging from a variety of evidence, the authorities also consider the website to be a good source of information.

Infoshop.org has long featured resources that are critical of the concept of intellectual property, which could be called the "divine right of kings" paradigm of the capitalist world. In addition to featuring a large amount of content in the public domain, it's also been aggressive on re-posting content from the copyrighted, commercial domain, in the interest of asserting the right to "fair use" in a world where DMCA is rapidly enclosing intellectual and artistic freedom. I've gotten my share of cease and desist letters from lawyers over the years. The first one came from the lawyers for Barricade Books, who have published the lucrative *Anarchist Cookbook* for several decades. They objected to the use of that book title on a webpage for a new cookbook being written by anarchists. More recently, lawyers from the publisher that publishes those yellow "for Dummies" books sent Infoshop a cease and desist letter in reaction to the *Black Bloc for Dummies* webpage, which includes information, pictures, and a FAQ on the infamous anarchist black blocs.

In many ways, keeping Infoshop up and running requires many library skills in addition to the regular webmaster and web design work. The project is really a big reference tool, but an interactive one that also links to many websites that aren't run by well-organized webmasters (or librarians). There are constant decisions which have to be made about organization of the information on the website, presentation of that information in a variety of helpful ways, development of new "subject" guides, and checking of information accuracy (especially those URLs).

Infoshop also functions as an anarchist and activist reference desk that is open 24 hours a day, 365 days of the year. Since Infoshop is seen as a big resource for activists, many people ask questions via email that can really be considered reference questions. The website is run by a small network of volunteers, which means that the volume of questions that come in can be overwhelming. Most of the questions involve the nature and definition of anarchism. These questions can be referred to the Anarchist FAQ, or various webpages and websites. There are many networking questions, such as: "Do you know of any groups here in Orlando, Florida?" The nature of the web allows many people with radical tendencies who live in isolated areas to seek out like-minded people. Many of the questions come from high school students who have had their rights abridged by teachers and administrators. Infoshop gets plenty of questions from students and researchers. The website also generates many queries from journalists and these requests have to be routed to the relevant people.

DOES TEAR GAS HINDER THE REFERENCE INTERVIEW?

Radical (and anarchist) librarians do a wide variety of interesting work that ties together their experience as library workers with their work as people engaged in social change. Sometimes these different roles come together in an actual job position. Given the long tradition of activism and social responsibility in the library profession, you might think that most librarians would be some kind of activists. I think some of us went into the profession thinking that most librarians were at least fierce opponents of censorship. Alas, the reality of the American library profession in the past decade demonstrated how much the profession has been captured by techno-weenies and corporate fetishists who want us to see every patron as a "customer." At least the ranks of radical librarians have been growing rapidly in recent years. Perhaps this, combined with the harsh realities of globalization in libraries, will turn around a profession that has lost it way and risks becoming irrelevant to the average working person.

We're the radical librarians and we like to shake things up a bit!

Websites:

Infoshop.org. <http://www.infoshop.org/>
Anarchist Librarians. <http://www.infoshop.org/library2/>

Further reading:

"Jessamyn West: Your Basic Anarchist Librarian...No, Really."
<http://www.themargin.org/interviews/011119_J_West.html>

MAIMONIDES IN THE STACKS; OR, DIGITIZE *THIS*!

George Lederer

Over 800 years ago, Rabbi Moses Ibn Maimon, the Sephardic philosopher that has come to be known as Maimonides, carved out this gem, embedded in his long-admired work *The Guide for the Perplexed*: "I do not seek to know the answer, but to more thoroughly understand the question" (trans. M. Friedlander, New York : Dover Pubs., 1956).

Maimonides was not a librarian, at least not by trade. But he did give his students, his readers, a license to use our distinctly human intellects, our unique points of view, in reaching decisions about what is worth knowing, and what is to be believed. And in this process, he reminds us, my sister and brother Wizards, of one of the central roles of librarians in his age, and in ours.

Answering questions is easy. Asking the right questions is much harder.

From my first job as a teenager in the '60s, as a library page, through years in school "media centers" (what was wrong with calling it a library?) and into my current incarnation as a corporate librarian here in the Silicon Forest, I have been aware that my job is to aid people in the use of collections. By knowing what may be available and where to look for it; by making judgments about the needs and interests of the user, the authoritativeness of the possible sources and the relevance, applicability, and relative believability of the spectrum of answers; by predicting, editing, and culling results, I compose questions.

"The volumes of trash poured forth daily, weekly, and monthly, are appalling. Many minds, which, if confined to a few volumes, would become valuable thinkers, are lost in the wilderness of brilliant and fragrant weeds." This picturesque description of the vast and uncharted Universe of Information is even more profound when one considers its source. It's from an 1871 *Study of Government*, by U.S. Representative (Kentucky) George H. Yeaman (cited by Klaus Mussman in *Technological Innovations in Libraries*, Greenwood Press, 1993).

Of course, the situation today is much worse, and computers have not helped. It is estimated that over a trillion bytes (10^9 KB) of data (mind you, that's not even information, really, much less knowledge, or — dare we say it?— wisdom) are added to the World Wide Web daily. The sheer tonnage overwhelms developments in "intelligent" processing. The Internet is like the ocean, I used to tell my students. In a cubic mile of seawater, several ounces of gold are dissolved. Do you have the means to refine it? It's a useful metaphor.

So, when gnarly web-surfers ask disdainfully: "What do we need a librarian for? It's all on the Internet," I smile ruefully. First, even if it were, retrieval is not automatic. There's never a guarantee you'll find what you are looking for, especially if you have no skill with Boolean logic operators, search syntax, and specialized vocabulary. Do you recognize, for example, that words have completely different meanings in different contexts, different disciplines? Acronyms and abbreviations are particularly nasty this way. Is ATM an automated teller machine, or is it asynchronous transfer mode? And in the information age, spelling counts, now more than ever. A sonnet is a poetic form, and no, it's not always 14 lines, but SONET is a synchronous optical network.

Suzanne Pilsk and her colleagues, in their article "Organizing Corporate Knowledge: The Ever-Changing Role of Cataloging and Classification," in the April 2002 issue of *Information Outlook*, gently chide: "Information that seekers seem to think they find serendipitously actually has an organized, purposeful structure created by professionals who use a variety of standards, systems, and rules meant to bring order out of chaos." Good plan. It's true that recent advancements in knowledge engineering, such as the semantic Web, have meant that some Internet-based documents carry more in the way of what we have come to call metadata. Of course, this is what librarians have always done. Metadata = bibliographic records. Knowledge Management = cataloging.

But we're way behind the curve here. The tsunami is overwhelming the best efforts of new-age digital knowledge brokers. Given the essentially democratic and equalizing nature of Internet publishing and dissemination, the idea of universal standards of metatagging is laughable. And who would enforce them, or how? Results of a search on Google are not transparent. They do not carry clear identification. Their contents are not self-evident. What's more, neither is the author, or even the publisher. No, a URL does not constitute a citation. The Internet is not a source, any more than the library is. It is a tool, and one that takes experience and skill to operate successfully.

And you don't have to hang around any kind of library very long to know that not everything is free on the Internet. Sorry. Vast resources of professional literature are reserved to proprietary, fee-based databases, and always have been, long before there were computers or CD-ROMs. And since the dot-com bubble has burst, or at least deflated somewhat, formerly free archives of popular newspapers and journals are now available only to paying customers—which, more often than not, include libraries: private, academic, or public. Need to see an article from last year's *Wall Street Journal*? You'll need a subscription. Your public library probably has one. Need to read a research paper on developments in microlithography, published in 1992? You'll need a subscription to the *IEEExplore*. Better head to your corporate or university library. Want some help deciding which database to search in, or how? You'll probably have to ask a librarian.

Am I preaching to the choir here?

Of course, not everything is digitized, nor can it be, nor should it be. In his 370-page tirade against the "assault on paper," *Double Fold* (New York : Random House, 2001), Nicholson Baker rails against the practice of destroying priceless antique books, newspaper, pamphlets and other documents, in the name of space-saving and "digital preservation," perpetrated by some of the nation's most prestigious, and presumably wise, librarians. What can compare, for example, with the joy of looking at your grandparents' wedding announcement on the original newsprint, redolent with the dust of decades? A microfiche? Or what digital image measures up to the thick rough-edged pages and full-color lithographs by N.C. Wyeth in an original edition of Howard Pyle's *The Merry Adventures of Robin Hood*?

No, the digital revolution is not all it's cracked up to be. Computer-based technological improvements in productivity, in libraries and elsewhere, are quantitative, not qualitative. "The potential of technology is always exaggerated, and its practical limitations ignored" (Cate T. Corcoran, "Are We Ready for the Library of the Future?," *Salon*, 12/02/97).

Here's the thing: Human experience, knowledge, the diverse and broad-based collected contents of all the world's libraries ... it isn't digital. It can't be defined as a series of discrete steps. It isn't either this or that. It's about context, and connection, and nuance, and individuality. Our uniquely-human higher-order thinking abilities to apply, to analyze, to synthesize, and to evaluate (thank you, Benjamin Bloom) are essentially messy and imprecise. They slide around. They are not digital. They're, well ... analog.

So we do our best to make collections that are more than mere heaps of documents. In building collections, we are conscious of both intellectual freedom and intellectual property. We endeavor to be tolerant and non-judgmental of the points of view of both sources and users, even as we dig for citations. And we apply whatever skills we can to help users navigate the still largely uncharted waters, with ease and with equity.

To some, all this may make me, and some of my sister and brother Wizards, "revolting" librarians, yes. But is it revolutionary? Hardly. In fact, I proudly wear the mantle of *reactionary* librarian. I favor cardigan sweaters. My half-glasses dangle on a cord around my neck. And I always keep a pencil behind my ear.

Shhhh!

DIARY OF A REVOLTING LIBRARIAN

Patricia A. Threatt

APRIL 2, 2001

I work at home. By "home," I mean my childhood home. I moved back in with my mother, "Mawmaw," and my dog, Hula Hoop. I know what people will say — another stereotypical nerdy librarian with no social life. Not true. I have a great social life. I'm a party animal. I lived in Austin when it was cool, before the techies moved in. I'm hip, damn it.

I left academia (well, the physical campus anyway) to move back home, into my old room, in my old neighborhood, with my old mother. I'm not sure I'm doing the right thing. I couldn't stand my job anymore. The world outside of academia doesn't understand how insane the world inside academia is. One of my favorite newspaper columnists, Dale Dauten, says that when an organization manages by committee, the outcome of the committee can only be the product of the least competent person in the group. He says, "You take a dozen lively, intelligent people, put them in a conference room, then leap out of the way of falling IQs.... What begins as a Meeting of the Minds soon becomes a Meeting of the Thoughtful Expressions." This makes me insane. The whole problem is that librarians shouldn't be administrators. We're no good at it. We're good at organizing, managing, and delivering information, but when it comes to running a library and its staff, we have no clue. We should be left alone to do our jobs. But the only way to move up in the library world is to become an administrator. Other professions have this problem, too. I have this fantasy of an academic library run by a corporation, like the campus food service. Oh, we'd still have bibliographic procedures committees and weekly public service meetings, but the final decisions would be made by some MBA type who would manage the funds and answer to the faculty and students. The librarians would sit in their offices working with the materials, doing research, and answering reference questions while the suits took care of the building, the budget, and the personnel. I'm sure this will never happen because librarians would never let a non-librarian tell them how to run a library, but it's a good fantasy.

So, I left a tenure-track position in the Special Collections Library at the state university for a short-term contract job. I love libraries too much to work in one. Everyone thinks I'm insane.

APRIL 16, 2001

Out of bed and into a pair of shorts and a t-shirt. Mawmaw and Hula Hoop wait patiently for me, reading the paper and chewing rawhide, respectively. We've established a morning routine. Wake up, drink coffee, scan the newspaper, and take a walk. We have to walk in the mornings because we live in South Louisiana. By 10:00 A.M., the heat and humidity will be stifling. You can't breathe, let alone walk.

Mawmaw carries a wad of plastic bags from the grocery store. They're not for what you're thinking. Well, one is, but the rest are for picking up litter. Mawmaw hates to see litter on the streets, which is ironic because the house being a mess doesn't seem to bother her. Mawmaw has a lot of odd quirks. She talks about death, misery, and suffering with ease, weaving it into her daily conversation. I've gotten used to this, but others seem surprised by it. I gently steer her out of the street as a car approaches. She reminds me, "If it comes down to me or Hula, save the dog."

We make it home, all three of us alive, which I'm sure surprises Mawmaw everyday. Hula heads for her pool while Mawmaw throws away the garbage she's collected and putters around the back yard. I settle in to work on the sun porch that I've converted to an office. Check the email, open up the online databases that I'll need, and get started. I'm cataloging a collection of photographs of the American Missionary Association. The photographers were regional superintendents of the AMA during the 1910s through the 1940s who carried their cameras with them as they made the rounds of their districts, visiting the young missionaries who worked to bring religion to the most remote regions of the country. The photographs document poor black communities in the South, urban immigrant ghettos in the East, isolated frontiersmen in the West, snowed-in Finns in the North, mountain people in the Appalachian Mountains, and the squalid border towns of the Southwest. The text accompanying the photographs documents the social attitudes of the day. Catholics must be converted, African-Americans must be educated, and Native Americans must relinquish their "savage" culture. Naturally, these attitudes appall the historians who use the collection. They want me to delete words like "Negro" and "squaw" and to re-phrase text written on the verso of the photographs, like "at last persuaded to give up the old ways, now a splendid worker." I leave it all in, since that's the whole point of documenting history. You have to take the good with the bad. The next generation needs a slap in the face to see how ridiculous racism is, then and now. I fancy myself a latter-day Archie Bunker.

MAY 23, 2001

I'm working. A friend of mine gave me a baseball cap to wear while I work. It's light blue with a pink crown embroidered on the front and "The Princess is working" on the back. This is my signal to Mawmaw that I'm working. Mawmaw has a very strong work ethic. She can't believe that I work at home, doing something I enjoy, and get paid for it. She has no idea what I do, but she tells people, "Pati Ann just *loves* to punch buttons." She means it both literally and figuratively, and enjoys the double entendre. So, when I have my hat on, she treats me like a real princess. With the hat, I've got unimaginable power — not spoken to unless I speak first, meals prepared to my specifications and brought to my desk, personal errands tended to, etc. Without the hat, we're back to our usual mother-daughter relationship — disapproval of my wardrobe, negotiations over the TV remote, and reminders to take care of the dog.

JUNE 12, 2001

I'm on my way to Baton Rouge today. I've got a meeting with the director of the Digital Library and the director of the project I'm working on. The project is progressing at a satisfactory rate. More smoothly than some projects, but not without setbacks. Getting this job was a struggle. The director of the project didn't want me to work at home, even though I have a good reputation in the library world and the previous cataloger worked remotely, too, but in an office. This is new territory for librarianship. For some librarians, libraries without walls is a strange and scary concept. These librarians got into the field because they love books. The idea that information and knowledge can be gained by any other means is as ludicrous as blood from a turnip.

Of course, some librarians envisioned my life a long time ago. Not just the techie librarians, but others, too, before computers were around. I like to think of librarians as either "old school" or "new school." It doesn't have anything to do with age or area of expertise, but with outlook, spirit, and philosophy. "Old school" librarians fret about what the committee will think. "New school" librarians do what's right and deal with the committee later.

After the meeting, I check into a hotel. This is the real reason for the trip. I lived alone for ten years and I really miss it. I miss being able to walk around naked. I miss the total control over my environment. I turn on the TV and shed my clothes.

AUGUST 3, 2001

Back at home to work. I'm plowing through these records with ease. 75% of them don't require any additional research. Portrait, Group; Children; African Americans. Not much more that the *LC Thesaurus for Graphic Materials* or the *Library of Congress Subject Headings* can say about it. I can't, of course, put in my own impressions of the photograph. That little boy has a runny nose. Why is that one wearing a sweater in the middle of summer in Alabama? Is she going through that childhood stage of wanting to dress herself, regardless of propriety? Is that all she has to wear? The photographer is too far away. Too much of the wall behind the children shows.

Sometimes I have to put a little more effort into the record. I'm more likely to tap into my network of knowledgeable friends and family than to consult the usual library resources. Using a physical library would mean changing my clothes, driving, and probably doing a few errands along the way. It's not laziness, though, that leads me to use people before books. It's just more fun.

I open up an online chat with my buddy at the State Library. "Look at this photo," I type, and insert the address. "Is that a donkey or a mule? I never can remember the difference." A coworker happens to be passing by my friend's desk and asks what she's doing. The coworker, who grew up on a farm, verifies that it's a donkey. So much more fun than consulting the encyclopedia.

Another photograph seems to be just some trees in a forest. I copy it into Adobe Photoshop and zoom in. There's a sign nailed to one of the trees. I call Mawmaw in to take a look. "Oh my god," she says, "That's a swastika!" and launches into stories from World War II.

Sometimes, though, I do have to make the trip to the library. I don't have a set of red books or the $800 CD-ROM. I usually save up all my questions, so I don't have to make daily treks to the library. Santa Claus? Yep, that's a good one. Crossed eyes? Use Convergent strabismus.

SEPTEMBER 10, 2001

I've discovered a better, more efficient way to work. From now on, I'm going to work assembly-line style. Enter all the geographic information first for all 100 records I'm going to complete this week. Then the description. Then subject headings. This way is much more efficient and it's easier to concentrate on one task. Plus, I don't have to keep 5 different browser windows open at one time.

OCTOBER 22, 2001

Mawmaw and Hula Hoop are whispering to each other. I hear snippets of the conversation. "Don't do that, Pati Ann will get mad." "Let's go see if we have any biscuits in the kitchen." These are my new co-workers.

I don't have a track record with getting along with co-workers. One time, I was managing several paraprofessionals. One was a young woman with a small toddler at home. One day, she brought her toddler in to work. She only works part-time, so she didn't think it would be a big deal. I discovered the toddler when I went to talk to her about some minor matter. A toddler. In the archives. Sharp instruments. Valuable documents. Not to mention the fact that she couldn't listen to me because she was keeping an eye on the toddler.

To make a long story short, things didn't turn out well. I made a new rule that children wouldn't be allowed in the office. Oh, the oppression! Child-Hater, Mother-Disrespecter, Single Woman! I admit, I could have handled it better. Like I said, librarians shouldn't be administrators, and I include myself in that list. Let me manage information and its dissemination. Someone else can be the Child-Hater.

November 22, 2001

Thanksgiving Day. No work today. I don't even check my email. Mawmaw, my sister, and I have our celebration at a restaurant. We're saving the big party for Christmas when the crowd arrives— siblings, in-laws, nieces, and nephews.

December 25, 2001

Christmas. The whole family is here, invading my space. The brothers-in-law are wallpapering the bathroom. The grandchildren are lined up for the computer. The younger ones want to play games, the older ones want to use email and chat with friends. I don't mind, really, it's just kind of strange to see someone else sitting at my desk. Worlds colliding.

January 7, 2002

The house (and therefore, my office) are back to normal. My contract for the AMA collection is over, so I'm feeling a bit lost. I've got plenty to do— work on this manuscript, overhaul the Digital Library's style manual, work on the house. For now, I'd rather just play computer games and take naps.

February 4, 2002

The lack of work is really starting to bother me. I'm lonely without it. I'm even starting to miss my former coworkers.

The thing that pushed me over the edge, that forced me to run screaming from the campus, was a library-wide fight over the staff email list. It still makes me angry to think about it.

At the library, there was an ultra-conservative staff member who habitually sent messages to the list spouting his philosophy and politics. Anti-gun control, homophobia, civilian militia rights, the whole stereotype. He sent these messages to the list for the library staff, so everyone received them. Everyone pretty much ignored them and the administration said there was nothing they could do. Free speech is sacred in the library.

One day, the Gun Toter sent a really hurtful, inflammatory, ugly message to the list. It really crossed the line. Since I was on the library's Automation and Systems Committee, I brought up the issue at the next meeting and said that I thought we should re-evaluate the list policy and start enforcing the part about "work-related messages only."

Well, that was a mistake. All hell broke loose. This time I was called a witch-hunter and a trampler of free speech. What are you doing calling yourself a librarian? I tried to explain that the staff member had every right to spread his message anywhere and any way he liked, except for the mandatory staff list of a public institution. No luck.

My boss called me in to her office and wanted to know what my problem was. She was particularly upset because I had said, "If I had known that I was going to have to listen to my coworkers' political views, I never would have come to work here." I did say that, of course, in a moment of frustration and happily admitted it. My boss said, "You can't say things like that!"

And that's when I knew. The absurdity of academia hit me like a ton of bricks. Homophobic gun nuts could say anything they wanted, but I couldn't. I was politically incorrect. Maybe I don't miss my coworkers all that much.

MARCH 29, 2002

The director of the Digital Library calls to discuss my next contract. This project involves cataloging images of materials from four different institutions in Louisiana. The main focus of the project is to train K-12 teachers to use primary resources in the classroom. I sign on for another three-year hitch working at home.

I tell Mawmaw all about the project. She has a million questions, still trying to understand what I do. I talk excitedly about how great the money is and how great the project will be.

Later, as I'm working at my desk, she enters my "space." She's tentative and her voice quavers a bit. She asks, "Does this mean you're moving out?" "Of course not," I tell her. Why would I go back to the library?

LIBRARY SERVICE TO THE INSANE

Cathy Camper

The Lost Language of Libraries

Pam North

There once was a word we all knew
to request keeping a book past the date due.
Now they ask to "extend"
or to "re-check-out again…"
What the hell happened to "renew?"

What *did* happen to renew? I knew it, my friends knew it, the neighbors knew it, even my parents knew what it meant!

Is it because our public schools can no longer afford to hire librarians, er, media specialists (whatever) and their "libraries" tend to be paltry collections of leftovers from a bygone era?

Is it due to parents too busy running their kids and their neighbor's kids from soccer to tae kwon do to swimming to horse camp to etc. to make time for visits to the local public library?

Could it be that these same parents were perhaps denied any library education, so they are ill-equipped to impart lessons in library use to their offspring?

I don't know the answer. All I know is the general public has lost the language of libraries and I have little hope that it can be recovered. After seven years at the front-lines of library customer service I have been exposed to some of the most exasperating misinterpretations and misuses known to libraryland. A few real-life examples to illustrate my frustration with this language gap are as follows:

Patrons call or come to the counter to renew materials and they just can't seem to come up with the word "renew." They ask to "extend," "re-check out," "re-check out again" (does that mean they already re-checked out once?) and my military favorite, "re-up." Really.

With the popularity of dot-com madness, I have had more than one patron ask how do I find a book with that "dot number thing," meaning, of course, the Dewey Decimal System.

The oft-confusing biography/bibliography quandary can be amusing. "I need a bibliography on Derek Jeter," the young boy asks. I question him as to how many books or articles he is looking for in the bibliography. "Just one, a short one," is the popular response.

When I have inquired if the patron has a citation for the book they are seeking I have actually been asked, "You mean like a traffic ticket?" Perhaps it is because municipal court meets in the building next door. I really don't know.

There are times that we actually screw up and refer to something in in-house library lingo. You should have seen the face on the patron that had asked for "Cook's

Illustrated" when I told him that the serials were in the boxes to his right. Honestly, I think he believed he might find some Cap'n Crunch on the shelf.

A recent favorite occurred while a young man was searching the OPAC. "When a book is L-O-S-T, what does that mean?" he queried. It was all I could do to keep myself from responding, "It means where you'll be in life if you don't learn to spell."

Sometimes it is not the wording but the process that is troubling for John Q. Public to grasp. At my library, in order for a patron to get a library card, we need to see a piece of photo ID and something showing a current address. Kids without said documentation need to be with a parent or guardian. The classic young person's response to "I'm sorry, you'll have to come back with..." is, "I don't have photo ID, but I can tell you my name and address." Well, you can probably tell me your grandmother's name and address, too, but that doesn't make you her, does it?! I want to give them a library card, really I do. Maybe they would check out a book on common sense.

In our consumer-crazed society "borrowing" a book seems incomprehensible. Patrons cannot believe that we actually "loan" materials freely, in good faith that they will be returned on the due date. They are constantly asking to "rent" or "buy."

And about that "due date." Yes, that is the date the material that is checked out is expected to be back in the library. It is not a mere suggestion as to general time period. Oh, and the fine that accrues when the material is late! If they had simply called to "renew."

DAMAGE NOTED: JOURNAL OF
A PUBLIC LIBRARIAN

Kate Pohjola

FRIDAY, FEBRUARY 9, 2001

I love my job, but it's so frustrating sometimes. My library recently underwent a minor facelift. We went from having five public access Internet computers to twenty-one. We quadrupled our public computing power, and we have definitely quadrupled in the numbers of people we have coming in to use the computers. However, we did not quadruple our staffing. It's just the two of us dealing with all of these people, and it seems that all I do is holler at kids all day. They really push and push and push and push, and by the end of the day, I'm usually ready to pull my hair out and/or kill someone.

I don't know if it's just me, or if it's kids these days, (and saying that makes me sound really freaking old and mean, which I'm **not**!) or maybe it's just the neighborhood that my library is in, but everyone is really fucking obnoxious. Nobody wants to wait for their turn, they all demand immediate service, and they're rude. I can be right in the middle of helping a patron and someone will interrupt to ask for something. More than once I've had to say something like, "Please wait your turn. You wouldn't like it if I stopped helping you because someone interrupted us."

Sometimes I worry that I'm being too harsh or too hard on the kids. I don't think that's the case, though. They're manipulative and obnoxious, and they seem to have learned it from their parents. Most, but not all, of the adults are exactly the same way!

I am frustrated. I adore my job and I can't imagine doing anything else, but I really despise the kids. If I acted like these kids, my mom would have smacked me silly. It really makes me wonder where the parents are.

MONDAY, FEBRUARY 12, 2001

I still hate kids. A tiny minority is so very respectful. It's amazing. I'd kill to have hundreds of kids who come in, actually say hello, and aren't rude to me and everyone else in the building.

The other kids are monsters, and they know it; they revel in their monstrosity. They're mouthy, they're disrespectful, and they can be just plain evil to each other. In between tattling on their friends, and having no qualms about booting someone when their time is up on a computer, they'll harass the good kids. And in their spare time, they steal books and write graffiti in the public rest room.

I remember when my mom was a Brownie leader and a couple of her girls were acting up. She made them call home and tell their parents why they were in trouble. I thought this was clever, and tried it with some kids here, but the parents just don't care.

The kids are, with a few noted exceptions, good kids. It's the parents, or lack of parenting, that really scare me. Parents drop their kids off at the library and expect us to baby-sit. These kids totally rule their parents, and the kids think they can rule me, too. I refuse to bow to their evilness. I won't hesitate to call the police when they're terrorizing my building. They get booted for picking on other kids, and any time I hear swearing or words like "nigger" or "fag," they're out. Sometimes I feel like a surrogate parent. Sometimes I'm a baby-sitter. There are those rare moments when I feel like I've made a friend. Regardless, I'm just a librarian, and I can only do so much. I am tired.

WEDNESDAY, FEBRUARY 14, 2001

As I was tearing around the building tonight, a patron told me she thinks I'm making a difference in some kids' lives. She said that my "laying down the law" with the kids is a good thing and that they'll appreciate it later in life. I have a hard time believing her. I'm tired of being a parent. I'm tired of being a baby-sitter. I'm tired of being a disciplinarian. I don't get to be a librarian anymore because I'm too busy chasing kids around my building.

MONDAY, APRIL 16, 2001

The library has turned into porn central. I don't dislike porn. Heck, some of it is downright appealing, but I still don't think it's appropriate for kids to be looking at it here in the library. I just booted a couple of 12–14 year old boys; I looked in the lab and a kid's screen had a very detailed photo of penetration. The kid was grabbing his friend to come check it out when I walked in. I asked him to leave, and he had *no* idea why! I know half the fun is sneaking and looking at things that you're not supposed to see — I did it all the time as a kid. But right out in public? Yikes.

FRIDAY, MAY 4, 2001

One of my regular teenage patrons came in last night, and after he used a computer for a little while, he stood by the desk and chatted with me. In the span of maybe fifteen minutes, he poured out his heart to me. I never, ever, want to be a teenager again. The kid told me that he was out on a pass from a mental hospital, and when I asked him why he'd been in, he showed me three large gashes on his arm. After he was taken to the hospital, the kid scratched two more welts into his arm. I just sat there and let the kid talk. I asked him why he cut himself, and he answered with, "I was depressed and so full of anger...." We talked more, and it was weird. All of a sudden I realized that I've made some kind of transformation from "mean library lady" to friend and confidante. It made me smile a bit inside. I'm worried about this kid though — he's sixteen and recently came out. He gets beaten up and harassed all the time, and he dropped out of school. I've been pushing him to go back, or to at least complete his diploma at night school. He's certainly not dumb by any stretch; he just really needs some help. I think he needs adults he can trust, too.

One of my other regulars, a fourteen-year-old girl, has all of a sudden become my buddy. She mentioned that she uses AOL's Instant Messenger, so I put her on my notify list and messaged her when I saw her online from the library. Now we chitchat all the time. It's mostly silly, goofy stuff, but I really feel like I've made another connection. She's another kid that definitely could use some positive adult role models in her life. It's weird to think this, but for better or worse, I'm a grown-up. I used to say that physically I was almost thirty, but mentally I was seventeen. I don't think that's the case anymore.

SUNDAY, MAY 20, 2001

It's interesting to me how many parents bring their children to the library and then let the kids run amok. The same dad comes here weekly always has his two little girls with him. He logs on and hits the Yahoo! personal ads, while his little girls run around attempting to amuse themselves. They get bored after a while and start running back and forth; the whole time they're here, Dad pays them little attention. I don't understand that mentality. It doesn't make sense to drag your kids to the library so they can sit and be bored. Dad should at least make a stop in the children's section to get books for the girls before he logs on to get his booty fix.

LATER

The dad I was whining about in my previous entry is still not paying attention to his kids, and now one of them is really bored and keeps applying and removing the Velcro strip on her shoes.

riiiiiip. riiiiiip. riiiiiip. riiiiiip. riiiiiip. riiiiiip. riiiiiip.
riiiiiip. riiiiiip. riiiiiip. riiiiiip. riiiiiip. riiiiiip.
riiiiiip. riiiiiip. riiiiiip. riiiiiip. riiiiiip. riiiiiip.
riiiiiip. riiiiiip. riiiiiip. riiiiiip. riiiiiip.

MONDAY, JULY 9, 2001

Today was a strange and frustrating day. We were totally swamped when we unlocked the doors. Kids were swarming in from everywhere, and everyone wanted a specific computer in the lab. No other machine would do. Sometimes I hate computers. Sometimes I hate kids. Sometimes I hate the Gates Foundation for giving us these computers, which bring in the kids. I just wish I had enough staff to really deal properly with all of the new patrons that come tromping through here on a regular basis.

THURSDAY, JULY 12, 2001

A patron returned three books this afternoon that were very stinky and covered in a gel-like substance. I knew the smell, but couldn't place it. I approached the patron and he explained that he was opening some canned cat food, stumbled and ended up dumping the freshly opened can into the bag with his library books.

"Really, it's cat food," he said, and held out his hand for me to smell. He tried again, even after I recoiled. "Sir, the books are unusable and you are responsible for replacing them." His reply: "Just bill me."

TUESDAY, JULY 24, 2001

Every kid that came in today was interested in the summer reading club. I've been after them all summer to sign up, and now that they've got a week left, they're finally getting involved. Better late than never, I suppose.

But, of course, it's not that simple. The kids are cheating. I never thought it was possible to cheat in Summer Reading Club. They're reading beginning readers' books instead of books at their reading levels, or, in a couple of cases, they're pulling books from shelves, writing down the titles, and turning in their book logs without ever having read a book. Amazing. I'm not sure if I should give them style points for creativity, or if I should be disgusted at their shrewdness.

TUESDAY, SEPTEMBER 18, 2001

Just when I think I really hate my job, I had a wonderful group of second graders come in for a class tour. I am on such a high! There were twenty of them, and they were so excited to be here. They asked all kinds of good questions, not a single one asked me about my pink hair, and nobody wanted to use a stupid computer!

The kids were energetic and enthusiastic and totally the breath of fresh air that I needed. Yeah, most people still suck, but the kids were fun. Days like today are totally career-affirming. Days like the rest just confirm that some people are total hose beasts.

WEDNESDAY, OCTOBER 17, 2001

I just went into the children's room and walked in on one kid whipping another kid with the stuffed snake.

WEDNESDAY, OCTOBER 31, 2001

I'm no longer looking for a job. I don't hate my job, I just hate the politics and policies that surround it. Politics surround anything and everything, and running from one place to another isn't going to solve anything. Despite the upheaval, I have it really damn good at work. I dress very casually, I can dye my hair any and all kinds of colors, I'm visibly pierced, and nobody seems to mind or care. I'm paid well, I have excellent health care benefits, and I'm guaranteed a 3% raise for the next three years since we settled on a contract extension last week.

Am I settling? I don't think so. I'm not always happy at work, this much I know. Right now, my staffing is the best it's been since I became a supervisor almost three years ago. I could still use another body to help with the lab, but we're mostly surviving. We've found a happy level of cooperation that works for us, plus we genuinely like each other, which I think helps immensely. The patrons and the kids drive us batty, but I think we've even made some strides with the kids. I'm actively striving to get more teen/young adult materials on the shelves, as well as other stuff that kids want to see and read.

FRIDAY, NOVEMBER 2, 2001

I agreed to arrange for the staff holiday party again. If I could get away with it, I'd have the party at Hooters.

WEDNESDAY, NOVEMBER 28, 2001

I did the inconceivable: I kicked everyone out of the lab and closed it. The lab will remain closed through the weekend, and most likely through next Tuesday. Over the past two weeks, a whole slew of the mouse balls have been stolen. It's hard not to laugh when the kids complain that they don't have any balls, either!

THURSDAY, DECEMBER 6, 2001

Today I caught a patron drinking a carton of chocolate milk while I was browsing the 700s. I walked up to her and said, "I'm sorry, but there's no food or drink allowed in the library. You'll need to get rid of that or go outside." She scowled at me, took her carton of milk, and left.

WEDNESDAY, JANUARY 23, 2002

For the love of god, please don't keep re-asking your question. It's not like I'll suddenly change my answer and tell you what you want to hear. That's certainly not going to inspire me to assist you any further than I absolutely have to.

Sample conversations I've had about 1,093,359 times today:

—"No, I don't know when the Michigan tax forms will be coming in."

—"Yes, we can download them for you."

—"It's __ cents per page for prints."

—"Yes, I understand the booklet is free."

—"No, we don't have any to give away yet."

—"They were mailed from Lansing last week."

—"Unfortunately, we won't know when they're supposed to arrive until they show up."

—"No, we don't have the list of places offering tax assistance for seniors."

—"No, I don't know when we'll get the list. It usually comes out in mid–February."

—"Sure, you can call back."

Tell me again why I'm a public servant. I keep forgetting.

MONDAY, FEBRUARY 4, 2002

Within the last half hour, I've had:

- A kid threaten to pee on my car —"Bitch, I'll piss on your car."
- Two girls call me a "stupid fat bitch" because I asked them to leave.
- Kids threw a bunch of eggs at the front windows.
- Teens fighting in the parking lot, too.

This doesn't even include the regular grief and back talk we get from regular kids on a regular basis. I'm tired and I'm frustrated. I'm still waiting for the police to arrive.

LATER

A couple of regulars stopped in and were waiting to use a computer when the egg throwing ensued. They went outside and rounded up the culprits for the police. One kid mouthed off to me, and one of regulars said, "Don't talk like that to Kate."

Color me shocked, and impressed. Granted, I think the regular and his friend are small-time drug dealers, but I can't prove it. And right now they're on my side and that makes me happy. He even offered to "take care of things," but I declined. I warned them to not start anything since I knew the police were on their way; I figured that was the least I could do.

This incident got two police cars to show up, and a third arrived while I was outside talking to the officers. The third car was the one that responded a couple hours ago when I called about the fight in the parking lot. They took names and numbers and asked me to identify the kids, which I did with glee. Okay, not quite glee, but I did point out which kids were mouthy to me, and the one who threatened to piss on my car.

The kids claim that some younger kids threw the eggs at the windows. Right. We used that exact same excuse as kids when the police showed up after we did something stupid. I know they're full of crap. The cops gave the piss-threatener and his buddy the duty of cleaning the front windows. I supplied a bucket of hot, soapy water, rags, rubber gloves, a broom, and a dustpan. I swept while they scrubbed the windows. It's very chilly out there, which was causing the egg whites to start to freeze. The boys did an okay job. The windows will probably need a good power wash in the spring. As they were leaving I said something like, "Thanks, guys. Hopefully we'll meet again under much better circumstances." One actually said, "I hope so, too."

TUESDAY, FEBRUARY 12, 2002

As I was leaving to pick up lunch today, one of the kids I booted out yesterday for running in the stacks was walking towards the door. I said hello, and he said, "I'm sorry about yesterday." I almost peed myself right there. Of course, later on in the evening, he was audibly farting whilst sitting on a wooden chair. Gotta love it.

WEDNESDAY, MARCH 6, 2002

I just caught two boys photocopying their hands whilst flipping the bird. I kept one for myself.

THURSDAY, MARCH 14, 2002

I am so evil! A salesperson just called here and asked for "Maybelle Burnette." I said "Maybelle is no longer with us. She's dead." The person on the phone became apologetic and started to try and hang up. I said, "May I help you with something?" She said that she was calling about a subscription for Maybelle. I interjected with, "Do you know where you're calling? This is a library named for Maybelle Burnette." The woman got upset and said, "I'll call back later when I can speak to a supervisor." I had the extreme pleasure of saying, "I am the supervisor." Then I asked her to take us off her call list and informed her that we do all of our subscriptions through a service. She got even huffier and hung up. Maybelle died in 1971. She ain't coming to the phone. Ever.

HIGH CALLING/LOW SALARY

Jenna Freedman

I am currently working as a librarian, and loving it, but only because the dot-com I worked at the job before this one went bankrupt. When I finished library school (December '99) at the University of South Florida in Tampa, I moved back to New York City and secured a job at one of the three public library systems for just over $32K/year.[1] I knew this wouldn't be enough of a salary to support even my austere lifestyle,[2] but I felt that my options were limited — the limitations being my lack of the additional academic credentials required by college and university libraries in New York, the fact that I didn't have any post–MLS experience, and my need to return to Rudy Giuliani's non-library-friendly New York City to be near my friends and family.

About a week before I was to begin my career in YA librarianship, a friend convinced me to interview at Pseudo Programs, an Internet television network. They were considering creating the position of production manager for me, based on my prior theater production management experience. (Neither my BA in theater nor my MLS were important.) The interview went well, and I was attracted by the vibrancy at Pseudo, the $42 grand they offered, and the 20-minute walk that would be my commute (instead of the hour-long multiple subway ride to the library job, the fare for which, incidentally, would raise my expenses by $1,200/year). This was a community I felt I could be a part of, and I did not have any such feeling about the library. For the most part, library school had not gotten me really excited about librarianship — especially public.

One of the biggest things standing in the way of my accepting the Pseudo job was that by doing so I would not be able to make good on my commitment to edit *the U*N*A*B*A*S*H*E*D Librarian, the "How I Run My Library Good Letter."* The publisher and editor-in-chief, who also happens to be my father, was extremely disappointed. He finally understood my choice only when I admitted that a large part of my decision in favor of a dot-com start-up was based on my desire to make enough money to live on for once in my life. Despite having had an 80% tuition scholarship and having worked as a graduate assistant, I also owed $8.5K in student loans. I figured I could get a library job once I paid off my library school debt.

In taking the Pseudo job I did make a dent in my IOU to Sallie Mae, thanks to the decent pay and then two substantial raises, but in April '00 tech stocks crashed, and by September I was applying for unemployment. I found myself in the same miserable position I'd been in eight months before. I couldn't afford to work in a public library in town, and I didn't have the proper credentials for academic library job. The library headhunter/temp agent with whom I interviewed didn't offer me much hope in special librarianship either. I couldn't sell out, even if I wanted to!

I applied for every academic library listed on the ACRL-NY jobsite, and was only asked to interview at one — Iona College in New Rochelle, which turns out to be an hour and forty-five minute commute from my apartment. I keep hearing and reading about a shortage of librarians, but my experience has revealed a shortage of jobs, at least where I live, due to hiring freezes and the restrictive hiring policies at many academic institutions. I consider myself lucky to have been hired at Iona, and I love working there, but the salary stinks almost as much as the commute. (Fortunately I spend so much time working and getting there that I don't have time to spend money on extravagances, other than utilities and train fare.)

As I look for work closer to home (I know I'm stubborn, but moving to Westchester County is not a possibility for me), I'm still struggling with the reality that I need to get further education in order to be eligible for work at city and state universities, and also at many of the private institutions. I don't know what getting another degree will do for me as a librarian, other than stress me out and draw focus from my work. I am already a good librarian, and I think that should be credential enough.

Many people in the progressive library community don't see salary and status as revolting librarian causes, but in order to attract and retain worthy practitioners, we need to make life more tenable for those of us called to this service. As NYPL librarian Zahra M. Baird said in a New York Times article, "I didn't choose this career to become rich, but I didn't take a vow of poverty, either."[3] We simply can't help others if we are struggling ourselves. I also realize that there are a lot of people much worse off than I am. The salaries offered for librarians at the New York public library systems are appalling, and it's not even the worst in the country. Furthermore, library support staffers are even more screwed.[4] How is that not revolting?

Notes

1. For those readers who don't live in New York, San Francisco, or Tokyo, understand that $32K is not a living wage for an adult. The rent on my 2-room studio is just over $1K, and I pay

nearly 1/3 of my salary in federal, state, and city taxes. My bi-weekly take home is about $20 short of my rent.

2. I mean it—I bring my lunch to work everyday, I rarely eat out or take taxis. I don't buy CDs or even books. I rarely buy clothes or shoes, and I don't have any luxuries like a cell phone, cable television, or air conditioning.

3. Greenhouse, Steven. "Forlorn and Forgotten in the Stacks; Low Pay Is Driving Many Librarians Out of New York City." *New York Times*, 14 March 2000, late ed., B1. Accessed from *Lexis-Nexis Academic Universe.*

4. I know my complaints are somewhat bourgeois. I don't wish to imply that I am experiencing any of the very real poverty from which so many people, in New York City and around the world, including library support staff, suffer.

"Being a Cataloger Is Better Than Gutting Fish for a Living Because…"

Catherine Clements

Lately, I seem to be having a personality crisis. Maybe it's because I'm creeping up on thirty. Maybe I have a mild case of schizophrenia. Maybe it's my job.

Occasionally, I am pleased that my identity is tied-up with this notion of "the librarian." And other times I want to burn my MLS degree, having first ripped it to shreds in a glorious fit of rage, and pretend like none of this ever happened. You see, I somehow ended up a cataloger.

When random people inquire as to my station in life, I usually state simply that I am a librarian and leave it at that. I am pleased when they tell me, "Funny, you don't look like a librarian." I am saddened when they say, "Oh, I can see that." I don't even mention the "c" word, since most sane people simply glaze over at the notion or desperately try to change the subject. It's just easier to leave the unspeakable unspoken.

For as long as I can remember, I've longed to have a calling, coveted some sense of destiny. After college, I thought I'd found it—and it was supposed to be librarianship. Lately, I've been wondering if maybe I didn't get the signals crossed. I don't feel like a librarian. I most definitely don't feel like a cataloger.

So, cataloging. It's probably the most misunderstood function of libraries. The patrons don't understand it, think it's all done by machines. Even our own kind don't always know quite what to make of it. Reference librarians perpetually alternate between questioning it and damning it. Friends and relatives just don't care; they may pretend to, but don't kid yourself—they don't. Hell, I'm a cataloger and I spend a good portion of my time simply loathing it. And if Martha Stewart can "catalog" her book collection in an afternoon, then she needs to share her secret with those of us who do it for a living.

But I've come to understand that cataloging is a science and an art, however archaic and bemusing it seems. It is a skill I have acquired, almost unwillingly. It allows me to bandy about terms like "database maintenance," "authority control," and "thesauri construction." And in certain circles that may even make me look smart. You might say that's a good thing, or you might not. I've even found what I consider a true nemesis in the form of NACO, the name authority component of the Library of Congress's Program for Cooperative Cataloging. But see, there's one of the problems. It would take me a virtual eternity to explain to the layman not only why NACO is my nemesis, but what the hell it is. Regardless, we all need a nemesis and my cataloger-self has found one. But what about destiny? Could this possibly be mine?

Several months ago I found myself working with a curious piece that caught my eye. Contrary to popular belief, a cataloger does not usually have the luxury of reading in its entirety every item that finds its way to her desk. But I took my time with this little gem and perused it at length. The title says it all: "You Can Win!"

To say I was intrigued would be a gross understatement, although, I do have a knack for taking an interest in the most mundane minutiae (hence the cataloging, I guess). This little booklet by Wilmer S. Shepherd, Jr. and published in 1939 purports to reveal "winning techniques for prize contests." These are contests of the complete-this-sentence-in-25-words-or-less variety, along the lines of: "I like P & G White Naphtha Soap because..." The book is dedicated to "Muriel, the girl of the red mittens." The girl of the red mittens?! I had to read on. And one of the great things about cataloging is that I could read on and be doing my job, the archetypal cataloger, pencil stuck in my bun and nose stuck in a crusty old book. Maybe I could even shuffle over to the last remaining card catalog in the building and look up something obscure. Right as rain.

Chapter One detailed something called the "red mitten technique." To briefly summarize, it seems Muriel worked in Mr. Shepherd's office, and during the dreary winter months, she donned the most fabulous, "softly bright," red angora mittens. Everyone took notice; they had no choice. These glorious mittens evidently represent the "gala symbol of a powerful secret of winning." They grab your attention and won't let go, enlist you in an "exciting conspiracy with yourself"— to take notice and find the beautiful, the unique, and the true. It all suddenly became very clear. That's what was missing in my tenure as a cataloging journeyman — the red mittens. I owned them once; I knitted them myself. Only now, I realized they had been unraveled and re-knitted into a pair of very unflattering hand-cuffs.

The rules, the rule interpretations, the coding, the strange math that goes into constructing a classification number, the bizarre local practice, the periods, the colons, the semicolons, x versus v — I'd let it all distract me from the real reason I was here: to reveal all this wonderful, odd, enlightening stuff to the world at large. To examine it, describe it, and simply revel in it.

Recently, I received an unexpected visit from a dear high school chum. I related the mysteries and treasures that could be found in the boxes and filing cabinets that line the dark and cold back rooms where I work. Tiny chromolithographs in the shape of cigarette cards, so bright and crisp you could eat them — hundreds of them. Broadsides with lovely woodblock prints, strong and firm after a hundred years. Travel brochures featuring ladies in movie-star pumps and kid leather gloves, having a lovely holiday. Proclamations for Arbor Day. All waiting to be cataloged and classified, to be revealed.

"Gee, it doesn't sound like you hate your job," she kindly pointed out.

It was quite balmy outside, but I seemed to have a pair of rather lovely mittens in my pocket.

I think I'll submit "Red mittens technique" as a subject heading proposal. After all, there's literary warrant.

VII. Unclassifiable

dear Melvil Dewey —
I really don't fit in your
decimal system
—Kathleen Kern

ASTROLOGY AND
LIBRARY JOB CORRELATION

Dean Dylan Hendrix and Michelle Wilde

Astrological skeptics claim that there is no real difference in the distribution of astrological signs within a given population. While we respect conventional wisdom and hard science, this is not what we found after evaluating the survey we conducted in late April 2002.

Before we begin our analysis, we have a few caveats to share. First of all, we do not purport to be professional astrologers. We are strictly dilettantes in the field. Moreover, due to the sample size of our survey (978 usable surveys), deadlines and the inherent complexity of astrology, there was no way to accurately read everyone's chart individually. Therefore, we consciously omitted vital information such as time of birth, place of birth, sign elements and cusp analysis for sheer practicality. To make the data accessible, we did not use statistical tests, relying solely on percentages. Our conclusions may seem cursory to some, but it is the best analysis of the massive amount of data considering the circumstances.

Finally, many colleagues felt it was their duty to opine that our jobs must be a joke, irreparable damage has been done to the image of librarians, and — surprise! — astrology is bogus. We are hardworking, salt of the earth librarians with real jobs at a real university. Our only crime is that we like to have a little fun with our profession. If we've irreparably damaged the insipid image of librarians along the way, we have done our job!

Astrology is no more invalid than someone's religious or spiritual beliefs. If you believe in something, it has relevance in your life whether Western empiricists have given it their OK or not. Even if physics is your religion, the energy that Einstein contemplated has many different names to people around the world: chi, akasha, tao, Over-soul, the Holy Spirit, vibes, etc. By our very existence, we are all creating curves in the space — time continuum. One can't help but think that massive entities like our sun, moons and planets are curving space time and, thus, affecting everything in close proximity, including the tiny neuropathways that form our personalities. Astrology, chaos theory, religion — it's all one and the same.

Now, on to the fun.

We began our study by soliciting responses on well-known library email lists; we made an attempt to include librarians from all walks of life, from catalogers to reference librarians, and public librarians to academic librarians. Unfortunately, a number of lists deemed our project an unworthy waste of time and refused to post our survey. We extend our deepest apologies to any group that feels underrepresented. PUBLIB and LIBREF are two of the larger lists that helped us with our research. In spite of limited exposure, we had unknowingly invoked the power of the Internet, and our little project was forwarded to librarians around the world. Completed surveys arrived in two forms: via email or via web survey. Due to limitations imposed on our survey by our university's Human Research Committee, we could not exceed 1000 responses. Over the course of a 9-day period, beginning on April 23, 2002, over 1000 librarians filled out our survey. On May 1, 2002, we disabled our web form and any surveys that arrived via email, snail mail or fax after that date were thrown out of the sample. Out of the responses, only 978 surveys provided adequate information for us to conduct an analysis.

Due to editorial requirements, our data and analysis regarding the correlation between Chinese astrology and library jobs could not be published in this volume. The data and analysis is on the Web at <http://lib.colostate.edu/news/astro.html>.

To ease discussion about astrology and library job correlation, we used two measures: overall percentage (OP) and percentage within a sign (PWS).

Overall Percentage (OP)

$$OP = \frac{\text{\# of respondents of a particular astrological sign}}{\text{total \# of respondents of all astrological signs}} * 100$$

For example, 10 Capricorns responded that they had serials duties and a total of 150 people responded that they had cataloging duties. The OP would be 10/150 = 0.0667 * 100 = 6.67%.

Since more Leos (105 responses) and Taureans (92 responses) responded to our survey more than any other astrological group, those signs rank consistently high on most OP calculations. Conversely, Aquarians (59 responses) responded to our survey less than any other sign, so they rank consistently low on most OP calculations. Therefore, it is worth noting that within the sample of each individual sign, there are significant findings. As a result, the PWS was born.

Percentage Within a Sign (PWS)

$$PWS = \frac{\text{\# of respondents of a particular astrological sign}}{\text{total \# of respondents of that same astrological sign}} * 100$$

For example, the same 10 Capricorns who responded that they had serials duties would be divided the total number of Capricorns that responded to our survey (74). The PWS would be 10/74 = 0.1351 * 100 = 13.51%.

Through analyzing OP and PWS data, we singled out the most significant correlations between astrological sign and library job duties. For example, in Table 3.3 — Cataloging Duties, Leos had the highest OP, 10.73%. This is a reflection that more Leos responded to our survey than any other sign. Scorpios rank right behind Leos with an OP of 10.30%, but the Scorpio's PWS is 31.58%, much higher than the Leo's 23.81% PWS score. Therefore, we find the link between Scorpios and cataloging duties extraordinarily more compelling. Please note that the correlations suggested by our data do not always match the ascribed characteristics for each astrological sign. Nonetheless, there are many extraordinary parallels.

Part I: Librarians in General

Dynamic. Authoritative. Fun-loving. Self-confident. These are words that describe Leos, and it makes one wonder who coined the stereotype of librarians as stodgy, spineless, and lacking in the humor department. It is no accident that there are lions standing guard at the top of the steps to the New York Public Library. Creative, organized, focused, and opinionated, Leos are willing to fight for what they believe in, and they are formidable foes to anyone who stands in their way. It is under the dynamic tutelage of Leos that libraries have remained a cornerstone of intellectual freedom. People born under this sign hate boredom and are independent to a fault. However, the Leo librarian must be careful not to be too controlling or demanding. Leos despise losing, and their stubborn opinionated side can make them seem like unpleasant know-it-alls. Picture the kid in school who sat at the front and wants to answer every question, constantly calling "I know, I know."

On the other end of the spectrum, Aquarians do not heed the call of Melvil Dewey. The humanitarian and philanthropic tendencies of the Aquarian and their kind and helpful manner make them ideal candidates for library work. However, libraries are the linchpin of order in the chaotic world of information. Thus, the rebellious and iconoclastic Aquarians prefer to create their own paradigms of organization. On a personal level, Aquarians do not like disruptions, can be very private and often appear distant to their fellow coworkers. Multitasking is impossible to avoid in libraries, and this is an additional deterrent for Aquarians. We believe that many Aquarians do not even consider librarianship due to the pervasive and damaging stereotypes of libraries as stagnating repositories of books. This is a tragedy, since many Aquarians are naturally gifted creatively and technologically. The library profession should be proactive in recruiting this astrological minority group.

Table 1.1— Western Signs of Librarians

Sign	OP
1. Leo	10.74%
2. Taurus	9.41%
3. Virgo	8.90%

4. Cancer	8.79%
5. Libra	8.38%
5. Pisces	8.38%
7. Aries	8.28%
8. Sagittarius	8.18%
9. Scorpio	7.77%
10. Capricorn	7.57%
10. Gemini	7.57%
12. Aquarius	6.03%

Part II — Librarians by Library Type

One of the first things that a new librarian learns is that outsiders to the profession have absolutely no idea what librarians do. We have all seen the slight smirk or look of bewilderment that many people give when they find out that librarians actually have Master's degrees. Popular culture perpetuates the stereotype of librarians as blue haired old biddies who love to shush people. Even the imaginative Star Wars saga is not immune, as evidenced by the bun-wearing Jedi archivist. Considering the misconceptions regarding the work of librarians, it is not surprising that most outsiders assume that all libraries are the same. However, as members of the library community, we know better. People who work in libraries feel that call to serve, but certain people who excel in public library work may loathe the idea of working with college students, and some academic librarians shudder to think of working with kids. Can astrology shed some light on these differences?

The largest percentage (47.5%) of respondents worked in academic libraries, and public librarians made up the next largest population, weighing in at 30%. Those who worked in special libraries comprised 10.7% of the population, and 15.7% of respondents classified their library as "other."

ACADEMIC LIBRARIES

Considering their strong belief that job satisfaction is more important than making money, is it any wonder that Cancers walk the halls of academia? The potent combination of innate tenacity and acute observational skills make Cancers crackerjack researchers who are well suited to ferreting out elusive references. These skills are complemented by a native ability to understand others, which is key to their success at the reference desk. Cancers adapt well to change, but they can also be overly cautious and conservative. Although they didn't drive the movement of information to the Internet, once Crabs saw the writing on the wall, they embraced the change and ran with it. Since Cancers are fascinated by the past, they are key players in the quest to preserve information, but they also have a tendency to be hoarders. This may account for the crowded stacks full of old materials that are so problematic in academic libraries.

Despite Aquarians making up only 6.76% of the OP in academic libraries, a whopping 49.18% have found their calling to be in academic settings. This comes as no surprise, since Aquarians are known for marching to the beat of their own drummer. Academia has traditionally been the bastion of freedom, both intellectual and personal. Thus, Aquarians, with their need for autonomy and activist tendencies, thrive in the collegiate environment.

On the other end of the spectrum, Pisceans, Virgos, and Sagittarians are much less likely to work in academic setting. Low-key Pisceans make up only 6.76% of academic librarians, and only 34.88% of Pisceans have thrown their hats into the academic arena. The linkages are not clear on why these Fish have not been hooked by academic libraries. The key to career satisfaction for a Sagittarian is travel, and lots of it. This restless sign loathes desk work, and finds the confines of an office to be suffocating. The academic culture of the never-ending meeting is too much for the antsy Sagittarian to bear. Although Virgos love research and very detail oriented work, they also have a tendency to be fussy and prudish, which puts them at odds with the permissive atmosphere of many universities. Of course, Virgos are also known as exceptionally hard workers who are notorious for putting in excessively long hours and staying at work until every last task is finished. Considering that university libraries are generally open from very early in the morning until the late hours of the night, perhaps the small number of Virgos in academia can be attributed to the fact that libraries have worked them all to death.

Table 2.1 — Academic Libraries

Sign	OP	Sign	PWS
1. Leo	11.49%	1. Cancer	53.33%
2. Cancer	10.81%	2. Aquarius	49.18%
3. Taurus	10.59%	3. Aries	47.62%
4. Aries	9.01%	4. Taurus	47.00%
5. Libra	8.56%	5. Leo	46.79%
6. Scorpio	8.11%	6. Scorpio	45.00%
7. Capricorn	7.88%	7. Capricorn	44.87%
8. Gemini	7.43%	8. Libra	44.19%
9. Aquarius	6.76%	9. Gemini	42.86%
9. Pisces	6.76%	10. Pisces	34.88%
11. Virgo	6.31%	11. Sagittarius	34.57%
11. Sagittarius	6.31%	12. Virgo	31.82%

PUBLIC LIBRARIES

Virgos are gentle, selfless, and good communicators who rule the roost in public libraries. They are the librarians who patiently toil over the questions of grade school students and drunken phone calls from patrons who need a librarian to step in and settle a barroom bet. Detail-oriented perfectionists, Virgos are the practical and efficient pillars of public libraries both large and small.

Sagittarians also find their niche in public libraries. These versatile adventurers can't stand to be stuck in a stuffy office, and public libraries offer an eclectic mix of work settings. Sagittarians love to travel on the job, so we suspect that these restless wanderers make up the majority of bookmobile drivers.

You will also be hard pressed to find a Gemini working in the public sector. Geminis are good at trivia and excellent communicators, but the nervous mental energy that is intrinsic to the Gemini personality makes it difficult for this sign to be patient with run of the mill questions. Remember the librarian who chased you out of the adult section when you were a little kid but worked endlessly to help you with your assignments once you were in high school? In spite of their versatility and love of working with people, Geminis are impatient with children; in public libraries, children are difficult to avoid.

Table 2.2 — Public Libraries

Sign	OP	Sign	PWS
1. Virgo	11.40%	1. Sagittarius	40.74%
2. Sagittarius	10.75%	2. Virgo	39.77%
3. Leo	10.42%	3. Capricorn	33.33%
4. Pisces	9.12%	4. Pisces	32.56%
5. Taurus	8.79%	5. Libra	31.40%
5. Libra	8.79%	6. Leo	29.36%
7. Capricorn	8.47%	7. Aries	28.57%
8. Aries	7.82%	8. Aquarius	27.87%
9. Scorpio	6.84%	9. Taurus	27.00%
10. Cancer	6.19%	10. Scorpio	26.25%
11. Gemini	5.86%	11. Gemini	23.38%
12. Aquarius	5.54%	12. Cancer	21.11%

SPECIAL LIBRARIES

Pisceans, Cancers, and Taureans are drawn to work in special libraries. Pisces are extremely sensitive and emotional, and they tend to work best in the background. The flexibility and diversity of job duties in the special library arena allow Pisceans to channel their creativity into areas not found in traditional library settings. They crave diversity in their job duties; since special libraries are often staffed by only one or two librarians, Pisces see the challenge of a one person library as a chance to stretch their creative muscles. Taureans, although deliberate and methodical, place the highest value on material comforts. The venue of the special library provides more opportunity for material gain, and this appeals to the Taurean personality. However, perhaps most importantly, special libraries give the Bull a safe environment in which he is king of the hill and run the library as he stubbornly sees fit.

Aries are fiery risk takers, and they are the sign least likely to be found in special libraries. Although they like to do things their own way, Aries are driven by ambition, and lack of competition in a small library with few staffers holds no appeal for the cutthroat Ram.

Table 2.3 — Special Libraries

Sign	OP	Sign	PWS
1. Pisces	13.95%	1. Pisces	13.95%
2. Cancer	13.33%	2. Cancer	13.33%
3. Taurus	13.00%	3. Taurus	13.00%
4. Leo	12.84%	4. Leo	12.84%
5. Aquarius	11.48%	5. Aquarius	11.48%
6. Gemini	10.39%	6. Gemini	10.39%
7. Sagittarius	9.88%	7. Sagittarius	9.88%
8. Virgo	9.09%	8. Virgo	9.09%
9. Capricorn	8.97%	9. Capricorn	8.97%
10. Scorpio	8.75%	10. Scorpio	8.75%
11. Libra	8.14%	11. Libra	8.14%
12. Aries	7.14%	12. Aries	7.14%

OTHER LIBRARY ENVIRONMENTS

The term "library" can be loosely applied to all sorts of settings, so it was only right that we include a catch-all category. This included: people who worked in government, prison, military, law, state, consortial, and medical libraries; and vendors, consultants, retirees, students, and the unemployed. It is also with a certain degree of regret that we must note that we also placed K–12 librarians in this category. Initially, we planned to include the school libraries as a separate category, but only 4.40% of our respondents identified themselves as school librarians.

Due to the diversity of information professions listed in the "Other" category, it is difficult to theorize why some signs are drawn to work in these alternative venues. However, it comes as no surprise that Geminis dominate the "other" category. Notorious for their mercurial personality and restless ways, Geminis thrive in diverse environments. They are expert multitaskers, and they have a hard time harnessing their nervous mental energy. The high number of Geminis working in non-traditional libraries could be seen as a testament to their versatility in the workplace. Then again, it could be chalked up to the fact that they keep changing their minds.

Table 2.4 — Other Libraries

Sign	OP	Sign	PWS
1. Gemini	11.25%	1. Gemini	23.38%
2. Virgo	10.63%	2. Scorpio	20.00%
3. Pisces	10.00%	3. Virgo	19.32%
3. Scorpio	10.00%	4. Pisces	18.60%
5. Libra	8.75%	5. Aries	16.67%
5. Aries	8.75%	6. Libra	16.28%
7. Taurus	8.13%	7. Sagittarius	14.81%
8. Leo	7.50%	8. Taurus	13.00%
8. Sagittarius	7.50%	9. Capricorn	12.82%
10. Cancer	6.88%	10. Cancer	12.22%
11. Capricorn	6.25%	11. Aquarius	11.48%
12. Aquarius	4.38%	12. Leo	11.01%

Part III — Librarians by Duties

Our survey allowed respondents to select multiple duties. Interestingly, 70.86% of responding librarians were involved in reference, 54.40% perform instruction and 51.33% develop collections. Contrary to the la-di-da bookworm stereotype, this evinces that a large percentage of librarians are actively involved with people, a trend worth mentioning.

ADMINISTRATIVE DUTIES

Before we started this project, we hypothesized that Leos and Taureans would be library administrators or, at the very least, have administrative duties. Oddly enough, this prognostication held true to form.

To successfully administrate any organization, those in managerial positions must exude self-confidence, focus, charisma and authority. To Leos, these qualities are as natural as beans are to chili. Leos are well known for selecting jobs that allow them some semblance of control. At their very best, Leos set the highest standards for their library and often motivate others to aspire to new heights with their charming and regal presence. Flourishing in positions that best use their innate organizational skills and creativity, Leos will pursue and even volunteer for administrative duties within libraries. On the flipside, Leos can expect too much from the folks they manage as their lives often revolve around their career. Do you remember that opinionated micromanager who wouldn't get off your back about the system migration? They are most likely a Leo.

The ambitious Bull is attracted to administrative jobs that allow them to use their natural stability and reliability to set a library on course. Taureans' unwavering patience works well for them as they ascend the ranks within an organization. Though not as flamboyant and visionary as the Leo administrator, Taureans rely on their natural stability and consideration to garner favor among their coworkers. On the negative side, many who feel that the library profession tends to stagnate might blame the abundance of Taurean leaders. The careful and security-conscious Bull personality is fiercely resistant to change. In the future library world, full of books, bots, and blogs, Taureans may find it harder to get promoted.

Table 3.1— Administrative Duties

Sign	OP	Sign	PWS
1. Leo	11.85%	1. Scorpio	32.89%
2. Taurus	10.10%	2. Leo	32.38%
3. Cancer	9.06%	3. Aquarius	32.20%
4. Aries	8.71%	4. Taurus	31.52%
4. Scorpio	8.71%	5. Aries	30.86%
6. Libra	8.36%	6. Cancer	30.23%
7. Sagittarius	7.67%	7. Libra	29.27%
7. Pisces	7.67%	8. Gemini	28.38%
9. Gemini	7.32%	9. Sagittarius	27.50%
10. Virgo	6.97%	10. Capricorn	27.03%
10. Capricorn	6.97%	11. Pisces	26.83%
12. Aquarius	6.62%	12. Virgo	22.99%

CATALOGING DUTIES

Scorpios are often characterized as intense, private and detached from the world — much like the archetypal cataloger. Scorpios prefer to stay behind the scenes rather than work directly with the public. Cataloging duties are a natural fit as their determined drive and imaginative problem-solving allow them the flexibility to handle anything from a batch of mundane MARC records to creating metadata for a cutting-edge digital library. It also must be noted that Scorpio is the most mysterious and sexiest sign in the zodiac. That explains your lascivious fantasies about Lucy the cataloger, even though you've never talked to her.

Table 3.2 — Cataloging Duties

Sign	OP	Sign	PWS
1. Leo	10.73%	1. Scorpio	31.58%
2. Pisces	10.30%	2. Pisces	29.27%
2. Scorpio	10.30%	3. Aquarius	27.12%
4. Virgo	9.87%	4. Virgo	26.44%
5. Libra	9.01%	5. Libra	25.61%

6. Taurus	8.58%		6. Leo	23.81%
7. Cancer	7.30%		7. Taurus	21.74%
8. Aquarius	6.87%		8. Gemini	21.62%
8. Aries	6.87%		9. Capricorn	20.27%
8. Gemini	6.87%		10. Sagittarius	20.00%
8. Sagittarius	6.87%		11. Cancer	19.77%
12. Capricorn	6.44%		12. Aries	19.75%

CHILDREN'S LIBRARIANSHIP DUTIES

Scorpio and Aries rank highest as far as respondents with children's librarianship duties. The qualities associated with these signs do not reflect an affinity for children. We were very surprised to see Leos and Pisces, children-loving signs, ranked remarkably low.

Table 3.3 — Children's Librarianship Duties

Sign	OP		Sign	PWS
1. Scorpio	14.67%		1. Scorpio	14.47%
2. Aries	13.33%		2. Aries	12.35%
3. Sagittarius	12.00%		3. Aquarius	11.86%
4. Virgo	10.67%		4. Sagittarius	11.25%
5. Aquarius	9.33%		5. Virgo	9.20%
6. Cancer	8.00%		6. Gemini	8.11%
6. Gemini	8.00%		7. Cancer	6.98%
8. Leo	6.67%		8. Pisces	6.10%
8. Pisces	6.67%		9. Libra	4.88%
10. Libra	5.33%		10. Leo	4.76%
12. Capricorn	2.67%		11. Capricorn	2.70%
12. Taurus	2.67%		12. Taurus	2.17%

COLLECTION DEVELOPMENT DUTIES

Notably, 67.80% of responding Aquarians have collection development duties at work. This is overwhelmingly significant as the next sign in the hierarchy is Scorpio with 57.89%! Obviously, Aquarians find collection development attractive, but we cannot figure out why. Water-Bearers desire to assist library users face-to-face, use their boundless creativity, and challenge convention, so this incredibly high correlation is puzzling. Perhaps the supervisors of Aquarians notice their gift for diplomacy and place them in liaison positions during budget crunches. Due to their successes in making libraries look good during materials and serials cancellations, maybe Aquarians are never allowed to relinquish those duties.

Pisces lag behind the other sun signs in collection management duties. They do not believe that collection management nurtures their creativity, so they never volunteer or apply for these positions. In a time of shrinking library budgets, many tough decisions must be made in regards to collections. Hostile user groups and their uninformed book challenges also scare Pisces away from collection development. The nervous and ambiguous Piscean has trouble with conflict resolution and decisiveness, resulting in the avoidance of collection development and its trappings.

Table 3.4 — Collection Development Duties

Sign	OP	Sign	PWS
1. Taurus	10.16%	1. Aquarius	67.80%
2. Leo	9.76%	2. Scorpio	57.89%
3. Virgo	9.56%	3. Taurus	55.43%
4. Scorpio	8.76%	4. Capricorn	55.41%
5. Libra	8.37%	5. Virgo	55.17%
6. Cancer	8.17%	6. Libra	51.22%
6. Capricorn	8.17%	7. Gemini	50.00%
8. Aquarius	7.97%	8. Aries	49.38%
8. Aries	7.97%	9. Cancer	47.67%
10. Gemini	7.37%	10. Leo	46.67%
11. Sagittarius	6.97%	11. Sagittarius	43.75%
12. Pisces	6.77%	12. Pisces	41.46%

INSTRUCTION DUTIES

At their best, Capricorns' enthusiasm, excellent organizational skills, and affinity for routine make them natural trainers. The Ram revels in repeating the same lesson to different classes. Additionally, they get off on the instant approval and status of being the "sage on the stage." However, be aware that having a large percentage of Capricorns doing instruction can lead to the quick stagnation of a library instruction program. At their very worst, they will fight any changes to instruction practices and complain vehemently to library administrators.

Though great communicators, Sagittarians hate lectures rife with minutiae, especially when dealing with academic subjects. The visionary Sagittarian would much rather discuss library instruction philosophies than how to use ABI/Inform. Hating predictability and routine, they would prefer to impale themselves on a sharp metal object (an arrow, perhaps?) than deliver the same lecture over and over. It is unfortunate because their playful and risk-taking approach could provide much needed makeovers for quiescent instruction programs.

Table 3.5 — Instruction Duties

Sign	OP	Sign	PWS
1. Leo	10.34%	1. Capricorn	63.51%
1. Taurus	10.34%	2. Taurus	59.78%
3. Virgo	9.77%	3. Virgo	59.77%
4. Cancer	9.21%	4. Cancer	56.98%
5. Capricorn	8.83%	5. Aries	55.56%
6. Aries	8.46%	6. Libra	53.66%
7. Libra	8.27%	7. Scorpio	52.63%
8. Pisces	7.71%	8. Aquarius	52.54%
9. Scorpio	7.52%	9. Leo	52.38%
10. Gemini	6.95%	10. Gemini	50.00%
11. Sagittarius	6.77%	10. Pisces	50.00%
12. Aquarius	5.83%	12. Sagittarius	45.00%

INTERLIBRARY LOAN DUTIES

Pisces are attracted to ILL duties much more than their astrological counterparts. Charity and sacrifice are valued by the Pisces personality, and this serves them well in ILL positions. To the dreamy Pisces, their patrons are not just the folks who walk through their doors, but rather the world at large. Not needing constant adulation, Pisces are content to work in the shadows while they quietly know they are fulfilling the grand mission of libraries: access to information. So the next time you receive an ILL request for an obscure documentary, you can be sure a Pisces is throwing in some "warm fuzzies" for free.

Table 3.6 — Interlibrary Loan Duties

Sign	OP	Sign	PWS
1. Pisces	11.49%	1. Pisces	24.39%
2. Leo	10.34%	2. Aquarius	20.34%
3. Cancer	9.77%	3. Cancer	19.77%
4. Aries	9.20%	4. Aries	19.75%
5. Capricorn	8.05%	5. Capricorn	18.92%
5. Taurus	8.05%	6. Leo	17.14%
7. Libra	7.47%	7. Scorpio	17.11%
7. Scorpio	7.47%	8. Gemini	16.22%
7. Virgo	7.47%	9. Libra	15.85%
10. Aquarius	6.90%	10. Taurus	15.22%
10. Gemini	6.90%	11. Sagittarius	15.00%
10. Sagittarius	6.90%	12. Virgo	14.94%

LIBRARY SYSTEMS DUTIES

Geminis are captivated by library systems work, as evidenced by the next highest PWS scorer, Virgo, trailing by nearly 5 percentage points. Geminis have an extreme distaste for boring job tasks and would rather work on challenging projects that require a variety of skills and their excellent logical mind. Library systems work provides the frenetic and fast-paced environment in which Geminis thrive. In most libraries, these techie folks are hard to retain. You may blame a competitive job market, but we would also point to the Gemini's itinerant nature as a cause. Similar to the semi-famous Gemini, Nick Burns (Your Company's Computer Guy), they are the systems gurus you are reluctant to call, due to their biting sarcasm, when your computer malfunctions.

Table 3.7 — Library Systems Duties

Sign	OP	Sign	PWS
1. Gemini	11.31%	1. Gemini	25.68%
2. Virgo	10.71%	2. Virgo	20.69%
3. Taurus	10.12%	3. Aquarius	20.34%
4. Libra	9.52%	4. Libra	19.51%
5. Cancer	8.93%	5. Taurus	18.48%
6. Scorpio	8.33%	6. Scorpio	18.42%
7. Aquarius	7.14%	7. Cancer	17.44%
7. Pisces	7.14%	8. Sagittarius	15.00%
7. Sagittarius	7.14%	9. Capricorn	14.86%
10. Aries	6.55%	10. Pisces	14.63%
10. Capricorn	6.55%	11. Aries	13.58%
10. Leo	6.55%	12. Leo	10.48%

PRESERVATION DUTIES

Virgos are so obviously drawn to preservation tasks by their personality type. Our initial prediction was confirmed by our survey results. Being meticulous and artistic perfectionists, Virgos love to repair library materials! Whether it's a simple tip-in or deacidification, Virgos are dedicated artisans. Their overly cautious nature is an excellent fit in preserving valuable or unique library resources.

People born under Aries, the sign least likely to be attracted to preservation, are rash, impatient and impulsive. If you've seen books in the stacks bound with duct tape, it's most likely the handiwork of an Aries.

Table 3.8 — Preservation Duties

Sign	OP	Sign	PWS
1. Virgo	15.79%	1. Virgo	17.24%
2. Leo	11.58%	2. Aquarius	16.95%
3. Aquarius	10.53%	3. Gemini	13.51%
3. Gemini	10.53%	4. Pisces	10.98%
5. Pisces	9.47%	5. Scorpio	10.53%
6. Scorpio	8.42%	6. Leo	10.48%
7. Cancer	7.37%	7. Cancer	8.14%
8. Libra	6.32%	8. Libra	7.32%
8. Taurus	6.32%	9. Taurus	6.52%
10. Sagittarius	5.26%	10. Sagittarius	6.25%
11. Aries	4.21%	11. Capricorn	5.41%
11. Capricorn	4.21%	12. Aries	4.94%

REFERENCE DUTIES

Taureans show a slightly stronger propensity for reference duties than their counterparts. Though Taureans see libraries changing a little too fast for their tastes, they find solace in traditional face-to-face reference, the cornerstone of library public services. Their impeccable patience allows Taureans to charm problem patrons and not become agitated. Bulls will always accept more desk hours when less patient sun signs are at their wits' end.

Table 3.9 — Reference Duties

Sign	OP	Sign	PWS
1. Leo	10.53%	1. Taurus	78.26%
2. Taurus	10.39%	2. Capricorn	75.68%
3. Cancer	8.66%	3. Aquarius	74.58%
3. Virgo	8.66%	4. Aries	72.84%
5. Aries	8.51%	5. Gemini	70.27%
6. Capricorn	8.08%	6. Cancer	69.77%
6. Pisces	8.08%	7. Scorpio	69.74%
8. Libra	7.79%	8. Leo	69.52%
8. Sagittarius	7.79%	9. Virgo	68.97%
10. Scorpio	7.65%	10. Pisces	68.29%
11. Gemini	7.50%	11. Sagittarius	67.50%
12. Aquarius	6.35%	12. Libra	65.85%

SERIALS DUTIES

Aquarian traits do not match very well with requirements of a serials job. Nonetheless, Aquarians are apt to work with serials more so than any other sign, as the data shows them to be quite an outlier at 27.12%. This unexplained phenomenon is akin to the Bermuda Triangle, the Nazca Lines, or Michael Bolton's popularity.

Table 3.10 — Serials Duties

Sign	OP	Sign	PWS
1. Leo	11.33%	1. Aquarius	27.12%
2. Aquarius	10.67%	2. Scorpio	17.11%
3. Libra	9.33%	3. Libra	17.07%
4. Aries	8.67%	4. Leo	16.19%
4. Scorpio	8.67%	5. Aries	16.05%
4. Taurus	8.67%	6. Virgo	14.94%
4. Virgo	8.67%	7. Gemini	14.86%
8. Cancer	7.33%	8. Taurus	14.13%
8. Gemini	7.33%	9. Capricorn	13.51%
8. Pisces	7.33%	10. Pisces	13.41%
11. Capricorn	6.67%	11. Cancer	12.79%
12. Sagittarius	5.33%	12. Sagittarius	10.00%

WEBMASTER DUTIES

Though no convincingly strong correlations exist, Aquarians, Geminis, Virgos and Pisceans tend towards taking on Web responsibilities over the other signs. When combined appropriately, your library has the recipe for a kick-ass Web team. First, stir in a Gemini and a Virgo, due to their love of technological challenges and methodical, detail-oriented work. Let these folks stew for a bit. Sprinkle in a pinch of Pisces for creative Web design ideas. Finally, add a healthy dose of Aquarian as team leader because of their natural technological aptitude and diplomacy. And voilà! A kick-ass Web team!

Our data suggests Aries and Capricorns stay away from Web duties in droves. Curiously, the personality traits of these two ungulate signs fit in well with the requirements of a webmaster.

Table 3.11 — Webmaster Duties

Sign	OP	Sign	PWS
1. Virgo	11.23%	1. Aquarius	27.12%
2. Cancer	10.16%	2. Gemini	24.32%
2. Pisces	10.16%	3. Virgo	24.14%
4. Gemini	9.63%	4. Pisces	23.17%
5. Taurus	9.09%	5. Cancer	22.09%
6. Aquarius	8.56%	6. Scorpio	21.05%
6. Leo	8.56%	7. Taurus	18.48%
6. Scorpio	8.56%	8. Libra	17.07%

9. Libra	7.49%	9. Leo	15.24%
10. Sagittarius	6.42%	10. Sagittarius	15.00%
11. Aries	5.35%	11. Aries	12.35%
12. Capricorn	4.81%	12. Capricorn	12.16%

OTHER DUTIES

The "other duties" text box was an extremely popular choice among survey respondents. Many respondents provided their résumé, vita and occasional comments à la "Scorpios rule!" on our web form. But seriously, we, as well as anyone, understand the true meaning of the phrase, "miscellaneous duties as assigned." With "other duties," we received a plethora of job tasks. These included, but were not limited to acquisitions, circulation, digital resource management, directorships, programming and public relations.

Despite showing only a slight correlation, the cooperative Libra is always ready to take on miscellaneous duties in the library. For example, their refined communication skills and diplomacy translates well in the public relations and outreach arena. Enjoying a variety of tasks, the Scales will attempt to help everyone with special projects as long as one doesn't take up too much of their time. Always be cognizant that Libras need their beloved balance more than anything.

Table 3.12 — Other Duties

Sign	OP	Sign	PWS
1. Leo	11.07%	1. Libra	31.71%
2. Libra	9.92%	2. Aries	30.86%
3. Aries	9.54%	3. Aquarius	30.51%
4. Taurus	8.40%	4. Scorpio	27.63%
5. Cancer	8.02%	5. Leo	27.62%
5. Scorpio	8.02%	6. Capricorn	27.03%
5. Virgo	8.02%	6. Gemini	27.03%
8. Capricorn	7.63%	8. Sagittarius	25.00%
8. Gemini	7.63%	9. Cancer	24.42%
8. Sagittarius	7.63%	10. Virgo	24.14%
11. Pisces	7.25%	11. Taurus	23.91%
12. Aquarius	6.87%	12. Pisces	23.17%

Due to small sample sizes and even distributions, no significant data was gathered about acquisitions, digital resource management, programming, and public relations. However, circulation duties correlated highly with Cancer. Protective of library materials, the security conscious Crab makes for a great circulation librarian. Furthermore, the combination of their strong sense of ethics and compassionate nature make them the ideal judges in fine disputes.

In addition, library directors or library deans who responded tended to be of the Leo (36.36%) and Taurean (27.27%) persuasion, though admittedly, the sample size was too small to seriously consider. However, this correlation matches the results from the administrative duties. So, the proof's in the puddin'!

Conclusion

What does it all mean? Do the stars and planets affect our library careers? Our data, culled from nearly 1000 respondents, shows that unique correlations exist between certain astrological signs and certain library positions. In many cases, those correlations fit very well with the ascribed personality characteristics of solar and lunar astrological signs.

We humans may never be equipped to fully understand our place in the cosmos. We librarians may never be equipped to fully understand our place in librarianship. However, we believe the mystery and divinity of our humanity to be a far more complex formula than any belief system a human can design, index or catalog. We like to think that fluttering butterflies over the Atlantic can eventually cause a tsunami in the Pacific. Or, more importantly, the position of Alpha Centauri can contribute to the transformation of a mild mannered civilian into a cocksure reference bandida.

Why *Librarian: The Musical* Is Doomed Before It Starts

David M. Pimentel

- Choreography exponentially complicated by the use of book trucks
- Characters who cry, "Renew me!" in moments of passion
- Inability of producers to gain accreditation from ALA
- Technical advisors insist that all books used as props be fully cataloged
- Few people can sympathize with the protagonist's tragic flaw: "list addiction"
- "Naughty Melvil" routine tied up in legal dispute with Dewey family
- Late fees assessed to audience members who don't arrive on time
- Lyrics that rhyme with "nonsectarian," "utilitarian," and "egalitarian"
- Constant IT upgrades for "Connect"—the software/salsa number—put the production horribly over budget

- Stage managers won't convert "fog machines" into "dust machines"
- Actors can't pronounce "festschrift"
- "Conference Ballet" sequence requires permission clearance from too many vendors
- Addition of a lengthy annotated bibliography makes the playbill weigh 8 pounds

STUCK BETWEEN A ROCK AND ANOTHER ROCK: JOB TITLE WORRIES

Dan Cherubin

They say that the capacity to adapt is the landmark of survival, and that we, as librarians, can work in any situation that requires our special abilities. No matter what we are called on the job, it's all the same.

I only wish that were true.

I used to wear my profession as a hip accessory. It clearly defined who I was. Now I carry it as a defensive shield. I must argue about my credentials daily. How did this happen? Much of it has to do with becoming someone with a new job title.

I want to talk about what still makes me a librarian. Regardless of any non-traditional library job I may hold, it is something to which I am forever drawn and quite possibly stuck with for the rest of my life.

I can safely say that none of the librarians I know, myself included, ended up in library school intentionally. Despite some bizarre altercations and the imminent closing of my school, I saw my time there as a perfect fit. Sure, I was certainly like many of my fellow contemporary classmates: loud, borderline obnoxious, wanting to change things, quite far away from the librarian archetype, but I also knew that librarianship was for me. I liked putting some kind of order to the universe, so that others would find the information they desired. I understood the rules of the bibliographic game, but I also knew that, in the proper hands, it could be made so much better and more relevant. I even understood that profound connection between cataloging and reference (which often seem like to go together like Mormons and tequila). I got huge amounts of satisfaction doing something I liked to do.

I was proud to be a librarian. That title was my badge of honor. I didn't need to argue as to why that was any different from being called an "Information Scientist" or "Research Specialist." I knew what I was, and I thought it was cool.

I worked as a librarian in not-for-profit institutions, philanthropic organizations and in the educational as well as the public library world. I loved saying I was a librarian and having people understood what that meant. They knew they could come to me to seek advice on how to find information or to explain how some form of classification works. I could negotiate with any client or customer as to what might be a better way of finding something. I chaired committees. I wrote articles. I developed subject headings. I saw people use my work and use it well. What couldn't I do, armed with this degree?

Well, I found there was one thing I could not do: make a living. After a decade as a librarian, I enjoyed the work immensely, but I was deeper in the financial hole that began when I enrolled in library school. For all the good I could do, I needed food and shelter.

I began to see my badge of honor as something that might be negotiable if I did some cosmetic surgery to it. Articles were popping up about how much librarians could make when they switched to the corporate world, and yet still worked as librarians. One such article[1] said librarians were making six figure salaries! (Note: as of this date, I've never met one of those librarians.) I thought a shift in jobs would be a quick and easy way to alleviate debt, possibly gain some new work experience, and still be a librarian. When a job offer came up, I decided to make the move. I took a job at a software company as their director of marketing. On paper, the job sounded similar to being a librarian. I would conduct research for the company, and present my findings. I would help the company better understand and utilize the arena in which they worked. And they hired me, so I figured I was correct.

Another assumption shot to hell.

Moving out of an actual library milieu into a software company was unsettling, at best. I had gone from a world of performing artists and librarians, intellectuals and esthetes, into one of greed, obtuse observations and misguided corporate drive.

My new work arena took a much different view on m experience than my previous venues. My credentials were no longer "real." Being a librarian carried some sort of stigma among the MBAs and techies, as if I spent the last decade sitting at a desk with a ficus and my lips in a permanent "shush" position. Never mind that I was the only one who could form a sentence. (I wrote all the collateral for the company.) Never mind that I spent 80 hours a week conducting primary and secondary research in a field (insurance software) that they all admitted regularly stumped them. My now defensive shield of librarianship became part of my daily makeup.

Every day I had to explain why we needed proper research, why we needed to negotiate that reference question when it came to providing analysis, why being able to do proper research would be just as good if not *better* than trusting one's "gut feeling" about the market, competition, clients, etc.

It is very likely that many of my colleagues in the corporate library world do not share this situation. Many of them seem very happy at their jobs. Maybe they don't have to defend themselves daily as to why being a librarian is a good thing. Then again, you can see that many in the corporate world don't exactly cherish this title bestowed upon us. The arguments against being something other than a librarian are fairly laughable. I guess maybe it's the non-librarians who have a bone to pick about the job title.[2] The thing is, during my time at the software company, whenever anyone I met would ask me what I did for a living, I would always preface it with, "Well, I'm actually a librarian, but right now I work at...."

As I was writing this piece, I was laid off from the software company. I survived 2 years there, which is pretty good for that type of work. I saw the layoff coming, so it wasn't a huge surprise. If anything, it may make for a happier ending to this piece. I get to do a wee bit of library "consulting" (cataloging mostly), and I'm looking to return full time to the profession.

But will my fellow librarians welcome me back? I've already been labeled a traitor because I had to take a job to pay off my debt. I was "selling out," "crossing the lines," giving up "all I worked for." In many ways, they were right. But I also knew I had to make some sort of move when I did. Perhaps if I had a rich boyfriend, or a corporate background or one of those fictional six-figure jobs, I could have continued as a librarian. But I didn't have that, so I needed to go.

And now that I'm unemployed, where will I go? Will I enjoy the fruits of another techie corporate job? I've already been told I don't quite have that "drive," which I can only take to mean I wear suits in designs other than Regis Philbin. The library job market is slim if you want to make a living and have over a decade of experience. Many folks stay in the plum jobs until retirement. Also, my most current offers, while interesting, are not doing anything remotely librarian-like.

I am no longer referred to as a librarian and, frankly, that worries me. What I have to offer is important, but the world doesn't want to hear it from someone who parlays that stereotype. (Even if being a queer tattooed skinhead type parlays a completely different one, it still doesn't sit well in corporate America.) I want to see myself back in some artsy, non-paying nook in the future. But can I survive that way?

I am a librarian, dammit.

Notes

1. Kelly Gates. "Librarians Are Finding Ample Opportunities." *Career Journal*, 2000.
    <http://www.careerjournal.com/salaries/industries/librarians/20001206-gates.html>.
    [Note: this URL is no longer available; check <http://www.archive.org> or <http://www.google.com> to retrieve a cached version.]
2. Ian Smith. "Beware of Becoming a Glorified Librarian." *Researcha*, 24 April 2001.
<http://www.researcha.com/pooled/articles/BF_NEWSART/view.asp?Q=BF_NEWSAR T_8216>.

HEY, BOOK WRANGLERS!

Cathy Camper

HEY, BOOK WRANGLERS!
MATCH the title with the LC
NUMBER It SHOULD HAVE:

1. BS431 ___
2. TP29 ___   4. PS835 ___   6. MT4973 ___   7 EZ115 ___
3. HA640 ___   5. MM71 ___   8. ET390 ___
                                                 9. BM5957 ___
                                                 10. PU695 ___

A — 1000 Truly Funny Jokes Told By Library Directors

B — The State of My Brain by I.M.A. Bordmember

C — Decorating Deciduous Trees in HIGH SCHOOL

D — ASVAB for MORONS

E — Addendums to Library Staff Memorandum 1845–2002

F — Bowel Cleansing MADE EASY

G — OUT OF THIS WORLD Droll Tales of Library Patrons I Have Known

H — THE FRAGRANCE OF PUBLIC READING ROOMS

I — MELTS IN YOUR MOUTH: TRUE TALES OF SEX IN THE STACKS

J — Shelving Books Made Me Rich

ANSWERS: 1J, 2C, 3A, 4E, 5I,
6B, 7D, 8G, 9E, 10H
8-10 correct = SHELVER Extraordineire!

4-7 correct = Substitute Library Aide
Kudos for finding books despite lack of
benefits.
0-3 correct - card carrying MLS! Now git
off yer BUTT + page A Book! CC©
2002

A Bit More Than a Year of Library Reading: A Revolting Bibliography

Jessamyn West

In preparation for this book, I decided to start reading obscure library literature. Since librarians seem to have a flair for getting published, the number of titles available, even in the "obscure" category, was somewhat amazing. I read books about librarian detectives and library humor books from ninety years ago. I found tiny pamphlets and massive volumes. I thrilled to similarities between the librarianship of yesteryear and the profession as it appears through literature today. I have included an annotated list of some of the titles I perused, and a list of those titles and URLs recommended by our contributors.

Caputo, Janette S. *The Assertive Librarian*. Phoenix: Oryx Press, 1984.
    "Assertiveness training for librarians is a really good idea. Teaching asshole patrons how to behave properly. Learning how to properly advocate for getting more funding for your libraries instead of just sucking it up and saying, 'Well, it's true, we don't have a revenue stream....'" It's all a great idea. This book was written in 1984, so I shouldn't be too harsh. And I did read it cover to cover. My problem is exactly the opposite: having been raised to be assertive, I've gone too far over the edge into being (sometimes) aggressive. This book carefully delineates the differences between assertive and aggressive and helps you to moderate your behavior. The downside to this book is that it seems like it's basically written for anyone in the service industry, or anyone with a job, really. I didn't see enough situations that pertained to librarianship specifically to make me think it was warranted to have a whole fresh assertiveness book for this profession. And did I mention it was written in 1984?

Cart, Michael, ed. *In the Stacks: Short Stories about Libraries and Librarians*. Woodstock, NY: Overlook Press, 2002.
    This book just came out a few months back and I signed up on the hold list at my library so that I could be the first to read it. Some of these stories are fairly familiar — Borges and Calvino have written about libraries in the past — and some are new to me. Only one of them didn't grab me and make me think in some way. One of the little delights of getting to read a lot of stories about librarians at once is that some of the stories can have bad libraries, some can have spinster librarians, and some can have a lady who lives at home with seventeen cats and you don't have to get your dander up about it; you can just enjoy the story without getting huffy about the author playing to type. This is an excellent collection with stories about all sorts of librarians and all sorts of libraries. Reserve it now.

Coutts, Henry. *Library Jokes and Jottings: A Collection of Stories Partly Wise But Mostly Otherwise*. London: Grafton, 1914.

I have a hard time laughing at contemporary attempts at humor. It may be that I find the authors trying too hard, or maybe they are assuming a frame of reference that I don't share. However, once I convinced the librarian to *please* let me take home this reference book just this once, I sat in the backyard with it and laughed. The funniest part, sadly, is that librarianship has changed so little in the last hundred years or so. We still have religious zealot patrons, and the guys who sit there all day long reading the newspapers. People still expect all sorts of entitlements because they are the taxpayers that keep the library open and children are still a constant threat and simultaneous delight. This books did not have the word "masturbator" in it, like a current library humor book might, but many of the situations were the same. Some of the jottings also included many humorous pieces that were in some ways quaint because they were not ribald or racy; plays on words with book titles, the amusement of dirty children not washing their hands, the plaintive yowlings of the patron who owes overdue fines. Find it through interlibrary loan if you possibly can.

Gellatly, Peter, ed. *Sex Magazines in the Library Collection: A Scholarly Study of Sex in Serials and Periodicals*. New York: Haworth Press, 1980

This book describes itself as a monographic supplement to the *Serials Librarian* magazine, but it looked like a book to me. I've been intrigued by some of the titles I've been seeing lately about librarians and sex, my favorite being "For Sex, See the Librarian" (about censorship, I believe.) This book is a collection of fairly scholarly papers dealing with how libraries deal with sex periodicals. The papers are easy to read survey types with no information that will knock anyone out, but some humorous parts. Most of the focus is on magazines such as *Playboy*, *Penthouse*, and *Oui*, but some of the writers explore more hardcore literature. The book wraps up with a long listing of sexually useful (as opposed to either LC's sexually backward) subject headings. Sandy Berman is always a delight and I think I would even enjoy reading his shopping lists. This article is no exception. Titling it "If There Were a Sex Index," he does an index — with his own subject headings, natch — of twelve sex magazines, ranging from the scholarly to the hardcore. The nomenclature becomes extra funny because, of course, all the headings are written in all caps, making all the smutty words seem like they are being shouted at you: GAY SOCIALISTS, SEX ON ROLLER COASTERS, SUCKING OFF, See FELLATIO. You can see how amusing this is.

Glozer, Liselotte F. *A Librarian's Cook Book*. Berkeley: Peacock Press, 1965.

My favorite of the bunch, this pamphlet, subtitled *How to Keep Your Mind on Classifying, Cataloguing and Doing Bibliographic Research and Yet Think of Food* contains a few recipes, some witty side commentary — including any research the librarian needed to do in order to properly prepare the recipe — and the LC and Dewey numbers for each.

Gorman, Michael. *Our Singular Strengths: Meditations for Librarians.* Chicago: American Library Association, 1998.

Michael Gorman gets libraries. In some ways, he seems wistful that he has advanced to a management position and no longer gets to deal with patrons on the front lines so much. This thoughtful book of koans celebrating libraries and librarianship can make even the most crusty librarian feel honorable about their profession and give them food for thought. Gorman offers topics—intellectual freedom, learning to be a librarian, the war of AACR2—and writes short paragraphs on them and ends each section with a final thought: "I will accept no substitute for the unique value of books and reading," "I will beautify my library to honor its guests," "I will do what I can to make my library a compassionate place." He delights in Ranganathan and even goes so far as to offer his own New Laws of Librarianship. While I don't always agree with Gorman, I respect the effort he made for the profession.

Harvey, Miles. *The Island of Lost Maps.* New York: Random House, 2000.

Wow, does this guy say some nasty things about librarians!

"...he sounded just as you might expect a librarian to sound, from the nasally voice to the precise, even persnickety, way of putting words together."

"Librarian—that mouth-contorting, graceless grind of a word, that dry gulch in the dictionary between libido and licentiousness—it practically begs you to envision a stoop-shouldered loser, socks mismatched, eyes locked in a permanent squint from reading too much microfiche."

This is another one of those adorable pop history books—this one about a map thief. Since Harvey had very little access to the thief, who refused to speak with him and even threatened him with a restraining order, he had to recreate much of the man's story, much like—he muses endlessly—a cartographer creates an approximation of a place. The book is a good solid read with just the kinds of tantalizing facts you expect from a history book written for the general public. The illustrations are reduced to grayscale selections from some of the maps in question and the bad guy does get caught and (more or less) punished. I ended up thinking, "Wow, that was an interesting topic, I'd like to go read a book about it...."

Kurzweil, Allen. *The Grand Complication.* New York: Hyperion, 2001.

Library mystery! This book follows a librarian with an almost obsessive love of lists and books as he gets gradually seduced into the arcane and book-based plots of an elderly gentleman who frequents his library. Delicious for those of us who love antiquarian books and the Dewey Decimal system. The librarian characters are three-dimensional but also quirky and smart in that odd way that librarians tend to be. I was sad when this book was over.

Lasky, Kathryn. *The Librarian Who Measured the Earth.* Boston: Joy Street Books, 1994.

This is a children's book about Eratosthenes, the librarian and mathematician who first thought out a way for measuring the circumference of the planet. The book has an intro that basically states that the author made up the parts of Eratosthenes' early childhood since no records survive of how he really lived. Drawing on historical account of the time, they paint a picture of their estimation of what a smart Greek child must have been like, and extrapolate from there. The book was well-illustrated and clearly explained the procedures that Eratosthenes went through.

Pearson, Edmund Lester. *The Librarian at Play*. Boston: Small, Maynard and Company, 1911.

More library humor from the early part of the last century. This one is a collection of essays, some inspired, some that seem more dated. My favorite essay deserves some discussion. It comes in the form of a letter found in a bottle. The writer is an essayist who recently had won a contest where he listed his 100 favorite books that he'd like to bring to a desert island. Well, he chooses all sorts of scholarly and erudite stuff. His prize is a cruise with these 100 books as his companions. Predictably, the boat sinks and he is marooned with nothing but the works of Plato and Homer while he wails about wanting to read something about knot-tying. His journal entries include such gems as "Aenid eaten by a goat," etc. This book, in addition to the one I read previously, highlight that while the library profession has been steadily evolving, the role of the library in modern society has stayed more or less the same. Annoying patrons are still weird in the same way; librarians are still stereotyped as overeducated and undersocialized. This book is a gem and worth tracking down at your local library archives.

Vogel, Betty. *A Librarian Is to Read*. Vancouver BC: Blue Flower Press, 1988.

Found this hidden on a shelf with the other books about libraries. Vogel used to be a Seattle Public librarian and her collection of short essays about libraries, library school and the job of being a librarian, will ring true to anyone who reads. Vogel covers such topics as "sex in the library" and "god in the library" with humor and a certain level of respect for even the craziest of patrons. It is clear that she loves her job, despite griping about low pay and low status. I am sorry I didn't get a chance to check out a book or two when she was working at SPL.

SEE ALSO: A COLLECTION FROM OUR CONTRIBUTORS

Books

Adamic, Louis. *Dynamite: A Century of Class Violence in America 1830–1930*. Seattle: Left Bank Books, 1984.

Atton, Chris. *Alternative Literature: A Practical Guide for Librarians*. Hampshire, England: Aldershot, 1996.

Bates, Mary Ellen. *Building and Running a Successful Research Business: A Guide for the Independent Information Professional*. Medford, NJ: Cyberage Books, 2003.

Berman, Sanford. *The Joy of Cataloging: Essays, Letters, Reviews, and Other Explosions*. Phoenix: Oryx Press, 1980.

Berman, Sanford. *Prejudices and Antipathies: A Tract on the LC Subject Heads Concerning People*. Foreword by Eric Moon. Jefferson, NC: McFarland, 1993.

Block, Marylaine, ed. *The Quintessential Searcher: The Wit & Wisdom of Barbara Quint*. Medford, NJ: Information Today, Inc., 2002.

Carlsson, Chris, ed., with Mark Leger. *Bad Attitude: The Processed World Anthology*. London: Verso, 1990.

Daniels, J. *The Adventures of Tintin: Breaking Free*. London: Attack International, 1989.

Dodge, Chris, and Jan DeSirey, eds. *Everything You Always Wanted to Know About Sandy Berman But Were Afraid to Ask*. Jefferson, NC: McFarland, 1995.

Eco, Umberto. "How to Organize a Public Library." In *How to Travel with a Salmon and Other Essays*. Edited by Diane Sterling, William Weaver, trans. New York: Harcourt, 1994.

London, Jack. *Iron Heel*. Westport, CT: Lawrence Hill & Co., 1990.

Manley, Will. *Unsolicited Advice: Observations of a Public Librarian*. Jefferson, NC: McFarland, 1992.

Plotnik, Arthur. *Library Life — American Style: A Journalist's Field Report*. Metuchen, NJ: Scarecrow, 1975.

Robinson, Spider. *The Callagan Touch*. New York: Ace Books, 1995.

Rugge, Sue. *The Information Broker's Handbook*. Blue Ridge Summit, PA: Windcrest/McGraw-Hill, 1992.

Schiller, Herbert. *Information Inequality*. New York: Routledge, 1996.

Scott, Randall W. *Comics Librarianship: A Handbook*. Jefferson, NC: McFarland, 1990.

Sprouse, Martin, ed. *Sabotage in the American Workplace: Anecdotes of Dissatisfaction, Mischief, and Revenge*. San Francisco: Pressure Drop Press, 1992.

Wheatley, Margaret J. *Leadership and the New Science: Discovering Order in a Chaotic World*. San Francisco: Berrett-Koehler, 1999.

Weigand, Wayne A. *Irrepressible Reformer: A Biography of Melville Dewey*. Chicago: American Library Association, 1996.

West, Celeste, Elizabeth Katz, et al. *Revolting Librarians*. San Francisco: Booklegger Press, 1972.

And more than a few people selected "anything by Sandy Berman."

Periodicals

Alternative Library Literature: A Biennial Anthology. Jefferson, NC: McFarland, 1984/85–2000/01 (Phoenix: Oryx Press, 1982/83 volume).

Booklegger Magazine. San Francisco: Booklegger Press, 1973–1976.

Counterpoise. Gainesville, FL: CRISES Press, 1997–

Websites

Anarchist Librarians Web.
    <http://www.infoshop.org/library2/stories.php>

Association for Independent Information Professionals.
    <http://http://www.aiip.org/>

Estate Project for Artists with AIDS.
    <http://www.artistswithaids.org/>

Independent Publishing Resource Center.
    <http://www.iprc.org>

A Librarian at Every Table.
    <http://www.cas.usf.edu/lis/a-librarian-at-every-table/>

Librarian.net.
    <http://www.librarian.net>

Librarians in the Movies.
    <http://www.lib.byu.edu/dept/libsci/films/introduction.html>

Library Stuff.
    <http://www.librarystuff.net>

LISNews.
    <http://www.lisnews.com>

The Modified Librarian.
    <http://www.bmeworld.com/gailcat/>

National Alliance for the Mentally Ill. *Stigma Alerts*.
    <http://www.nami.org/campaign/stigmabust.html>

NewBreed Librarian.
<http://www.newbreedlibrarian.org>

New England School of Law. *Color Index.*
<http://portia.nesl.edu/screens/well_its_red.html>

Spunk Library.
<http://www.spunk.org>

Street Librarian.
<http://www.geocities.com/SoHo/Cafe/7423/>

ABOUT THE CONTRIBUTORS

Tara Alcock is the public services librarian at the farthest north library in the United States, Tuzzy Library in Barrow, Alaska.

Karen Antell is an MLIS student at the University of Oklahoma, a reference librarian at the Norman (OK) Public Library, and an active participant in the Oklahoma Library Association's Social Responsibilities Round Table. She also teaches water aerobics to (mostly) older adults at the local YMCA.

Paul Axel-Lute has worked at the Rutgers–Newark Law Library ever since he got out of library school. He did eventually publish his book on Lakewood, N.J.

Reva Basch wrote *Researching Online for Dummies* (2nd edition with Mary Ellen Bates), as well as *Secrets of the Super Searchers* and its sequel, *Secrets of the Super Net Searchers*, from which sprang the Super Searcher series she now edits for Information Today, Inc. She lives on the northern California coast with her husband, several cats, and satellite access to the Net.

W. Beauchamp is an information specialist at a nonprofit, progressive research center near Boston, and writes the zine *Subject to Change*.

Alison Bechdel has been drawing the comic strip "Dykes to Watch Out For" since 1983. Nine collections of her award-winning cartoons, including the most recent, *Post-Dykes to Watch Out For*, have been published by Firebrand Books. Her strip appears biweekly in 70 publications in the US and Canada. She lives in Vermont.

Sanford Berman, former Head Cataloger at Hennepin County Library (1973–1999), co-edited *Alternative Library Literature: A Biennial Anthology* (Jefferson, NC: McFarland), writes a quarterly column for *Unabashed Librarian*, pickets and demonstrates for just causes, and is invariably beaten at tic-tac-toe by his 5-year-old granddaughter, Jasmine, who cheats.

Barbara Bourrier-LaCroix received her MLS from Emporia State University in 1996. She lives in Winnipeg, Manitoba, with her partner Gord, her daughter Aimée and their three cats. When not performing amazing feats of reference work, she does other related library things for the Canadian Women's Health Network, sometimes even cataloguing. She authors a regular Q&A column in *Network/Le Réseau*. The proudest moment of her life was when her daughter grabbed a stack of books and announced she wanted to play library.

Tracy Brennan is a librarian at a large research university in a city where azaleas bloom at unexpected times of the year. When not planning Cooperative Results-Areas Paradigms or serving as co-convener of a Structural Hierarchy Interexplorational Taskforce, Tracy provides reference services to business school students who hope to be future captains of industry.

Keith Buckley has been the reference librarian at the Indiana University Law School Library since 1980. He also writes music, fiction, poetry, historical studies, as well as being the owner and engineer of a recording studio in Bloomington, Indiana.

Cathy Camper has worked for years at the Minneapolis Public Library. She has just recently published a book with Simon and Schuster called *Bugs Before Time: Prehistoric Insects and Their Relatives*, about giant prehistoric bugs. She did the cover art work for *Alternative Library Literature 1998–1999*.

Jennifer Camper is a cartoonist and graphic artist living in Brooklyn, NY. She has published a collection of her cartoons, *Rude Girls and Dangerous Women*, and a graphic novel, *subGURLZ*. She spends a lot of time in libraries.

Dan Cherubin (aka The Ska Librarian) received his M.S.L.S. from Columbia University. He has worked as a senior music librarian at the New York Public Library, among other places. He was at a software company, which was very bad, and now is a consulting librarian at large. He lives in NYC. You can check out his life or offer him a job at <http://www.geocities.com/ska_librarian>.

Catherine Clements is a cataloger at the Library of Virginia. On a good day, she can find beauty and truth in the cataloging rules. On a bad day, she may be found banging her head against a copy of AACR2.

Emily-Jane Dawson is a library assistant at the Multnomah County Library in Portland, Oregon. She received her MLS from the University of Maryland, College Park, and is a member of Portland Copwatch and AFSCME Local 88.

Piers Denton started working in libraries a long time ago putting books on shelves, stamping them out and then putting them back on the shelves again. Since completing her library studies in 1992, the author has done more inspiring work as a librarian in public and educational libraries across Australia. Currently working mostly with online materials, she strives to bridge the digital divide created by poverty. Her interest and activism these days are generally based on the issues of gender politics, the environment, and developing strategies of conflict resolution both on a intergovernmental and a personal level.

Chris Dodge watches birds, writes poetry, feels joy and pain, talks with strangers, eschews television, manages a collection of nearly 1600 periodicals at *Utne Reader* magazine, and maintains the *Street Librarian* website. From 1980 to 1999, Dodge civilly served in the employment of Hennepin County Library, Minnesota, most of those years energized by the presence of benevolent boss Sandy Berman, during that time co-editing with Jan DeSirey *Everything You Always Wanted to Know About Sandy Berman But Were Afraid to Ask* (McFarland, 1995) and 99 issues of *MSRRT Newsletter* (a centenarian final edition of which was published in early 2000).

Naomi Eichenlaub graduated with her MLIS from the School of Library, Archival and Information Studies (SLAIS) at the University of British Columbia, spring 2001. She is currently employed at Royal Roads University Library, Victoria, BC, where she does work in reference, cataloguing, government documents and collection maintenance.

Karen Elliott is a Neoist (look it up) pseudonym for a jaded queer library student turned jaded genderqueer librarian. Most of her 1999 observations have turned out to be depressingly accurate, though she draws solace from the groups of like-minded library workers she keeps meeting.

Jenna Freedman finally earns a living wage as Coordinator of Reference Services at Barnard College. She publishes an annual zineletter, [the] *Lower East Side Librarian Solstice Shout-Out*. If you track her down and mail her a stamp or a trade, she'll send you a copy.

Moe Giust is a burr under the saddle of Academic Librarianship at a major research institution, where he or she served many years as a paraprofessional before finishing an MLS as this volume went to print.

Judy Hadley, eternal paraprofessional, finds herself thirty years later once again working in the library world. Dogged and determined, she has never quite given up her dream of a totally free, grassroots library.

New to the game, **Dean Dylan Hendrix**, *aka* Menudo Terremoto "Dank" Williams, is a hardcore Aquarian from SAY-town, Texas. A graduate of Handsome Boy Modeling School and Howard Elementary, Dank loves to ball and visit the Planet Red Called Love.

Cindy Indiana has been a librarian for almost 20 years, working in government documents, general reference, arts reference, and library administration. Her favorite film about librarians is *Desk Set.* She believes that Bunny Watson would enjoy reading library erotica in the privacy of her own home and, of course, after making sure her library was in order.

Bruce Jensen has been a library clerk, a reference librarian, a teacher, a hod carrier, and a freelance malcontent. He writes regularly for *Críticas Magazine*, and his *Spanish in Our Libraries* website <http://www.sol-plus.net> has been opening its electric arms to librarians nationwide since 1998.

Elizabeth Katz, co-publisher and co-editor of the original *Revolting Librarians*, lives with the woman of her dreams in Lake Oswego, Oregon, and works for both the Lake Oswego Public Library and the Congregation Beth Israel library. She established a library and library services for inmates at the Washington County (Oregon) jail.

Kathleen Kern left cooking school to pursue the far sexier career of librarian. A born public services person with the heart of a cataloger, she worked at several business and academic libraries pre- and post-MLS. She is now an assistant reference librarian at the University of Illinois at Urbana-Champaign. Kathleen prefers the title Libraryun.

For **George Lederer**, librarianship may be an inherited condition. His mother was a university librarian, and he began working as a page in the New York Public Library while still in high school. When the original *Revolting Librarians* was published, he was a student at the University of Oregon in the People's Republic of Eugene, studying cataloging, storytelling, and a broad-based curriculum of cultural diversity. He has been a journalist, a treeplanter, a theater director, and a school librarian. Still trying to figure out what he wants to be when he grows up, he currently manages a corporate technical library for an electronics firm in Hillsboro, Oregon.

A. Librarian is on the faculty of a small university library in a metropolitan area and looks forward to the day when A. can openly discuss A.'s library education and use gender-specific pronouns. Thanks and love to Ed, Moose, Alex, and Ellen for all that they do.

Rory Litwin is a reference librarian at the California State Library in Sacramento, CA. He is an elected SRRT Action Councilor, editor/publisher of *Library Juice*, webmaster at Libr.org, and review editor for *Progressive Librarian*. At deadline time he was on the ballot for ALA Council. He likes sushi.

Biblio l'Teca is the cowardly nom de plume for a public librarian who resides somewhere in the Midwest. Normally, she doesn't trouble to hide her opinions behind phony-baloney names, but is feeling a mite bit skittish about having a white supremacy group on her ass. Aside from her paid duties at the library, she writes for library publications and is involved with wage, equity, and status issues. In her spare time, she gardens, herds children and cats, and wonders what TeenChat and on-line casinos have to do with the Digital Divide.

Owen Massey is a diffident Englishman surprised to find himself working with rare books. His favorite medical subject headings are CULTURE MEDIA and BLAST CRISIS.

Marilyn Gell Mason now lives with her husband (after several years of commuting) who is chair of the Management Information Systems Department in the College of Business at Florida State University. Their children are all over the world and she laughs about installing clocks to keep track of the time zones. Mike is a writer in San Francisco, Don is a businessman in Seattle, and Charlie is a geologist and computer software specialist in Kuala Lumpur. They all offer abundant opportunities to travel to wonderful places. And all five, in some way or the other, are now in the information business.

Chuck "Chuck0" Munson is an anarchist librarian and webmaster who currently lives in Arlington, Virginia. When he isn't keeping his numerous websites up and running, he edits two magazines: *Alternative Press Review* and *Practical Anarchy*. He is currently working with a collective of local activists to open an infoshop called the Brian MacKenzie Center.

Jess Nevins received his M.L.I.S. from Simmons College in January 1996. Since that time he has been a contract librarian and has worked in public, academic, corporate, and special libraries. He is currently an assistant professor and reference librarian at Sam Houston State University in Huntsville, Texas.

Following a thankless decade as a technical writer, **Pam North** returned to school and started her library career in 1995. She is currently deputy director at the Sherwood Public Library in Sherwood, Oregon. Pam serves as the editor of the *Oregon Library Association Hotline* and is a contributor to the *OLA Quarterly*. She resides in West Linn, Oregon, with her husband and their Bernese Mountain Dog.

Erica Olsen, known in librarian circles as the "Librarian Avenger," is an interface designer from Michigan. Her first essay, titled "Why You Should Fall to Your Knees and Worship a Librarian," earned her a lifetime supply of paperclips at reference desks across the country. She spends her free time hanging around children's sections teaching kids how to look up swear words on LexisNexis.

Noel Peattie was editor of *SIPAPU: a newsletter for librarians*, between 1970 and 1995. In addition, he has published a novel, and three poetry books (and is working on a fourth). He also co-authored *The Freedom to Lie: A Debate About Democracy* (McFarland, 1989), with the late John C. Swan. His current publisher is Regent Press, 2040A Oakland, CA 94608.

David M. Pimentel remembers first finding *Revolting Librarians* in 1998 — while browsing the Zs at library school — and thinking it was a yearbook by hippie MLS students from the sixties. Since he typically imagines his life as a musical, it seemed only natural to envision his career in the same way.

Art Plotnik led two lives after "No Silence:" As an ALA publishing exec (editor, *American Libraries*; editorial director, ALA Editions; executive producer, *Library Video Magazine*) and as a writer — six books, ranging from language to biography to nature guides. At ALA, his reform efforts focused on bringing image-busting, kickass librarians (of all shapes and colors) to light as authors or as subjects of profiles and news stories. Now, as a full-time writer, he hangs at the local library and bugs the staff to break rules.

Kate Pohjola, the "bastard librarian from hell," is a tattooed, book slinging, ass-kicking, foul-mouthed librarian with a cat and a dog, a house, and a love for all things Detroit.

Elspeth Pope received her first library degree from McGill in 1951. After 15 years as a reference librarian, she taught technical service courses at SUNY-Geneseo, University of Pittsburgh and University of South Carolina. Taking early retirement in 1983, she married Jim Holly, and moved to Olympia and later Shelton. She now has a freelance indexing business.

Katia Roberto spent all week cataloging for Southern Illinois University Carbondale until leaving in May 2003. Non-work time is spent staring at the computer, reading zines, and trying to get out of doing the dishes and laundry.

Katharine Salzmann swears that she has never encountered problem patrons such as the ones described in her poems. Everyone that she has served at the University of Texas, Howard University, and in her current position as archivist/curator of manuscripts at Southern Illinois University Carbondale, has behaved perfectly and professionally.

Toni Samek is associate professor in the School of Library and Information Studies, University of Alberta, where she teaches courses in information access and intellectual freedom. Chair of the Canadian Library Association's Advisory Committee on Intellectual Freedom, she also speaks and publishes widely on related subjects. She lives in Edmonton.

C. M. Stupegia is a revolutionary yet sometimes psychotic librarian who resides in southern Illinois. A graduate of Dominican University, she has been a proud member of the library profession for five years. Her piece was written during a moment of crisis of faith; she has, however, recovered nicely and is responding well to regular manicure/pedicure and massage sessions. She lives by the credo, "Librarians Unite."

Diana Brawley Sussman has worked with populations who've endured great adversity — refugees, people who are poor, or going blind. She finds the fortitude of people — that they laugh, smile, and say thank you — amazing. She is currently director of the Southern Illinois Talking Book Center, a National Library Service library for the blind and physically handicapped.

Polly Thistlethwaite is the coordinator of instruction at Colorado State University Libraries, soon to be the associate librarian for reference and access services at the

Graduate Center, City University of New York. She's a former member of ACTUP/New York and the Lesbian Herstory Archives Coordinating Committee.

Patricia A. Threatt is a contract cataloger for digital projects, small business entrepreneur, companion to Hula Hoop and Mawmaw, teacher of adult learning courses, and woman about town. She is the author of numerous articles on a wide variety of subjects, such as "Toole's Louisiana Voice in the Neon Bible" (Part of *Songs of the New South: Writing Contemporary Louisiana*), "Give the Patrons What They Want," and "Connecting the Ivory Tower and City Hall: How University Special Collections Use the Internet to Document Local History."

Daniel C. Tsang is politics, economics and Asian American studies bibliographer, and social science data librarian at University of California, Irvine. He also hosts *Subversity*, a radio program on kuci.org, and writes for *OC Weekly*.

Jana Varlejs is associate professor, Rutgers Library and Information Science Department, where her courses include outreach services and user instruction. Before joining Rutgers to direct the LIS continuing education program, she was outreach consultant for the state library development agency in Massachusetts, and AV/YA librarian at Montclair (NJ) Public Library.

Celeste West is a cheerful verbivore who welcomes you to the gateless gate of the Zen Center Library in San Francisco. Her latest book is *Lesbian Polyfidelity*. She is now learning to toss three religions in the air and keep them up there for an upcoming novel, *Laughing Buddha Maria, Lumine Us, Good Faeries All*.

Jessamyn West is the charismatic yet perpetually unemployable Virgo webmaster of librarian.net. She lives in Seattle and Vermont.

Michelle Wilde is a proud representative of the Taurean contingent of academic librarians.

Jennifer Young is a Sagittarian serials/non-book cataloger at Saint Louis University in St. Louis, MO. When not providing superb access to library materials and defending librarians ("Yes, you need a master's degree"), she likes chocolate, martinis, and funky nail polish.

Chris Zammarelli is a librarian assistant at a mid-sized law firm in Chicago. He and his wife Jennifer Berktold have a website called *Lemur Love* <http://www.lemurlove.com>, at which he houses a censorship and library science news site called *The Pernicious Librarian* <http://www.lemurlove.com/perniciouslib>.

INDEX